Education for Transformation:

Implications in Lewis Mumford's Ecohumanism

For

Sally

and

Susan

Education For Transformation:
Implications in Lewis Mumford's Ecohumanism

by
David R. Conrad

An ETC Publication
1976

Library of Congress Cataloging in Publication Data

Conrad, David R.   1937
    Education for transformation.

    Includes bibliographical references and index.
    1. Education - Philosophy.   2. Mumford, Lewis,
1895 -   I. Title

LB885.M722C66   370.1   75-25867
ISBN 0-88280-030-2

Copyright © 1976 by ETC PUBLICATIONS
                    Department 1627-A
                    Palm Springs
                    California 92262

Printed in the United States of America

✿ contents

❧ foreword

Lewis Mumford is a giant of the twentieth century. Yet by no means is he the only such giant whom many of us fail to recognize. Altogether too frequently we are deluded and distracted instead by multitudes of little people — little people who talk much more shrilly, divert us more adroitly by means of public relations and inflated self-images, and thereby deceive us the more easily by quick-buck, patent nostrums for our ailing age.

Far more persuasively than any other educational interpretor, David Conrad has placed Lewis Mumford where he rightly belongs: as a giant among pygmies. Although Mumford has long been recognized among architects and city-regional planners as a world authority, Professor Conrad is the first to recognize in depth the educational dimensions of Mumford's panoramic interpretations of time and space — more so, perhaps, than Mumford himself may care to admit as willingly as would a specialist in educational practice and theory. The author of this book is competent in both scores: he is a grassroots innovator at the University of Vermont as well as a careful student of contemporary ideas, including prolonged study of Mumford himself.

There are several reasons why this book appears at an importunate time. It coincides closely with Mumford's eightieth birthday. It recognizes him as an educator of importance as well as a cultural historian, critic, visionary planner, and philosopher of humankind. Above all, it jars us at a moment in human evolution when, not only as educators but as responsible citizens, we severely need jarring.

For the lifelong, focal contribution of Lewis Mumford reawakens us to a desperate paradox. This is the paradox that civilization itself is fraught both with fearful omens of global destruction and with magnificent opportunities for global reconstruction. Unlike mere contradictions or dichotomies, a genuine paradox invites far-reaching resolution and transcendence. Mumford's work is filled with forebodings and warnings. Equally, it is radiant with the potentialities of a humane life of love, creativity, and comradeship among all peoples. I do not think I misrepresent him, or Conrad's perceptions of him, when I suggest that in this paradox is to be found the epitomization of Mumford's "life force" and indeed of his permanent contribution to the history of civilization.

Conrad's way of strengthening his interpretation is heightened by exhaustive knowledge of Mumford's prolific writings as they are listed at the close of this book. It is strengthened still further by close acquaintance with many other writings that reflect both favorably or unfavorably upon Mumford's own work. Certainly the author refuses to draw a worshipful or glamorized portrait; on the contrary, he raises sharp questions and disagreements influenced both by other critics and his own independence of mind.

In any case, Mumford emerges in this book as the foremost advocate of a radically transformative philosophy of education. Thus he indignantly rejects, either forthrightly or inferentially, any kind of complacency, timidity, or defeatism that infects so many teachers, students, and administrators of the contemporary educational establishment. His work is a thorough antidote against this infection. It proves, as Mumford demonstrates by his own persistent dedication, and as Conrad reconfirms so brilliantly, that the single most compelling commitment of our time is to the conduct of life and the transformations of man.

Theodore Brameld
Professor of Philosophy
of Education Emeritus
Boston University

✦ preface

This book evolved over the last ten years as I explored Lewis Mumford's many books and articles. During my exploration, I became increasingly aware of the wealth of implications in Mumford's philosophy for educational theory and practice. It grew apparent to me that his philosophy of wholeness and interrelatedness deserves a much wider hearing than it has received. Few have spoken more eloquently on behalf of human rights and a humanizing environment during the past half century than Mumford.

In the introductory chapter, ways that Mumford's ideas relate to contemporary educational concerns like "humanistic education," "career education," and "accountability" are suggested. Chapter Two deals with the concepts "biotechnic society" and "biotechnic education" which Mumford offers as alternatives to the present profit-oriented social order and tunnel-visioned educational system. In the third chapter, attention turns to Mumford's notion of an organic technology which supports human growth and potentiality rather than blocking it. Educators and others are urged to be wary of the "megamachine" (or oversized, overpowered technology) which threatens us all through overproduction of weapons, excessive bureaucracy and other forms of giantism.

Chapter Four is concerned with organic architecture or architecture that provides a nurturing, aesthetically pleasing environment for men and women at a time when greed and expediency seem to outweigh humanistic values like cooperation and human warmth. Among other ideas, the monumentalism and monotony of much modern architecture is suggested as a ripe topic for critical investigation by teachers and students.

In the fifth and sixth chapters respectively, the focus shifts to Mumford's view of the city as a microcosm of the world and to urban-suburban alternatives. Educators are urged to help their students create a life-affirming environment for every urban resident. Balanced new communities are offered as a way of relieving the congestion of cities, as well as a way of assuring integrated housing and services. Implications for education in the New Town movement are also explored in Chapter Six.

Chapter Seven moves from the city and new communities to the larger region which Mumford has always found important. Regions contain many cultural differences as well as encourage a sense of unity. Regional survey is offered as a movement toward synthesis in education and educational implications are developed at some length.

Moving from study of the region to study of the planet, the eighth chapter looks at Mumford's notion of "One World" or world community that is both diverse and unified, full of cultural variety yet cooperative and sharing. Transformation to such a world order will not be easy, but survival with life-affirming quality may depend upon it. Once again, Mumford's ideas are related to educational theory and practice.

The Appendix contains a biographical study of Lewis Mumford. His life and work are analyzed in order to help the reader become more familiar with this twentieth century Renaissance man. The reader may wish to review the Appendix first for background information.

This study of Mumford's ideas with implications for education owes much to Theodore Brameld who inspired and encouraged me continually. I genuinely appreciate the assistance of Kenneth Benne, Richard Olmsted, Eugene DuBois, Shigeharu Matsuura, and Walter Creese. Lewis Mumford's hospitality during two personal interviews is warmly acknowledged. I am especially grateful to Sally Conrad who has been a tremendous help in many ways during my research and writing.

I wish to thank Herbert L. Leff, Robert J. Nash, Nobuo Shimahara, David A. Shiman, and Jay M. Smith for reading my manuscript in its entirety. Their constructive comments and suggestions for improvement were of great value. Of course, final responsibility for the contents of this book is mine.

Most of Chapter Four, "Organic Architecture: Symbolic and Functional," appeared originally in *The Journal of Aesthetic Education* and Chapter Six, "Education and the New Town Movement," in *The Teachers College Record*.

David R. Conrad
University of Vermont

✸ chapter 1
introduction:
toward a
visionary education

OF VARIOUS Americans who might be chosen during the bicentennial celebration to represent America's most worthy values, very few educators would choose Lewis Mumford. This is unfortunate since Mumford has spent his entire life advancing human, life-affirming values which many teachers and administrators today are beginning to embrace. Professional educators committed to "humanistic education," "confluent education," "open education" and other kinds of human-centered education will be intellectually and emotionally challenged by Mumford's ideas.

Mumford, of course, is not known as an educator, but he is not known exclusively as an historian, sociologist or philosopher either. Mumford is proud to be a generalist in a time of specialization, an interdisciplinary thinker when many academics still lock themselves into narrow disciplines, a humanist when behaviorist-oriented psychology and philosophy tightens its grip in educational circles. He never received a bachelor's degree, but has taught in numerous colleges and universities. He is probably the world's most distinguished authority on cities, the most respected historian of technology, and one of the more famous living moral philosophers. Yet, his ardent warnings have not been heeded nor his profound message heard by more than a fraction of people.

Young people have begun to appreciate Mumford's writings published during the last half century, but educators have still to recognize this giant in their midst. The purpose of this work is to help educators and others appreciate Mumford's many contributions to American and world culture. It is hoped that a discussion of Mumford's ideas and an exploration of educational implications in these ideas will encourage educators to look closer at Mumford's publications and introduce some of his ideas into their own personal and professional lives.

Lewis Mumford is a radical thinker in the sense that he gets to the roots of problems and issues. He is not content dealing with symptoms; he digs deep into the malaise of American society and calls ardently for fundamental reforms. He pleads for self renewal and social renewal, for a fuller-bodied person and revitalized group experiences. Mumford calls for nothing less than transformation of the individual and transformation of American and world culture.

This book will explore ways that education in schools, universities, adult education centers, and less formal settings can help transform human beings and societies from hatefulness to love; from ugliness to beauty; from compulsive competitiveness to freely-chosen cooperation; from destructive power to constructive, life-enhancing power. The time for education for transformation is now during the celebration of the two hundredth anniversary of a nation supposedly dedicated to peace, social justice, and individual liberty. Mumford, himself steeped in American culture and a leader in the development of American studies, leads the way toward a transformed world which guarantees freedom and justice to every inhabitant of the planet.

The term "ecohumanism" suggests an active philosophy emphasizing the human capacity for social-self-realization and inter-relationships with the natural environment. Educational philosopher Theodore Brameld defines social-self-realization as " . . . the ever-growing fulfillment of the powers of man in communion with other men."[1] "Ecohumanism" combines the humanism of social-self-realization as a process and a goal with ecology, "the science of the relationships between organisms and their environments."[2] Mumford is a humanist who has great faith in the creative potential of men and women individually and in groups, though he also recognizes human limitations. He has always been concerned with environments which people experience, whether the environment be wild, landscaped, or constructed. Mumford's "ecohumanism" is his all-encompassing world view, his organic philosophy of man/

woman and nature, his ecological approach to human beings, to knowledge, to life.

A visionary education is needed today more than ever and Mumford helps articulate it. Pedestrian reforms or panaceas will not be adequate to meet the compounding crises that face humankind. An education that questions the status quo, that provokes government officials, that challenges industry, that fosters self-governance, that develops the ability to criticize as well as to construct is necessary. An education centered on environmental studies broadly conceived, on aesthetic experience, on peace and conflict resolution, on problems of racism, sexism, and poverty is vitally needed. Educators must consider the future and help plan the future without forgetting the past. At the same time, they need to utilize the present more creatively, remembering that what affects a student right now in a personal way probably affects him in a meaningful way.

Educators will have to face the fact that "open education" and "individualized instruction," for all of their virtues, are not answers to the monumental problems of either school or society. "Open education" is often so open that it closes options for children, options that deal with intensive investigation of root problems. "Individualized instruction" often stresses individualization to the extent that individuals become cut off from interaction with others and group cooperation takes a back seat to individual competitiveness.

Other "innovative" movements have been encouraged lately in education. Career education has been offered as a response to the failure of schools to investigate career alternatives. But career education, in pumping career knowledge into students at an early age, fails to give adequate attention to non-career-oriented concerns and, worse, trains uncritical students to fill slots in the present social order. Environmental education has been treated too often in a narrow, encapsulated way. To many, it means little more than cleaning up refuse along dirty river banks or pinning dead butterflies on an identification board.

A rabid interest in accountability has swept departments of education in a number of states. But a number of educators are beginning to realize that accountability has been treated in a much too restricted way. Accountability is fine, they argue, but let us be held accountable for advancing values like sharing, caring, loving, and helping, rather than mastery of basic skills alone. Let us be accountable for doing our part to develop whole persons who probe skillfully, think deeply, and feel intensely. In teacher education, many are questioning the whole notion of "performance-based" or "competency-based" education, recognizing that mastery of a long list of behaviorally-defined competencies does not necessarily connote a qualified, competent teacher-human being.

Some movements or curriculum developments that point to more substantive change than the previous include high schools "without walls," peace and global awareness education, aesthetic education, urban education and values education. It remains to be seen whether the possibilities latent in these and other movements become reality. Certainly if Mumford's views are embraced by educators and educational institutions, they will.

Implications for education in Mumford's philosophy are vast. Environmental-aesthetic education, for instance, would become a keystone in the curriculum. Students and teachers would undertake ecological surveys of neighborhood and region, learn to look more intensely at natural and man-made environments and develop political skills to combat visual blight and corporate exploitation. Peace education would center on peaceful ways to resolve conflict, values and attitudes that either promote or block world peace, similarities that bind all human beings together, and cultural differences that make life more interesting. World order education would concentrate on global issues like social justice, economic well-being, ecological harmony, population, food and political participation. Urban education would revolve around problems of living in rundown cities, of chronic unemployment and crime, of historical growth and development of world cities. Proposals for new towns or communities as urban alternatives would be given prominence.

Mumford would not discard terms like career or consumer education, but would deal with them in a manner very different from that now being proposed. In the case of career education, Mumford would have children and youth discover the pleasures and satisfaction of the craft tradition rather than remain hooked on depersonalizing, mass production-oriented jobs and careers. Consumer education would focus on the production-consumption spiral of American society, helping students become selective buyers of quality goods rather than promiscuous purchasers of cheaply-made merchandise hawked by seductive discounters. More important, students would be encouraged to question the need for every purchase and exposed to the ecological consequences of a wasteful society. They would explore the economics of Capitalism and Communism, of anarchism and democratic socialism. Greed and exploitation by industry and government, misery and suffering in mines and factories would not be sidestepped; neither would happiness and joy at moments of leisure, the warmth of family and friends at home, and the satisfaction of doing meaningful tasks at work. Alternative life-styles that offer greater personal freedom, closer group cooperation, and drastic cuts in goods consumed would be treated seriously.

The social sciences would focus on men and women as symbol-creators and tool-makers, on the environment that is constantly shaped and fashioned, on historical precedents and future aspirations. The sciences would concentrate on the biosphere, on human relationships to plants and animals, on the moral responsibility of science and scientists to promote a safer, more healthful world. The language arts would center on the development of language as a creative act, on literature of past and present which expresses the tragedy and glory of life, on themes which help individuals understand themselves and their fellow creatures more profoundly. The arts would express the most positive, promising aspects of culture, becoming active agents of cultural transformation rather than reactive agents; fashionable "movements" like pop art, op art and electronic music would not be neglected, but the arts would help define a better world as well as comment upon the ills of the present world.

Mumford's ideas have implications for educators at all levels and in all disciplines. In elementary schools, Mumford-inspired teachers and children would spend considerable time exploring neighborhood and community. In their classrooms, they would confront issues usually overlooked or considered too sophisticated for young children. As persons, teachers would become active in politics and demonstrate their social responsibility in numerous ways. As individuals with diverse backgrounds, experiences, and interests, educators would display both intellectual and emotional competence.

Implications in Mumford's ecohumanism for secondary, university, and adult education especially stand out. His notion of biotechnic culture oriented to organic needs and human-centered technology suggests that education be concerned primarily with creating such a culture. Other concerns suggest that architecture as a social art, as a home for men and women, be given further attention. The desperate need for global understanding and world community implies that educators devote greatly increased effort to this endeavor. World education centers, peace studies offerings, and global order workshops and in-service programs might be established more widely. Peace intern programs similar to those organized by the World Without War Council would be expanded.

Unique secondary programs like the one sponsored by the Oceanics on board the 316 foot long sailing ship *Statstraad Lehmkuhl* are consistent with Mumford's concerns. Male and female students and faculty help to work the ship and participate in an interdisciplinary academic program when off duty. On land, they make lengthy field trips under difficult conditions in remote parts of Africa, South America and Asia, living in close contact with local people, and becoming participant-observers in cultures different from their own. The Oceanics includes students from many economic, religious, social, and racial backgrounds, as scholarship funds permit. Mumford would approve of the integrated composition of this school as well as its emphasis on integration of intellectual and activity-based learning. Students in the Oceanics and thousands of related programs not yet conceived gain valuable knowledge and understanding of the language, arts, customs, and traditions of people across the world, hopefully working toward peace and the resolution of global problems throughout their lives.[3]

Mumford might find the School and University Programs of the Institute for World Order promising approaches to the creation of world community. These programs introduce world order studies into schools and universities, providing help to teachers, students, and administrators involved in planning and operating curricular programs on world order issues and values; publishing innovative teaching materials and scholarly studies; and sponsoring workshops and colloquia. The Institute prepares books and anthologies, research monographs, and teaching tools of various kinds from a film on "Population and Quality of Life" to a periodical called "Ways and Means of Teaching About World Order." Mumford's hope for transformation from "post-historic man's starvation of life"[4] to "One

World"[5] man's/woman's love for the wholeness and richness of life may become reality through the endeavors of groups like the Institute for World Order and countless individuals committed to world brotherhood.

Teacher education has much to learn from Mumford's life work. A few implications have already been mentioned and others will follow. It should be clear already that teacher education centered around Mumford themes would be radically different from today's teacher training. One clear example of the difference is mentioned in *The Transformations of Man*. "One World" man (or "One World" teacher) rejects mechanical efficiency and fragmentation; "he is," Mumford asserts, "just the opposite of the competent technician."[6] And yet much of teacher education is geared toward training the "competent technician," the expert in classroom management and behavioral objectives. The industrial or factory model is revered as teachers are trained to chisel learning into bit parts.

Instead, teachers of teachers ought to make connections between aspects of knowledge, to widen personal-social perspectives, to facilitate development of the thinking, feeling, willing, acting human being.[7] As long as teacher educators view their role as nothing more than training competent technicians, they will remain enemies of wholeness and social-self-realization. Teacher preparation will remain fixated at the stage of "post-historic" or "machine-made" man who considers scientific intelligence supreme and emotion, feeling, and fantasy superfluous.[8] If Mumford's notion of "One World" man is adopted by teacher educators, teachers will be prepared as generalists more than specialists, internationalists more than nationalists, humanists more than mechanists.

Frequently arguing that education is a life-long enterprise, Mumford sees education as much more than formal schooling. Education gained through involvement in community affairs, political campaigns and regional projects is of great value. He admires self education that involves travel, exploring a city, and researching an area of special interest. Adult education that makes creative use of spare time appeals to him since he believes strongly in the self-renewing, regenerative potential of leisure activities. Informal education taking place in family and neighborhood settings is important for its intimacy and warmth. The entire process of enculturation holds significance for Mumford and therefore implications in his writing could be endless. However, this study will concentrate on implications for formal education while not forgetting Mumford's own broad conception of education as "paideia," the ancient Greek term meaning "education looked upon as a lifelong transformation of the human personality, in which every aspect of life plays a part."[9]

Education as "lifelong transformation" of the person as well as of human society is the major theme of this book. After consideration of many of Lewis Mumford's ideas, inferences will be made which demonstrate the richness and depth of his vision. By not only describing and analyzing key elements in his philosophy but also freely expanding upon them, drawing them out, and applying them to contemporary social-cultural problems and educational theory and practice, it is hoped that Mumford will be recognized as the outstanding thinker, prophet and educator that he is.

Mumford's strong tendency toward dialectic — toward synthesis growing out of opposing forces like the individual and the group, the rational and irrational dimensions of life, passive contemplation and active participation — is a constant theme of this book. Relatively few though they are, Mumford's explicit references to such educational concerns as curriculum reform, the teaching-learning process, the control of schools and the preparation of teachers are discussed. But much more important, educational ideas and concepts implicit in Mumford's ecohumanism are examined and elaborated upon in order to make his dynamic philosophy more relevant and useful for educators. With Mumford as a guide, education can be transformed from narrowness and provincialism to wholeness and world consciousness.

---

[1]Theodore Brameld, *Education As Power*, (New York: Holt, Rinehart and Winston, 1965), p. 59.

[2]William Morris, editor, *The American Heritage Dictionary of the English Language* (New York: American Heritage Publishing Co., 1971), p. 413.

[3]For further information on the school ship *Stratsraad Lehmkuhl*, write to the Oceanics, 145 East 74th Street, New York, New York 10021.

[4]Mumford, *The Transformations of Man*, (New York: Collier Books, 1962), p. 131.

[5]Mumford, *The Transformations of Man*, p. 139.

[6]*Ibid.*, p. 180.

[7]See "Foundations of Education: The Restoration of Vision to Teacher Preparation," by David Conrad, Robert Nash and David Shiman. *Educational Theory*, XXIII (Winter, 1973), 42-55.

[8]Mumford, *The Transformations of Man*, pp. 118-19.

[9]*Ibid.*, p. 179.

✌ chapter 2
biotechnic society
and
biotechnic education

THE TERM "biotechnic" is one of several terms used originally by the Scottish sociologist, Patrick Geddes, but adopted by Mumford in several of his own volumes. Biotechnic refers to an emergent economy and social order following the neotechnic (an economy based on electricity and the lighter, sometimes rare metals), which follows the paleotechnic (a mutation of the eotechnic with coal and iron supreme) which in turn follows the eotechnic (an economy based on wind, water and wood for power and dominant in Western Europe from the tenth to the eighteenth century).

To replace the neotechnic which has dominated industrialized countries since the eighteen-eighties, Mumford envisions "a civilization in which the biological sciences will be freely applied to technology, and in which technology itself will be oriented toward the culture of life."[1]

In a biotechnic order:

> . . . the biological arts and social arts become dominant: agriculture, medicine, and education take precedence over engineering. Improvements . . . will rest upon a more organic utilization of the entire environment, in response to the needs of organisms and groups considered in their multifold relations: physical, biological, social, economic, esthetic, psychological.[2]

Biotechnic culture is oriented to the cycle of life, with its continuous processes of birth and growth, renewal and death.[3] Biotechnic economy represents a radical departure from the "pecuniary economy" centered on profit that developed during the past five hundred years.[4] Mumford's concept of biotechnic culture, which is unabashedly utopian,[5] is based upon the primacy of human personality and human community; it substitutes life-values for those of a power and profit economy.[6]

A fine example of the failure of a money economy or pecuniary economy to satisfy human needs can be seen in urban housing. In *The Culture of Cities*, Mumford argues that as housing standards rise the opportunity for profit through renting or selling drops and production turns elsewhere, creating grave housing shortages and over-crowding. Housing becomes more and more expensive for working people and less and less adequate for a healthy life. In a biotechnic economy, however, "instead of wages and income directing demand, vital demand determines the level of income and directs production into socially useful channels."[7] Minimum standards for housing based on biological needs and modified by social factors which both tradition and research indicate are desirable for bringing up children would be drafted. These standards would also set a minimum level for wages in any given region at any given time.[8] A biotechnic economy would reverse the priorities of a pecuniary economy by assuring good housing for everyone.

The goal of a biotechnic economy, stated succinctly, is the creation of "the best possible environment for human nature and culture."[9] Such a life-embracing economy puts great stress on the qualitative standards not only in housing, but in jobs, consumer goods, education, and personal relationships. Social services become more important than private profit making, cooperative processes more respected than parasitic and predatory processes which have ruled so long.[10] Gross inequalities are removed in the shift from a producer's economy to a consumer's economy, and organic limits to growth are established.[11]

In the late thirties Mumford stated that he was quite optimistic about an emerging biotechnic economy. He viewed the increase of collectivism. The expansion of consumers' associations, and the building of better communities for workers since the third quarter of the nineteenth century as deep changes even where the profit system was operating.[12] However, the Second World War dampened his hopes. Later came the post-war boom with a surge of private enterprise, an obsession with consumption, an almost wholly uncontrolled mass exodus to suburbia. Accompanying these developments were serious reservations by Mumford about the direction of American and Western society, a nagging sense of despair, but not a giving up.

In the late sixties, Mumford exhorted Americans, perhaps more urgently but no less earnestly than before the war, to reckon with the liabilities of mass consumption — the overproduction of automobiles which leads to despoliation of land and air, for example. He flatly asserts: "What we have unthinkingly accepted as brilliant technical progress too often results in biological and social regression." [13] Compulsive expansion which callously disregards human health, safety and welfare, he warns, causes "the forces of life, if they break out at all . . . [to] do so in the negative form of violence, crime, and psychotic disturbances." [14]

As anti-life forces tighten their grip in the nineteen seventies, aid to troubled cities withers and urban expressways, faceless office buildings, and apartments for the rich spring up everywhere. Education is largely neglected, health and welfare funds are pinched severely, and poor people are gouged by greedy landlords. But the forces of life are indeed breaking out among Blacks, Puerto Ricans, Native Americans, Chicanos and other minority people who have long been denied their right to equal opportunity. Mumford's biotechnic economy has not evolved, but his conception of the culture which might yet evolve is as relevant today as it was almost a half century ago.

A new social order centered on life-needs and a technology which respects rather than defies organic demands is even more imperative today because life-destroying elements from racism to atomic weaponry constantly threaten human survival. Educators must be held accountable for preparing children, youth, and adults to live in a biotechnic society. Even more fundamental, educators and the education profession should be held responsible for helping them create a biotechnic culture based on what Mumford calls:

> . . . the realities of life itself, on human growth in a biologi-
> cally sound and socially stimulating environment, on
> sexual maturation and a good family life, on disciplined
> emotional expression in the arts and in daily practice, on
> constant citizen participation in the public affairs of the
> community . . . [15]

Mumford's "basic communism"

How can we make this biotechnic dream become a reality? What can schools as institutions and educators as teachers and parents do to humanize and equalize our society? To begin, we might look closely at the ingredients of Mumford's biotechnic order, especially at a provocative term he introduced in *Technics and Civilization.* Arguing for a scientific economy in which all standards of consumption would be established, with gains beyond those calculated going to the whole community, Mumford claims that "basic communism" would normalize consumption and mark the "end of those princely capitalistic dreams of limitless income and privileges."[16]

The term "basic communism" stirred considerable controversy in the United States, as might be expected, with one critic commenting that "the phrase he uses may be accurate in the etymological sense, but will shed more heat than light in quarters where the latter is most acutely needed."[17] Because of the almost pathological fear of "communism" among Americans, reaching a peak in the McCarthy era of the 1950's, perhaps this critic's point was well taken. Tactically, use of the expression "basic communism" may have been unwise and may have alienated some otherwise friendly critics, but as a system of distributing wealth to the community as a whole, it had been proposed many years earlier by the American utopian Edward Bellamy in *Looking Backward* and *Equality.*

In the paperback edition of *Technics and Civilization* (1963), Mumford explains that he wishes to retain the word "communism," but wants to set the record straight by noting that his "communism" is post-Marxian because it does not depend upon the paleotechnic values on which Marx based his theories. Marx put too much stress on the material needs of man and not enough on the spiritual needs to which Mumford gives prominence. "Basic communism," then, neither implies the particular nineteenth century ideology and militarism of some Communist nations nor the imitation of political methods of the Soviet Union.[18] In Mumford's "basic communism:"

> ... the claim to a livelihood rests upon the fact that, like
> the child in a family, one is a member of a community: the
> energy, the technical knowledge, the social heritage
> of a community belongs equally to every member of it,

since in the large the individual contributions and differences are completely insignificant. [19]

The claim that individual differences are "completely
insignificant" is startling and not at all consistent with Mumford's
usual respect for individuation: if he means that the individual
becomes totally absorbed into the community, then he should be
criticized for grossly disregarding the varied needs and
achievements of individuals. Though he probably would not want to
be taken literally here, from an educational point of view this
comment is disturbing because it suggests that Mumford may not be
as alert to differences and problems ranging from mental retardation
to reading difficulties, from emotional disorders to speech
impairment, as he might be. Such a rash statement is difficult to
justify, even in light of the following modifying comment: "Differentiation and preference and special incentive should be taken into
account in production and consumption only after the security and
continuity of life itself is assured." [20]

Criticism of Mumford's over-emphasis on group solidarity,
however, should not obscure the important implications in his
assertion that the essentials of life belong to all members of a
community instead of to an elite coterie. In a planned economy, vital
wants like food, shelter, and medical attention would be guaranteed
for all but would necessarily be limited because "healthy activity
requires restriction, monotony, repetition, as well as change, variety
and expansion." [21] How these would be limited fairly he does not
say, but presumably the entire community would make decisions of
that nature and then abide by them. He does recommend a
minimum income for everyone with incentives for hard work and
outstanding contributions. [22]

Vital wants cannot be restricted to the barest amount of food,
clothing, or shelter to sustain life, however. Life also requires goods
and services that might be classified as "luxuries" — books, music,
painting, drama, play — and these, too, must be provided in "basic
communism." [23] To this list we might add as much formal and
informal education in as many areas as anyone might desire and a
great variety of recreation alternatives which would satisfy canoeists
and cross-country skiers, gardeners and hikers, motorcyclists and
professional sports fans.

Necessary for these developments, of course, would be broader
financial support for education and recreation. Greater emphasis on

educational alternatives like the Minneapolis-based Education
Exploration Center designed to help parents and students find
the best ways to learn is needed.[24] And more experimentation with
educational television and alternatives to television like the Boston
Polyarts group that sponsors impromptu puppet shows, fiddling
contests, yoga lessons, and street fairs for people of all ages in the
city is desirable.[25] For diversified education, state and federal
governments must financially underwrite education in
unprecedented ways, encouraging research and imaginative
learning proposals, and discouraging education geared to
acceptance of the status quo or development of competent
technicians but incompetent human beings. For diversified
recreation, community, regional, and world organizations must work
together and plan now for single-use and multi-use urban and rural
areas, as well as wilderness tracts that will remain forever free from
encroachment.

Mumford is convinced that a community should control and
distribute its own resources rather than depend upon the faulty
capitalist contention that consumption must become greater in order
to fatten stockholder profits. Normalizing consumption means
providing for the vital wants of everyone but cutting down on the
number of goods produced, attacking waste, and denouncing an
economy of superabundance. It means setting up norms by people
themselves for a good life in a life rather than a goods-oriented
society. Certainly this is a utopian idea today, as it was in the thirties,
but Mumford knew then as we know now that it can be
accomplished if people everywhere focus on this long-range goal
and the means needed for its achievement. In expressing a visionary
opinion in 1934, Mumford verbalized a life-long theme that merits
serious consideration today:

> When we have such a norm our success in life will not be
> judged by the size of the rubbish heaps we have pro-
> duced: it will be judged by the immaterial and non-
> consumable goods we have learned to enjoy, and by our
> biological fulfillment as lovers, mates, parents and by our
> personal fulfillment as thinking, feeling men and women.
> Distinction and individuality will reside in the person-
> ality, where it belongs, not in the size of the house we
> live in, in the expense of our trappings, or in the amount
> of labor we can arbitrarily command.[26]

The foundations of "basic communism" already exist, we are told, in schools, libraries, hospitals, museums, parks and playgrounds which are supported by the whole community, as well as in police and fire services. Other forms appear in unemployment and old-age insurance.[27] Mumford could not have foreseen over forty years ago that many residents of inner cities would no longer feel that schools and parks, police and fire services, are controlled by the communities in which they operate, even though supported financially by them. Increasingly, inner city residents are demanding a larger voice in the policy and operation of their schools which all too frequently are controlled by remote downtown school board members more interested in higher political office than in the education of children. Community control of police and fire departments is also being sought, and with good reason since hostility between largely white policemen and firemen and black residents has been an important factor in civil disturbances.[28]

If Mumford's "basic communism" has partly taken hold in the United States in some watered-down but nonetheless beneficial programs like social security, food stamps and Medicare, it has not by any means become a strong commitment on the part of the American government. Needed more than ever is community control of schools, land, and other community resources — not only in urban areas but elsewhere. Community residents should not only seek greatly expanded federal aid for schools, parks, and social services, but should also insist upon and be granted a large degree of local control as long as basic human rights are not violated. Communities should welcome and respect professionals, be they educators, doctors, or police, for their special skills; professionals, in turn, should recognize that they are part of a community which expects them to involve community members actively in decision-making and in implementation of mutually agreed upon plans. The community has a responsibility to guarantee freedom to experiment with new ideas and professionals have a responsibility to serve the community as resource individuals with special abilities. Neither group should claim superior authority.

Community control of production could be achieved through cooperatives, although cooperation as a substitute for competitive capitalism has generally failed both on the farm and in the city in the United States. A major reason for this failure has been inadequate assistance by the state and federal governments; most cooperatives need low interest loans and other protective forms to survive. [29] Still, a growing number of cooperatives like the Acadian Delight Bakery, an offshoot of the Southern Consumers Cooperative, are thriving today. A color film on this and other southern cooperatives called "The Quiet Revolution" has been made to bolster burgeoning cooperative efforts across the South.[30] In the North, food co-ops like the Onion River Co-op in Vermont which serves hundreds of families have been organized in many areas. Cooperatives and non-profit public industries represent a very real hope for bringing production under direct control of workers and giving the consumer much lower prices and higher quality merchandise.

Common Ownership of Land

In *The Culture of Cities*, Mumford argues forcefully for the communal ownership of land. Stating that a bad land policy "which confused stable occupation and security of tenure with the irrelevant concept of individual ownership, should be obliterated,"[31] he proposes instead a "sound land policy which shall vest ownership in the community, and guarantee tenure, for definitely assigned periods, to those who work the land thriftily and pay their communal taxes."[32] The land originally derived from the community and that is where it belongs again, he asserts. Almost ten years earlier he had noticed great tracts of land suffering from exploitation by private interests, and he wanted to make sure even then that natural resources, especially land, are returned to the community.[33]

One of the most pressing reasons for communal ownership is the possibility of planning with all the needs of the community in mind rather than depending upon the impulses of individual owners. Because of the many misuses of land, some of them tragic, public control — that is, control by the people themselves, not by a handful of businessmen or by a domineering government — should become a goal of every community. This is the policy of community land trusts now operating in Maine, Vermont, and other states. It is commonplace in many parts of Sweden.

In school, students could examine the positive and negative aspects of communal ownership, studying its possible impact on private enterprise, the community and all inhabitants. With community control, would "block busting" by disreputable real estate agents be possible? Would the average citizen have more or less influence on proposed expressways or seizure of park space for commercial purposes? How would people feel about leasing land, for a guaranteed tenure, from a community controlled public authority? Could individuals learn to accept communal ownership and maintenance as a sensible alternative to wasteful development and over-development of land by greedy speculators? How could those who believe private ownership of land is constitutionally guaranteed be convinced that it may not be? Historically and culturally, how has land been used and abused in this country and abroad? How can it be better used in the future? Finally, why is land a valuable resource and why does it become more valuable as population increases?

Students and teachers could discuss ways to find answers to these and a myriad of other questions which would emerge as the search intensifies. Interviewing and questioning parents and neighbors might be instructive. Reading might suggest new directions and filming might result in a different level of awareness of the land as a priceless though steadily shrinking resource. Group and panel discussions on such topics as "The Social and Economic Implications of Returning Land to the Community" might be followed by visits to businesses affected by such a move and to social institutions already in public hands. The study might lead to larger problems like the best ecological uses of land and the kind of society which could be created if exploitation of the land — and exploitation of people — were eliminated.

As in virtually all of Mumford's ideas, no definite limits can be set to contain the questions, problems, and proposals growing from such a comprehensive study. To be most effective, schools would stimulate problem-solving reaching far beyond traditional textbook or discussion methods. Perhaps the best "schools" would be those without walls or institutional rigidities; certainly the ringing of bells to signify changing periods, daily confinement to a crowded classroom, and petty restrictions now imposed would need to be eliminated. Sharply fragmented subjects as we know them today would dissolve in favor of problems or questions like: "Who has the right to own land?" and "What can we learn from American Indians about the earth?" A future-oriented study of land-use and air-use in the year 2000 might trigger the imagination of many young people and pave the way for future planning of all resources.

Students, granted new responsibilities, would learn from the earliest years how to use their time constructively and why some regulations, which they would help establish, are necessary for cooperative work. Boys and girls would "teach" each other and learn from each other continuously. Teachers, given more freedom to innovate, would work with individuals and small groups much of the time. Paraprofessionals — young men and women, mothers, retired people — would assist with clerical work, demonstrations, and projects in the school, and guidance and supervision on outside ventures. The classroom itself would lose its sanctity as groups meet frequently in museums, libraries, churches, homes, offices, storefronts and hospitals instead of in formal school settings. Children with special physical and psychological needs, though possibly continuing to meet in the school proper, would join others in active community involvement whenever circumstances or health permitted. The school would thus become less a building or container for education than a dynamic process leading toward fuller personal and community development.

Biotechnic Versus Capitalistic Economy

Mumford's concept of a biotechnic economy is directly contrary to the capitalistic economy of the United States and other capitalistic nations. Viewing capitalism as more than an economic system, rather "as a tissue of values and purposes, which largely displaced the immaterial goals of a transcendental religion,"[34] Mumford sees capitalism dominated by the "accountancy of numbers" — timing, measuring, counting, labelling, ticketing — which appear in education as marks, examinations, annual inventories, and the like.[35] As capitalism concentrated on the symbols of power and the means of power it "tended to displace the values of art, religion, friendship, parenthood. These goods, the only goods that the poor majority of mankind had ever securely called their own, were despised and belittled."[36] Much to his displeasure, pride and aggression became the central virtues of capitalist morality and acquisition a major impulse.[37]

In the late twenties and into the thirties Mumford was particularly vigorous in his attacks on capitalism, agreeing largely with George Bernard Shaw's criticism of capitalist society[38] and charging that the "qualitative aspect of civilization has no meaning for capitalism, which translates all its values into financial counters."[39] Declaring that capitalism "as a system represents a wholesale perversion of human activities and purposes quite as sinister as any perversion *within* the system,"[40] he optimistically reported in the mid-thirties that capitalism was dead and that attacks on it were therefore wasteful. All effort, he insisted, should be concentrated on creating a new order rather than gloating over the death of an old order. [41] Mumford's premature judgement was repeated later in the same decade when he claimed that the era of expansion was over. Since capitalism belonged to that era, capitalism "as a complex of values, methods, purposes, and means" had become an anachronism. [42]

By the late forties and early fifties with capitalism more powerfully entrenched than ever, Mumford toned down his criticism. He saw capitalism being modified by "more democratic processes, which share out responsibility and thus widen the realm of freedom,"[43] a very different kind of capitalism from a century before. Though the more dramatic faults of this system — child labor, closed shops, and miserable wages — had indeed been rectified, it is puzzling that Mumford seemingly became tolerant toward a capitalistic system that continued to breed inequalities.

In 1968 Mumford admitted that his biotechnic society could not be capitalist even though capitalism continues to change for the better.[44] He has not backed away entirely from earlier criticism of capitalism, but it would appear that his views have become tempered as he has grown older. Mumford remains opposed to the philosophy of capitalism, but in the final analysis seems naive to believe, as he did in 1951, that even with changes capitalism can "widen the realm of freedom" when minorities are still discriminated against in jobs and housing, the poor become poorer and the rich richer, and industry tied to the military seeks bigger, more wasteful weapons of destruction.

A biotechnic economy and biotechnic culture rejects capitalism in favor of democratic socialism which strives for justice and equality not only in word but in deed. Just as Mumford hoped for a post-capitalistic, post-militaristic, post-nationalist era in 1939,[45] we must work toward that end today. In doing so, democracy must become a dynamic process which pervades the day-to-day activities of every person and institution. John Dewey prepares the way when he writes that democracy means:

> . . . a way of living together in which mutual and free
> consultation rule instead of force, and in which co-
> operation instead of brutal competition is the law of life;
> a social order in which all the forces that make for
> friendship, beauty, and knowledge are cherished in order
> that each individual may become what he, and he alone,
> is capable of becoming.[46]

For all his biting comments about Dewey's style of writing, Mumford
has not expressed the essence of democracy more cogently.

Means Toward a Biotechnic Order

Though Mumford devotes much more thought to documenting
the ills of capitalist society and outlining the features of a biotechnic
order than he does to strategy for discarding the old and adopting
the new, he does turn his attention to a few means of achieving the
new order. One vital need is a "quickening of the direct I-and-thou
relationship," an expanding of opportunities for intimate relationships in the family, neighborhood, and community.[47] Though basic
group formations may take new forms in the future, "the intimacies
that they share, the co-operations that they pledge are essential to
the development of man's basic humanity."[48] These survivals of
aboriginal village life are still necessary, Mumford contends, because
without such close relationships among family and friends men and
women will become absorbed into an amphorous mass, losing their
self-identity and capacity to love.[49] Mumford fears a trend away
from interpersonal relations in face-to-face groups and a trend
toward mechanical or electronic devices like television which do not
permit talking back.[50] Global communication and transportation,
no matter how highly developed or instantaneous, will not make the
world a neighborhood if the neighborhood as a center for primary
personal transactions is permitted to languish.[51]

Mumford cannot be faulted in his appeal for deeper, expanded
I-thou relationships within a small enough circle of friends to be
feasible. But his assumption that the neighborhood, as the particular
place where one lives, is of over-riding importance in promoting
personal relationships seems exaggerated and disproportionate to
the real situation in modern life. As theologian Harvey Cox
observes, one's close friends in the city no longer need to live next

door or in an adjacent apartment.[52] The neighborhood as a unit is not as important as it once was since increased mobility has made new alternatives possible. Many people select friends with whom they can relate at varying interpersonal levels, no matter where they happen to live, rather than force themselves upon neighbors in physical proximity.

As long as Mumford stands by his conviction that a biotechnic order demands closer, more honest relationships among families, friends, and fellow workers, it is easy to agree. But when he places so much stress on close-knit neighborhood groups and relationships which could become ingrown and foster provincialism, issue can be taken. Certainly the neighborhood is an important place to stimulate I-thou relationships, but it is only one of many. Mumford relies heavily on the neighborhood concept without fully appreciating its drawbacks: the possibility of increasing isolationism through total preoccupation with immediate local issues and the possibility of perpetuating neighborhood prejudices. In short, his narrow conception of the neighborhood seems no longer adequate.

In another area, Mumford is not only perceptive but ahead of his time when he recognizes the significance of the social sciences in *The Condition of Man:*

> An active knowledge of the social environment and of the behavior of men in social partnership, their needs, their drives, their impulses, their dreams is just as indispensable for working out the new social order as reading, writing, and arithmetic were for those trained to capitalism. And so equally for the arts of society: the art of politics, the arts of enlightened behavior and orderly communication, must become the main field of new inventions.[53]

Though effectively outlining the vital needs of the new order, Mumford typically fails to discuss measures necessary to execute these vital needs. However, sociologists and psychiatrists like David Riesman, Erik Erikson, Robert Coles, Kenneth Keniston, and Philip Slater have been developing during the last two decades the kinds of studies which Mumford feels are vitally necessary.[54] Today the vital needs of society which Mumford mentions as requiring solutions are those being sought by large numbers of young people in high schools and colleges. Book stores abound with volumes of social criticism. Students are returning to Freud to understand better their own childhood and are studying those contemporary sociologists, psychologists, and anthropologists whose investigations have marked and promoted the quickening tempo of social change.[55]

Though Mumford was in the forefront with ideas which today excite many students, it was not until scholars tested them in the field that these potent ideas became educationally significant. It is heartening that Mumford's worthy suggestions have been followed with research and more rigorous analysis than he ever attempted, but regrettable that it took so long for the social sciences to become as significant as they are today in educational theory and practice. How prophetic is his 1940's statement that: "The progress of the biological and social sciences will result in a shrinking of the province of the machine. Here, I believe, is a fact of deep significance: its implications have still to be grasped."[56] Its implications are just now being grasped, although a humanized technology truly in the service of humanity is still distant. If there is more reason for hope today than three decades ago, however, it is because a number of young people seem starkly aware of the dangers of rampant technology. These young people are keenly alert to the potential of humanistically-oriented social-behavioral sciences for social-self-realization.

"Paideia" As Biotechnic Education

Mumford is explicit about some ways of educating for a biotechnic order and about certain aspects of education in a biotechnic culture. He writes that the aim of education is achievement of the maximum variety compatible with the maintenance of order.[57] In spite of his stress on unity in personality and in world culture, Mumford favors as much diversity as possible as long as such diversity can be reconciled with the good of all men everywhere. Deploring sameness and compulsive habits, he believes that education has a responsibility to achieve a dynamic self-renewing social order:

> ... an order in which harmony shall be achieved by the expression, rather than the repressive regimentation, of social diversity, and in which cooperation will take the place of one-sided dominance by despotic individuals, classes, or nations.[58]

An education designed to achieve this new order would be life-long;[59] adult education would be as important as child or youth education. In a biotechnic society, education "will constitute the principal business of life."[60] A new term is needed, however, to distinguish education as continuous, active, and more than schooling from the customary definition of "education" as formal training or from expressions like "self-development" or "character formation"[61] Mumford adopts the Greek word *paideia*, reintroduced by Werner Jaeger in his famous study of Greek ideals,[62] to represent this broader conception of education: "*Paideia* is education looked upon as a lifelong transformation of the human personality, in which every aspect of life plays a part." [63] The lesson of *paideia* is twofold: growth and self-renewal cannot be delegated and development of the whole individual is paramount. [64]

Educationally, this means that each person is given considerable freedom to choose and follow his/her own lifestyle. "Students" of all ages make personal decisions about their present activities and future plans. Individual citizens, not the least students and teachers, have increased opportunities to participate in community political activities and bureaucrats are stripped of much of their power;[65] if Mumford has his way, public life will embrace from one third to one-half of one's time. Upper class education of the past and narrow vocational education of the present are antagonistic to biotechnic education which accents visual and tactile explorations of the environment, group "happenings" or projects centered on themes or areas of interest and relationships between lovers, mates and friends.[66]

As a focus on the whole man, *paideia* seeks to develop the flexible and many-sided personality of the amateur. Biotechnic economy with its normalized standard of consumption and its harnessing of technology for human ends makes leisure time available to everyone, not just to the wealthy, and leisure in turn increases educational possibilities. Mumford sees great value in introducing crafts and skills back into the household[67] as well as in more formal schooling which expands the horizons of individuals beyond the confines of professionalism and vocationalism. But he does not deny the value of vocational education, even if he sincerely thought some progressivists in the twenties and thirties paid unquestioned homage to the unquenchable appetite of industrialism. In fact, he is convinced that every person should participate in the routine duties of workshop, factory, farm or office as a valuable part of their education.[68] Work and the discipline of work should not be divorced from play or leisure or learning; all, he feels, are essential ingredients of *paideia*.

Mumford asserts that schools "must provide a curriculum not aimed at producing more technicians, more engineers, more mathematicians, more scientists, but at producing more whole men and women, at home in *every* part of the environment."[69] Whole men and women can only be "produced," a dubious choice of words to be sure, through a balanced program of hard work and spontaneous play, of vocational training and social responsibility. *Paideia* will seek to create a new type of person who willingly accepts the duties required in a biotechnic order: duties that include communal participation and a holistic approach to one's self and one's world. If it is successful, *paideia* will lead to a One World man who is "no longer the incarnation of his class, his trade, his profession, or his religious faith, any more than he is the incarnation of his exclusive national group."[70] One World man belongs to humankind; he or she is a world citizen first and citizen of a particular nation second.

Paideia as One World education, education for an emergent person and emergent social order, radically differs from education in the past and most education at present. *Paideia*, as Mumford conceives of it, incorporates many ideas of Dewey and Kilpatrick, as well as earlier thinkers going back to Plato, Aristotle, Rousseau, Pestalozzi, and Froebel. But its search for unity and synthesis in the individual and in the world makes it especially close to the reconstructionist philosophy of education. Like perennialism, *paideia* is historical and intellectual, but unlike perennialism its teleology is not based on Thomism nor its practices on abstract learning divorced from experience. Like essentialism, it shows respect for rationality and the acquisition of significant knowledge, but unlike essentialism it is more actively concerned with social change and the integration of learning and doing. Like progressivism, *paideia* is experimental, naturalistic, and flexible. But unlike progressivism, *paideia* emphasizes goals like world community and the need for normative commitment. Like reconstructionism most of all, *paideia* is future-oriented more than past or present-oriented, although historical roots and present realities are never neglected.

Mumford and reconstructionist philosopher Theodore Brameld are similar in their quest for wholeness and synthesis; neither is satisfied with a supposedly "objective" or "purely rational" approach to human problems because both recognize the significance of the "sociology of knowledge" and the importance of subjectivity — of feelings, sensuality, artistic creation. Neither philosopher accepts the notion of an authoritarian deity, preferring instead to rely on a person's potential as a human being capable of becoming a fuller, more integrated personality. Neither accepts the current social system with its inequities and oppression; rather, radical reform through education is posited to change the present direction and priorities of societies that neglect the biological and spiritual requirements of individual people. For both, education cannot be divorced from culture, nor the self from society. Humans create culture and culture creates humans; both continuously interact with each other and with education as a cultural process.[71]

One World man, a long-range but nevertheless possible goal as long as One World is never considered a final or completed goal, is the common goal of *paideia* and reconstructionism. Both philosophies appreciate the futility of men and nations continuing to live as they do today in a world armed to the teeth with devastating intercontinental weapons of war. But even more than recognizing this folly, they are convinced that the resources of life must be distributed more equitably, that developing nations must be granted self-government, that oppressed peoples everywhere from the Indians of North America to the *burakumin* of Japan must be given their due share of material necessities and freedom to decide their own destiny.

For One World man and world community to have a chance of success, every individual will need to undergo self-renewal; in intensive self and social analysis every person will need to question hatreds and fears, racism and prejudice, in himself or herself, and in society. Attitudes, judgments, biases must be rooted out and questioned. In the place of long-held, often stubborn beliefs hopefully will grow a new comprehension of — a new compassion for — every living being. Neither *paideia* nor reconstructionism holds any illusion that the task will be quick nor easy, but neither will settle for less. Education will hold the key to progress in this direction, but not the kind of education so often perpetrated on children and adults by traditional schools and timid teachers.[72]

Paideia, like reconstructionism, requires humanistically innovative schools and socially aware, self-confident, courageous teachers. It expects much of students in terms of self-responsibility to learn and to try different ways of learning; it demands more than superficial familiarity with a subject and more than cursory observation of social phenomena. *Paideia* demands thorough, cross-discipline study as well as participation in the affairs of community, region, and world. As an ongoing process, *paideia* encourages and makes use of human relations techniques and communication skills which lead to more satisfying human relationships. Above all, *paideia* and reconstructionism seek social-self-realization through maximum development of individual abilities within the framework of a social order that guarantees fundamental human rights to all. *Paideia's* goal is nothing less than the attainment of biotechnic civilization.

---

[1]Lewis Mumford, "Glossary," *The Culture of Cities* (New York: Harcourt, Brace, 1938), p. 495.

[2]*Ibid.*, p. 496.

[3]Mumford, *The Culture of Cities*, p. 438.

[4]*Ibid.*, p. 458.

[5]Lewis Mumford, *The Conduct of Life* (New York: Harcourt, Brace, 1951), p. 235.

[6]Lewis Mumford, "The Unified Approach to Knowledge and Life," in *The University and the Future of America* (Stanford: Stanford University Press, 1941), p. 115.

[7]Mumford, *The Culture of Cities*, p. 461.

[8]*Ibid.*, p. 462.

[9]*Ibid.*, p. 463.

[10]Lewis Mumford, *Men Must Act* (New York: Harcourt, Brace and Company, 1939), p. 25.

[11]Mumford, "The Unified Approach to Knowledge and Life," p. 114 and *The Urban Prospect*, (New York: Harcourt, Brace and World, 1968), p. 221.

[12]Mumford, *The Culture of Cities*, p. 464.

[13]Mumford, *The Urban Prospect*, pp. 222-23.

[14]*Ibid.*, p. 222.

[15]Mumford, *The Urban Prospect*, p. 5.

[16]Mumford, *Technics and Civilization*, Harbinger Books (New York: Harcourt, Brace and World, 1963), pp. 399, 404.

[17]Clarence Marsh Case, "Closing in on the Machine," Review of *Technics and Civilization*. *Sociology and Social Research*, XIX (February, 1935), 216-17.

[18]Mumford, *Technics and Civilization*, p. 403.

[19]*Ibid.*

[20]*Ibid.*

[21]*Ibid.*, p. 394.

[22]Mumford, *Technics and Civilization*, p. 403.

[23]*Ibid.*, p. 395.

[24]Stephen Silha, "Communities of People in Touch with Each Other," *Christian Science Monitor*, Jan. 14, 1974. p. 5.

[25]"Group in Boston Does Free Shows," *New York Times*, Sept. 30, 1973, p. 52.

[26]Mumford, *Technics and Civilization*, p. 399.

[27]*Ibid.*, p. 404.

[28]*Report of the National Advisory Commission on Civil Disorders* (New York: Bantam Books, 1968), pp. 299-309.

[29]Sidney Lens, *Radicalism in America* (New York: Thomas Y. Crowell Company, 1969), pp. 101-2.

[30]Jan Hillegas, "Southern Cooperatives," *The Southern Patriot*. December, 1969, p. 4.

[31]Mumford, *The Culture of Cities*, p. 330.

[32]*Ibid.*

[33]Mumford, *Sticks and Stones*, 2nd Rev. Ed. (New York: Dover Publications, 1955), p. 207.

[34]Mumford, "The Social Responsibilities of Teachers and Their Implications for Teacher Education, *Educational Record*, XX (October, 1939), p. 473.

[35]*Ibid.*

[36]Mumford, *Faith for Living* (New York: Harcourt, Brace, 1940), p. 25.

[37]Mumford, *The Condition of Man* (New York: Harcourt, Brace, 1944), pp. 167, 181.

38Lewis Mumford, "Bernard Shaw's Case for Equality," review of *The Intelligent Woman's Guide to Socialism*, by G.B. Shaw, *New Republic*, July 4, 1928, p. 178.

39Mumford, "The Need for Concrete Goals," in *Challenge to the New Deal*, ed. by A.M. Bingham and S. Rodman (New York: Falcon Press, 1934), p. 225.

40Lewis Mumford, "The Waste Land," *New Republic*, July 10, 1935, p. 258.

41Mumford, "The Need for Concrete Goals," pp. 225-26.

42Mumford, "The Social Responsibilities of Teachers," pp. 474-75.

43Mumford, "Toward a Free World: Long-Range Planning Under Democratic Control." Address delivered at a Conference on World Order, Rochester, N.Y., November 13, 1951.

44Mumford, Private interview, Leverett House, Harvard University, March 29, 1968.

45Mumford, "The Social Responsibilities of Teachers," p. 498.

46John Dewey, "Education and Social Change," *Social Frontier*, III (May, 1937), p. 238.

47Mumford, *The Transformations of Man*, p. 147.

48*Ibid.*, pp. 145-46.

49*Ibid.*

50Mumford, Private interview, Leverett House, Harvard University, November 14, 1967.

51Mumford, *The Transformations of Man*, p. 146.

52Harvey Cox, *The Secular City* (New York: The Macmillan Company, 1965), pp. 38-54.

53Mumford, *The Condition of Man*, p. 412.

54See David Riesman, *The Lonely Crowd*; Erik Erikson, *Childhood and Society*; Kenneth Keniston, *The Young Radicals*, Robert Coles, *Children of Crisis*, Philip Slater, *The Pursuit of Loneliness*.

55See Mark Gerzon, *The Whole World is Watching: A Young Man Looks at Youth's Dissent* (New York: Paperback Library, 1969), pp. 149-96.

56Lewis Mumford, "Looking Forward," in *Science and Man*, ed. by Ruth Nanda Anshen (New York: Harcourt, Brace and Company, 1942), p. 354.

57Mumford, "The Unified Approach to Knowledge and Life," p. 124.

58Mumford, "The Social Responsibilities of Teachers," p. 481.

59Mumford, *The Culture of Cities*, p. 474.

60Mumford, *The Transformations of Man*, p. 178.

61*Ibid.*, pp. 178-79.

62Werner Jaeger, *Paideia: The Ideals of Greek Culture* (New York: Oxford University Press, 1939). I.B. Berkson, a reconstructionist-inclined philosopher of education, has also been influenced by Jaeger's study of *paideia*. See *Education Faces the Future* (New York: Harper, 1943), pp. 21, 263-64 and *The Ideal and the Community* (New York: Harper, 1958), p. 214.

63Mumford, *The Transformations of Man*, p. 179.

64*Ibid.*

65Mumford, "The Social Responsibilities of Teachers," p. 495; *Values for Survival* (New York: Harcourt, Brace, 1946), p. 160.

66Mumford, *The Culture of Cities*, p. 473.

67Mumford, *Faith for Living*, p. 250.

68Mumford, *The Culture of Cities*, pp. 473-74.

69Lewis Mumford, "Closing Statement," in *Future Environments of North America*, ed. by F. Fraser Darling and John Milton (Garden City: The Natural History Press, 1966), p. 728.

70Mumford, *The Transformations of Man*, p. 180.

71See Theodore Brameld, *Patterns of Educational Philosophy* (New York: Holt Rinehart and Winston, 1971), pp. 345-563.

72In calling for heroic perseverance in teachers, Mumford once bemoaned: "Timid people, slack-willed people, cagey people — let us confess it freely among ourselves — we have lured too many such people into the school system and have made their way too easy." See Mumford, "The Social Responsibilities of Teachers," p. 498.

✂ chapter 3
organic technology:
in the service
of human beings

AS A CRITIC of dehumanizing technology, technology uncontrolled by human effort and uncontained by human purposes, Mumford is unsurpassed. For many years, he has pleaded for a technology or "technics" sensitive to organic, biological, and aesthetic needs and desires. An organic technology gives power to people themselves for personal and social betterment whereas modern "advanced" technology gives almost unlimited power to an elite group of military, political, financial, and labor leaders. Technological control by this latter power-hungry group has not been achieved by a consensus of humankind, Mumford argues, and therefore does not respect the accumulated values of human history.[1]

A recent critic of technology includes Mumford as one of the "post-industrial prophets" he studies.[2] Though demonstrating a reasonably good understanding of and appreciation for Mumford's reservations about technology in the context of human cultures, Huhns claims that "In the 1970's Mumford's historically grounded humanism may seem quaint, even romantic, studded with unabashed manifestoes."[3] He criticizes Mumford for not being in tune with present technological realities and positive future possibilities. But it may well be that other "post-industrial prophets" like Jacques Ellul with his fatalistic attitude toward technology, Marshall McLuhan with his overreliance on the medium as the message, and Buckminster Fuller with his quantitative bias and grandiose technological fantasies, are out of step with the organic needs and potentialities of human beings. Mumford may be the soundest, most humane, most realistic interpreter of all these "prophets." Rather than being quaint, his humanism may be precisely what modern technology needs in the 1970's and beyond.

Like a number of contemporary critics, Mumford deplores the increasing mechanism and technological extremism of present-day society and the resulting alienation and depersonalization. "Many vital human needs," he observes, "have been frustrated by our one-sided overemphasis on the quantitative and the mechanical; this is true both in thought and in social and personal development."[4] As a symbol, the machine[5] may have represented accurately the crude industrial culture of the mid-19th century, but at least by the mid-twentieth century we ought to have realized that the machine "represents only a fragment of the human spirit."[6]

It would be incorrect to maintain that Mumford is totally opposed to modern technology because of the serious reservations he holds about the historic and present uses of it. Mumford does hope to alter the relatively positive treatment of technology in *Technics and Civilization* when he criticizes the early book as naive and written by a young man.[7] At the same time, he is as critical of those who would retreat entirely *from* technology and its potential benefits as he is toward those who would retreat *to* the machine as some kind of grace-bestowing instrument. Neither damning technology as utterly hostile to man, nor praising it as man's salvation in an ever more complex world, will suffice. Romanticism as "an emotional oasis in the desert of industrialism"[8] has much to offer with its emphasis on feelings and emotion, playfulness and spontaneity, but so too does technology with its "promise of release from compulsory labor and every form of external slavery."[9] The fundamental question to be asked of any technological device or proposal should be: "What essential human need, viewed in historic perspective, is being fulfilled or is being sacrificed?"[10]

This question needs to be asked constantly by educators, whether of the architectural design of a proposed school building, the choice of a "teaching machine," or the computerized schedule of class time is at stake. Does this building plan satisfy the organic criteria of sunlight, warmth in feeling as well as temperature, flexibility with some degree of permanence, proper scale for a child, and a sense of freedom? Or does it look more like a warehouse than an inviting learning center? Are impersonal, antiseptic hallways featured rather than airy, friendly passageways; splendid intercoms, buzzers and bells but few spaces for informal face-to-face discussions; plenty of expensive electronic marvels like closed-circuit television but very limited funds for extending class experiences beyond the building proper to the community, region, and world outside?

Does a particular programmed learning device perpetuate the cramming of facts and the acquisition of knowledge rather than help a student learn how to learn and how to function as a social being? Should a school or university accept the same premise of the factory, as Mumford has charged, "the belief that fragments of mechanical production or fragments of knowledge are real, are significant, and are valuable in themselves?"[11] Should accountability schemes be based upon an industrial model? Should the purpose of education be to train children to fit into and promote an acquisitive society? Or, rather, should the purpose of education be to prepare children to question acquisitive, mechanistic values and to discover morally responsible personal and social values?

Should educational institutions be tightly structured time-wise as well as subject-wise and thereby lend themselves to efficient operation, or should they be loosely organized and loosely structured thereby permitting maximum experimentation by students and teachers? How much or how little structure is necessary for creative endeavor in the arts, humanities, social sciences, physical sciences? How can a school best be organized to encourage interdisciplinary study and maximum social-self-actualization?

No one has any final answers to these and other questions, but no educator should therefore avoid serious inquiry of this kind. To shrug off questions revolving around personal or depersonal instruments, attitudes, and approaches is to acquiesce in the face of an ever more complicated and demanding technology. Educationists cannot afford to turn the other way when surrounded by the latest array of technological hardware and software accompanied by eager hucksters. Neither should they look away when confronted with new school construction, centralized educational parks, and radical proposals for decentralized facilities in factories, libraries, churches, and museums. If Mumford's fundamental question regarding the fulfillment or the sacrifice of human needs is consistently acted upon in favor of humanistic rather than mechanistic goals, the school would become a much stronger humanizing force in a highly mechanized society.

New World and One World Education

Characteristically examining technology from an historical perspective, Mumford considers a few implications in technological development for education. The discovery of printing, for instance, brought great losses as well as gains: printing made reading and writing accessible to all members of the community, not just to an elite minority. But with mass production of books, he observes, came a demand for "mass production of suitable standardized minds."[12] Education, conceived as book-learning, "was supposed to abbreviate the slow necessities of life,"[13] and this led to a wholesale systematic education which Mumford has always deplored. Anything that smacks of wholesale or systematic learning is immediately suspect whether prompted by the printing press or by so-called "teaching machines."

Teaching machines threaten "to abbreviate the slow process of life,"[14] he feels, creating negative alienation and lessening rather than increasing opportunities for human contact. Mumford has called B.F. Skinner a kind of Buckminster Fuller of the educational world: a mind like Skinner's is dangerously fanatic even though clever and seemingly humane.[15] Behaviorism may successfully reinforce the status quo and Skinner may achieve certain learning "successes," but what kind of person is being developed or encouraged? Mumford's harsh and sweeping denunciation of Skinner is another expression of his belief that education is a slow organic process which emphasizes the giving and receiving of human love more than the accumulation of abstract or concrete knowledge.

Mumford credits John Amos Comenius, the Moravian teacher and philosopher, with pointing out the revolutionary implications of a systematic universal education and lauds him for placing manual exercises and drawings on a par with verbal learning. Still, Comenius held an essentially mechanical world view, speaking of the will as a wheel and desires and affections as weights in his description of the movements of the soul. Mumford is critical of Comenius, too, for inventing the monitorial system of teaching very large groups as a way of reducing costs.[16] To his own credit,

Mumford recognizes the disturbing paradox in the principal of mass education: "From the beginning, the humanitarian ideal of a systematic education for all was combined with a mechanical pedagogy that invalidated it."[17]

This weakness of mass education appears in the present mechanization of education through regurgitating knowledge in examinations, especially through evaluation based on objective examinations corrected by machines. Much of the difficulty stems from New World ideology, he believes, an ideology centered on capitalist cupidity and mechanistic models. Because of the anti-personal, anti-communal bias of the New World ideology, virtually all the means of liberation — including technology — tended to work against rather than for liberation.[18]

The underlying aim of New World education is:

> . . . the fabrication of Mechanical Man: one who will accept the mechanical world picture, who will submit himself to mechanical discipline, who in thought and act will enlarge the empire of the machine.[19]

Mumford thoroughly rejects New World education in favor of One World education which emphasizes education for actualized whole men and women who adopt an organic world picture rather than a mechanical one. The alternative to New World ideology is profound concern for the basic rights of every human being; the alternative to New World education is One World education based on love of all mankind, love as:

> . . . the central element of integration: love as erotic desire and procreativeness, love as passion and aesthetic delight, lingering over images of beauty and shaping them anew, love as fellow feeling and neighborly helpfulness, bestowing its gifts on those who need them, love as parental solicitude and sacrifice, finally, love with its miraculous capacity for overvaluing its own object, thereby glorifying it and transfiguring it, releasing for life something that only the lover at first can see.[20]

"Loving underlies effective learning . . . No teaching machine can supply this,"[21] Mumford writes in The Myth of the Machine. Can anyone who accepts his assumptions about love and learning deny the fact that "teaching machines" (or computer-assisted instruction) totally fail to supply or inspire love? If loving is as central to learning as Mumford claims, can any technological device fulfill the need for love and loving even in part? Mechanical and electronic apparatus cannot give or receive love and for this reason, above all others, educationists should soberly debate every possible application of technology.

Educational institutions in a biotechnic order would make use of only those mechanical devices that increase freedom not decrease it, that humanize learning not dehumanize it, and then only after prolonged scrutiny. The criteria would always be: does this or that "machine" (device, contraption, piece of equipment or apparatus) interfere with, retard, or come into negative conflict with humanistic values like love, emotion, sharing, social intercouse? Is this or that learning device necessary and, if necessary, is it desirable? Does it infringe upon or limit the possibilities for loving as outlined so eloquently by Mumford?

Technological instruments should not be discarded simply because they do not and cannot hold the promise of love or because they slight subjective qualities and accent the objective. But neither should they be used if they monopolize the learning process or replace direct contact between students and teachers and students and other students. Opportunities for love and feeling, participatory democracy and cooperation, should be vastly increased in educational settings, and opportunities for knowledge gathering through technological means alone should be lessened. Mumford's most important charge to educators is to question and weigh the implications of technology on the person and the social group before adopting one means or another. In this he has provided a great service for professional educators who notoriously make impulsive moves without thoughtfully considering consequences or analyzing implications.

The Person and the Megamachine

In his outstanding volume on the history of technology, *The Myth of the Machine*, Mumford discusses two basic aspects of the machine: one negative, coercive, destructive and one positive, life-promoting, constructive.[22] In many ways, he was more interested in the latter aspect in his youth, but as Mumford felt increasingly that technology was grossly misapplied,[23] he criticized the negative, dangerous, threatening aspects of technology. More and more he discounted the claims of those who maintain that technology holds the key to man's survival, even though he continued to look at both the positive and negative possibilities of technology.

In his recent wide-ranging analysis of the role of technology in human history. Mumford challenges the popular over-emphasis on early man as tool maker and tool user. Ritual, language, and social development were just as important — or more important — than material "tools;" dreams, images and sounds, symbols of all sorts played a significant part in the evolution of human cultures. [24] Mumford explores the contributions of early man in terms of domestication and social organization, leading to his important concept of the megamachine or, simply put, the "Big Machine" which includes all of the components — political, economic, military, bureaucratic — of the machine. The technical equipment derived from the megamachine he calls "megatechnics" in contrast to the "technics" of a smaller-scale, more diversified, more organically-based technology. [25] From the building of pyramids with slave labor to rocket and missile building in our own age, the megamachine has had — and continues to have — a powerful hold on civilization.

In the second volume of *The Myth of the Machine,* titled *The Pentagon of Power,* Mumford continues his comprehensive analysis of technology from the fifteenth century to the present. It is a vast, alternately depressing and encouraging volume which further defines and dissects the megamachine and megatechnics. *The Pentagon of Power* has much to say to educators; early in the first chapter, for instance, Mumford observes that American colonists who justified their overthrow of English rule in the name of freedom, equality, and the right of happiness retained the institution of slavery and put steady military pressure on the Indians whose lands they seized by deception and force. [26]

How many social studies teachers and their students explore the "New World dream" and the nightmare which it became? "Wherever Western man went, land robbery, lawlessness, culture-wrecking, and the outright extermination of both wild beasts and tame men went with him," [27] Mumford claims. This condemning statement alone could form the basis of a provocative study of American history. To what extent is it an accurate and fair indictment? What examples can be cited to both defend and attack this accusation? Why did New World man adopt Old World institutions and practices? What can be done today to rectify some of the travesties of the past? What kinds of action should be taken to fulfill — rather than negate — the ideals of freedom, equality, and love which the American dream professes? These and other questions could play a significant role in a human-centered curriculum.

Mumford suggests a number of other ripe topics for study. The notion of "the more rapid the movement the greater the improvement" which fascinated the frontiersman as well as the "mechanical pioneers" of the past and present could be explored. [28] This notion or assumption has been embraced unquestionably by American highway builders whose interstate highway system slices up city and countryside. The gross disfiguration of the landscape, as well as the social cost to people, has been documented well by Kenneth Schneider in a lively book that deserves attention: *Autokind vs. Mankind: An Analysis of Tyranny, A Proposal for Rebellion, A Plan for Reconstruction.* Schneider quotes Mahatma Gandhi who shares Mumford's belief: "There is more to life than increasing speed." [29]

One of Mumford's chief criticisms of the megamachine is the predominance of order, regularity, predictability, and centralized power. Complex phenomena must be reduced to the measurable and the repetitive. But "the actual world occupied by organisms" — particularly human beings —" is one of literally indescribable richness and complexity," he asserts, and only a small part of the transformations that take place are visible or can be reduced to mathematical symbols. [30] Form, color, odor, tactile sensations, emotions, feelings, dreams would suffer qualitatively from any attempt to quantify them.

Mumford develops this theme at length and condemns those who take a narrow, deterministic, mechanical view of man; Fuller, Johnson and Masters, and Skinner all come in for scathing criticism. Writes Mumford: "To dismiss as non-existent what happens to be indescribable is to equate existence with information." [31] Clearly, existence is a great deal more for Mumford than the observable and measurable. Educators might well heed his warning which relates directly to the growing trend toward "accountability" and "behavioral objectives" in education. Rather than separating learning into a series of minute parts and depending upon rigid "pre-tests" and "post-tests" for measurement as if a physical system were being studied, educators ought to do the opposite with children and youth:

> ... assemble more and more parts into a pattern of organ-
> ization that, as it approaches more closely to living
> phenomena reacting within a living environment,
> becomes so complex that it can only be reproduced and
> apprehended intuitively in the act of living, since, at least
> in man, it includes mind and the infra- and ultra-
> corporeal aspects of mind.[32]

Equating organisms with machines as Descartes and his counter-parts did or reducing human beings to machine-like objects is dangerous folly.

Mumford's discussion of the polytechnic tradition, the tradition of a mixed technology which respects subjective feelings as well as muscular strength and mechanical skill, is important for educators. Aesthetic expression is an integral part of the polytechnic heritage, especially in terms of handicrafts, but the aesthetic dimension has not been given a chance to flourish in today's megatechnic-oriented society. Nevertheless, some individuals recognize the value of the aesthetic and have built upon the polytechnic tradition in the small craft enterprises they have started. The back-to-the-land movement, the flowering of backyard and community gardens, the development of cottage industries, and the growth of "farmers' markets" as outlets for crafts and organically grown vegetables have been reactions to an over-industrialized, over-automated society. So, too, has been ex-perimentation with alternative technologies: windmills, methane generators, and solar energy. In all of these efforts, the aesthetic quality of working the soil with a hand tool, building and observing a graceful windmill, or constructing a small house with one's own hands is an important ingredient in each experience.[33]

One ingenious individual, an army lieutenant who served in Vietnam, has designed a simple irrigation pump driven by bicycle or motorcycle that the Vietnamese people themselves can build from discarded war materials.[34] Inspired by Vietnamese peasants, he has spent many thousands of hours designing and testing his idea. Convinced of the pump's practicality in areas that depend upon irrigation, the lieutenant sought development funds from a number of sources, but without success. Especially disheartening was the response from the Agency for International Development through

Ellsworth Bunker, U.S. Ambassador in Saigon at the time. Bunker called the pump "inefficient, unwieldy, and unstable," asserting that the Vietnamese people were not interested, and claiming that gasoline-driven pumps were superior.[35] Bunker's conventional, megatechnic-oriented response is indicative of a prevailing attitude toward simple machines which may do a better, more economical, certainly more ecologically sound job if given a chance.

Are teachers exploring the polytechnic tradition with their students, going back to the use of simple machines and examining the handicraft tradition restored in the nineteenth century by William Morris and renewed once again in the 1970's? How often are teachers questioning values implicit in mass production and considering the aesthetic quality — or lack of it — in different kinds of work? Have teachers taught about food and food preparation, for instance, not just by visiting a modern bakery and reading propaganda from giant food processors but by questioning the way food is grown, examining the nutritional content of foods, and exploring the world food crisis and how it affects many children and adults? Mumford believes that a great wealth of knowledge about regional foods and food preparation has been lost; foods today have become more and more sterile looking and tasting. This is another example of the abandonment of a mixed technology:

> Here again, the polytechnic tradition stands for variety and esthetic discrimination as essential conditions for heightening organic activity. In cooking, clothing, bodily ornament, and gardening, as in painting and sculpture, no culture had to wait for the 'industrial revolution' for endless modifications and qualitative improvements.[36]

One of the richest concepts for educators in the *Pentagon of Power* is that of "technological compulsiveness: a condition under which society meekly submits to every new technological demand and utilizes without question every new product, whether it is an actual improvement or not."[37] Teachers and administrators should be held accountable for helping students become more aware of the presence of "technological compulsiveness" in America and in other parts of the world. This would mean launching a probing critique of highly industrialized nations in general and American culture in particular. In what ways do Americans succumb to "technological compulsiveness" in terms of consumer products like electrical appliances and recreational vehicles? How many resources do Americans waste and what are the alternatives to wasteful consumption of goods? How do corporations foster "technological compulsiveness?" What attitudes do people have toward the development of new weapons systems? How can ecologically anachronistic attitudes toward new technological devices — whether for military, space or civilian use — be altered? What role does the media, especially television advertising, play in the promotion of "technological compulsiveness?" In what ways does the capitalist system of the United States or the Communist system of the Soviet Union depend upon this phenomenon for its survival?

Examples of "technological compulsiveness" would be relatively easy for students to identify and research if educators have the will to encourage such investigation. Perhaps they should start by focusing on their own lifestyle: have they themselves been manipulated by advertisers or by cultural institutions to want more than they need? Have they accepted unquestioningly the growth of deadly atomic warheads, the use of napalm to incinerate human beings, and the continuing research on ever more sophisticated anti-personnel weapons? With their students, they could explore the many dastardly, life-denying aspects of technology and then seek life-affirming, life-fulfilling alternatives.

Most important would be the search for workable ways to dismantle the megamachine that erodes the safety, health and well-being of humankind. Petitions, boycotts, strikes and other means of peaceful civil disobedience could be promoted as legal and desirable rather than as taboo strategies. Learning political skills, organizing skills, and skills of cooperation would become fundamental. So, too, would be action research carried on by means of interviews, practicums, and direct involvement in political, labor, and governmental organizations or agencies.

Never would ongoing contact with others in value clarifying, consciousness-raising, intimate groups in an educational setting be neglected, however. In fact, the development of a support group whose task is criticizing American culture and finding ways of improving it would be vital. Teachers, students, and community people together could openly share their disagreements and differences as well as similarities in a skillfully led group. Though the exploration might begin with an analysis of the notion of "technological compulsiveness," this study, like the regional survey and plan Mumford often recommends, would lead far afield with no apologies. Some of the most provocative, lasting learnings would occur as a result of unexpected encounters. Instead of the usual loathing of this kind of teaching-learning by some accountability addicts, opportunities for spontaneous, incidental learning would be enthusiastically welcomed.

Mumford considers war "the body and soul of the megamachine."[38] War or the threat of war, he argues, "is the ideal condition for promoting the assemblage of the megamachine[39] and the staggering waste which results from war leads to huge profits for some and a social deficit for many. The twentieth century megamachine has grown steadily since the First World War, he believes, when military conscription was introduced in England and the United States and industrial conscription in England. Scientists were put to work everywhere to develop destructive weapons and governments controlled information being given to their own people. Stalin's Russian megamachine was similar to the ancient megamachine in its dependence upon coercion, terrorism, and suppression, and Hitler as "the chief agent in the modernization of the megamachine"[40] enlisted most Germans in his totalitarian mission. Besides restoring the most diabolical aspects of the ancient megamachine, the Nazis also developed sophisticated procedures for mass control, procedures which Mumford believes are being perfected today by corporate and government megamachines with the help of spying devices, market research, and computerized files or data banks on the private lives of individuals.[41]

The mass extermination of civilians in London and Rotterdam by the Germans or in Dresden and Tokyo by the United States showed the megamachine at its totalitarian worst. Finally, the creation of the atom bomb brought fragmented parts of the megamachine together and stimulated further development of the ever-more-lethal war machine. In Mumford's view, both the ancient and the modern war-oriented megamachine are oriented toward death, but the new megamachine knows no bounds since it is commanded by remote control and keeps its bosses physically and emotionally detached, high above the clouds or deep in a missile silo.[42]

The military megamachines of the world are growing in number and in power. France and China have been testing nuclear weapons and recently India joined the ranks. Other countries may follow suit. Mumford envisions several possibilities: that the United States and the Soviet Union will destroy each other or that these giants will coalesce with smaller megamachines on a global basis. "The only rational alternative" to these possibilities, he indicated, "is to dismantle the military megamachines."[43] This is indeed a radical alternative, but one that ought to be weighed seriously. It is an alternative that might become a focus for study in schools and universities.

A number of organizations are now providing resources to help teachers and students confront complexities of the military megamachine. Among these are the Center for War/Peace Studies which publishes *Intercom*, a journal featuring various strategies (games and simulations, especially) and helpful background information for teachers. The peace education division of the American Friends Service Committee prepares materials on current issues, organizes workshops, and trains peace organizers-educators. A third group, the Institute for World Order, has developed a school program which provides information about curriculum materials, teaching methods, and practical approaches for implementing the study of world order issues and values. Peace and war prevention is a major world order value goal of the Institute and its school program publication, *Ways and Means of Teaching About World Order*, often features articles on this subject. The school program makes constructive use of technology through an assortment of books, booklets, pamphlets and individual lesson plans; films, filmstrips and tapes; and simple to complex games and instructional simulations which generate participation and make real issues come alive.

Teachers might center their exploration of the modern military megamachine on a series of pivotal questions: How can conflict, a part of life, be resolved without violence?[44] How do you resolve conflicts in your own life? What new weapons system is the United States developing or hoping to develop in the future? What effects will new weapon development have on the natural environment, on the economy, on social problems? How can disarmament be speeded up? What manifestations of the military megamachine do you see around you? How can you present your ideas to legislators, parents and others most effectively? How can nations cooperate rather than compete? What kind of global order will be necessary to assure peaceful relations rather than war among nations? How can such a world order be achieved? What can individuals do toward this end?

The military megamachine could and should become a central theme in education of the present and future; no other concern is literally as threatening to human health and safety as this and none has been more neglected in the schools and universities of America. Mumford should stir every educator to redirect his energies toward an investigation of what he calls the "megatechnic wasteland" [45] whether that be manifested in military extravagance, space rocketry, nuclear power development, super-highway building, skyscraper production, or any other form of the "pyramid-complex."

Fellow Critics of the Megamachine

Ben Seligman, author of *Most Notorious Victory: Man in an Age of Automation*, shares Mumford's growing fear that technology ominously threatens essential human qualities. Not unlike Mumford, he contrasts modern man's disintegrative predicament with primary man's striving to integrate work, ritual, play, and leisure into a significant whole. [46] Seligman, influenced by experts on technology like Siegfried Giedion, Jacques Ellul, Norbert Wiener, Erich Kahler, and Herbert Marcuse as well as by Mumford, agrees with all of them that "technology has emptied work of significance and that such a development is bound to create conditions in which a sense of estrangement flourishes." [47]

Robert L. Heilbroner, a distinguished economist and authority on technology, calls for public control of "the technological invasion" in a foreword to Seligman's book, warning that "the coming generation — the children who are now in school — will be the last generation able to seize control over technology before technology has irreversibly seized control over it." [48]

Recently, Theodore Roszak, like Mumford, has been attacking what he calls the technocracy, "the regime of experts — or of those who can employ the experts." [49] The central goal of the technocratic society "is to keep the productive apparatus turning over efficiently." [50] Roszak has more faith in the young to protest expansion of the technocracy than Mumford; Mumford claims that many young dropouts, members of the counterculture, are addicted to "megatechnic primitivism." [51] At the same time, Mumford joins Roszak in praising the revolt of some young people against an overpowered technology. [52] Overall, Roszak seems to have a better understanding of contemporary youth culture than Mumford who seems quick to attack youth for "barbarism" and the excesses of some. But both scholars appreciate the dangers inherent in a "technocracy" or in "megatechnics" and both are hopeful that a more humane technology will be created. "The technocracy will not be overthrown," Roszak writes. "It will be displaced — inch by inch — by alternative realities imaginatively embodied."[53] Mumford asserts:

> Though no immediate and complete escapement from the ongoing power system is possible, least of all through mass violence, the changes that will restore autonomy and initiative to the human person all lie within the province of each individual soul, once it is roused.[54]

Erich Fromm, who has remarked that future historians will consider Mumford's *The Myth of the Machine* "one of the prophetic warnings of our time,"[55] observes that the present technological system has two guiding principles: "that something *ought* to be done because it is technically *possible* to do it" and "maximum efficiency and output" is imperative.[56] Fromm, like Mumford, has been writing about a more humanized technology for years and both hope desperately that men and women will make it happen.

Authoritarian and Democratic Technology

Mumford, clearly, is not alone in his troubled concern for the implications of technology on our lives. In many ways he has been the forerunner of those now expressing serious reservations and anguished fears about the machine and machine-dominated culture; in 1940, for instance, he observed that the counterpart of the soldier in the industrial world is the robot — the worker who becomes a cog in an impersonal machine that runs him.[57] Almost thirty years later, John Kenneth Galbraith arrived at virtually the same conclusion: "I am led to the conclusion, which I trust others will find persuasive, that we are becoming the servants in thought, as in action, of the machine we have created to serve us."[58]

The tendency in mass production, Mumford wisely states, is for the machine to operate the worker instead of the other way around. The worker becomes de-rationalized under such a system and can only assert his human qualities by "non-participation, by resistance, by throwing a monkey wrench into the works."[59] A feeling of impotence, of powerlessness, of alienation grows out of what Mumford calls "authoritarian technics,"[60] technology on a giant scale, overbearing, immensely powerful, and controlling rather than controlled. "Democratic technics" which has existed side by side with "authoritarian technics" since late neolithic times is by contrast a small scale method of production "resting mainly on human skill and animal energy but always, even when employing machines, remaining under the active direction of the craftsman or farmer."[61] Mumford sees hope for enriching man's working hours as well as his leisure time in "democratic technics" which places him in charge of technological processes and brings him in closer touch with fellow workers and with the products of his labor. We should be instructing our technology to adhere to social and ethical principles, and not be intimidated by it, he insists.[62]

Historian Merle Curti observes that the machine has been an enemy to those who believe that traditional craftsmanship is still a worthwhile value[63] and to a great extent this applies to Mumford. The machine, particularly the megamachine, is an enemy not only to the craft tradition but to hopes for a more rational technology which satisfies pressing social responsibilities instead of swallowing up millions of workers and billions of dollars in the desperate production of arms and space vehicles. The modern megamachine may be curbed in the future through small, personalized organizations like mystery cults, friendly societies, churches, guilds, colleges, and trade unions, Mumford believes, adding that no wonder sovereign states historically have tried to suppress such threatening organizations.[64] To this list might be added citizen groups developing from George McGovern's candidacy for President, Appalachian mountain groups fighting strip mining and demanding political power, and groups like Friends of the Earth which question the prevailing socio-economic system and its devastating effects on the natural environment and the quality of life in general.

The megamachine can be slightly restrained as a group of senators are demonstrating in terms of military extravagance and as Ralph Nader is proving in the industrial arena, but mere beginnings have been made in this direction. Some young people are justifiably rebelling against the megamechanical qualities of overgrown universities and high school students are starting to reject the impersonality and irrelevance of conventional schools in favor of schools like the Milwaukee Independent School which emphasizes individual projects tied to a student's own interests.[65] More and more people are fighting the "megamachine" of interstate highways which divide cities into isolated camps and displace literally thousands of people. And increasing numbers of individuals are turning to old and new arts and crafts as a way of combatting the "megamachine" and its manifestations in terms of negative alienation and impotence. Many new craftsmen might agree with a one-time engineer in Virginia, now a maker of clay pots, who reflects on his former job: "I was punching someone else's clock."[66]

Educational institutions could fight the tendency toward bigness exemplified in the megamachine by expanding opportunities for dialogue and individual attention and by creating environments which accent the personal rather than the bureaucratic. They could recruit democratic teachers whose role is more one of enabling or facilitating; in turn, teacher education colleges could shift from training educational technicians to preparing teachers with both competence in their area of specialization and competence in viewing young people as individuals capable of effecting both personal and cultural change.

Cognizant of both transmissive and innovative cultural factors, teachers ideally would encourage students to be independent yet in need of others, individualistic yet cooperative, historical-minded yet tuned to the future, technologically aware yet rejecting technology as a final answer to any social or cultural ill. Above all, teachers would be personal and personable in all their dealings with each other and with students, staff, and community: attacking the impersonalism of electronic equipment when face-to-face meeting would do just as well or better, encouraging respect for opinions which collide with their own, and curbing tendencies toward automating or streamlining learning when such tendencies lean toward standardizing rather than personalizing learning.

An organic, "democratic" technology would fulfill the criterion for the positive, life-promoting, constructive side of technology, in Mumford's view. Such a technology would not hamper human values, but would contribute to them, in some cases even make them possible. New means of food production might be discovered and new kinds of insect control developed to permit worldwide abolition of toxic pesticides. Nuclear medicine, making use of radioactive isotopes in cancer therapy, would be expanded and new ways of providing sight to the blind, hearing to the deaf, mobility to the paralyzed would be investigated. In these and many other ways affecting human health and welfare, technology could become one of humankind's great blessings.

An organic technology is a technology with social controls placed upon it. For example, snowmobiles, trail bikes, swamp buggies, and power boats would not be permitted to invade wilderness areas, upsetting delicate ecological balances, disturbing wildlife, destroying habitats, annoying men and women who seek a respite from the business pressures of their daily lives. New motorized vehicles which today invade once-remote areas will surely turn one of the last refuges from technological society into a haven of mechanical paraphernalia unless severely curbed. A study of the implications of these and other technological inventions on human beings and all organic life would be a worthwhile addition to the high school curriculum, a curriculum which sorely needs to focus on social controls for technology.

Long convinced that man has not achieved the greatest social good from the technological means available to him, Mumford urges that technology be applied to eliminate work which is degrading or involves unwilling drudgery.[67] Technology has brought radical change in the human condition — a "promise of release from compulsory labor and every form of external slavery."[68] The human question — how many lives might be lost without it? — what does it contribute to the worker? — should always outweigh the question of expense or mechanical feasibility when it comes to deciding the value of technology.[69] Questions of value should be addressed to technology in its every form, questions like: Is the saving of a few minutes' commuting time worth the human costs involved in building an expressway across downtown Philadelphia? If a gas-lamp is brighter than a candle, does this mean a gas-lamp is a better source of light? Mumford aptly writes that "it is only in terms of human purpose and in relation to a human and social scheme of values that speed or brightness have any meaning."[70]

Technology is not necessarily good or bad in itself; it is the use to which technology is put and the relationship of that technology to human values which determines whether a particular aspect is beneficial or harmful to humankind. Technology, as Mumford well knows, can provide the means to rebuild old cities and build new ones, create medical breakthroughs, develop safer contraceptives, clean up rivers and lakes, filter the air with mechanical scrubbers, solve waste disposal problems with devices like the auto crusher and fusion torch, and build schools which are less like factories or office buildings and more like aesthetically pleasing community centers.

In short, technology can help provide a decent standard of living for everyone on earth. But Mumford's caution about relying too heavily on technology to solve all of our problems, or to consider it outside the framework of human ends, or to give up one's decision-making capacity to a technology which sometimes makes human choice seem superfluous, is justified and should be heeded. Only an organic technology based on humanistic goals is acceptable to Mumford and nothing less should be acceptable to educators. Mumford would be in full agreement with the anthropologist Ashley Montagu who dramatically asserts:

> If mankind is to be saved, it can be done only by replacing the values of industrial technology with those of humanity, of cooperation, of love. It is only when humanity is in control, that technology in the service of humanity will occupy its proper place in the scheme of things.[71]

Looking into the future, Mumford would also concur with a distinguished ecologist he admires very much, Rene Dubos:

> I am inclined to believe that emphasis in the future will be less on the development of esoteric technologies than on the development of a conservatively decent world, designed to satisfy those needs of human nature that were woven in our genetic fabric during our evolutionary past.[72]

---

[1]Mumford, "Closing Statement," p. 724.

[2]See William Huhns, *The Post-Industrial Prophets* (New York: Harper and Row, 1971), pp. 32-64.

[3]*Ibid.*, p. 34.

[4]Mumford, "Looking Forward," p. 356.

[5]When Mumford uses the term "machine" he uses it as a shorthand reference to the entire technological complex. See *Technics and Civilization*, p. 12.

[6]Lewis Mumford, "Function and Expression in Architecture," *Architectural Record*, CX (November, 1951), 110.

[7]It is interesting to note that one scholar studying Mumford's machine aesthetic at some length fails to recognize his growing scepticism of the machine. See Thomas Reed West, *Flesh of Steel: Literature and the Machine in American Culture* (Nashville: Vanderbilt University Press, 1967), pp. 102-3.

[8]Mumford, *The Conduct of Life*, p. 234.

[9]Mumford, *The Transformations of Man*, p. 177.

[10]Mumford, "Closing Statement," p. 727.

[11]Mumford, "The Unified Approach to Knowledge and Life," p. 122.

[12]Mumford, *The Condition of Man*, p. 256.

[13]*Ibid.*, p. 257.

[14]Mumford, private interview, March 29, 1968.

[15]*Ibid.*

[16]Mumford, *The Condition of Man*, p. 257.

[17]*Ibid.*, p. 258.

[18]*Ibid.*, pp. 258-59.

[19]*Ibid.*, p. 259.

[20]Mumford, *The Transformations of Man*, p. 176.

[21]Mumford, *The Myth of the Machine: Technics and Human Development* (New York: Harcourt, Brace and World, 1967), p. 42.

[22]Mumford, *The Myth of the Machine*, p. 191.

[23]Mumford, *In the Name of Sanity* (New York: Harcourt, Brace, 1954), pp. 35, 23.

[24]Mumford, *Myth of the Machine*, pp. 14-15.

[25]*Ibid.*, pp. 188-89.

[26]Mumford, *The Myth of the Machine: The Pentagon of Power* (New York: Harcourt, Brace Jovanovich, 1970), p. 8.

[27]*Ibid.*, p. 9.

[28]Mumford, *The Pentagon of Power*, p. 22.

[29]Kenneth R. Schneider, *Autokind vs. Mankind*, (New York: Schocken Books, 1971), p. 209.

[30]Mumford, *Pentagon of Power*, p. 54.

[31]*Ibid.*, p. 71.

32Mumford, *The Pentagon of Power*, p. 87.

33For further discussion of the relationship of aesthetics to energy, see "The Science Teacher As Energy Analyst and Activist" by Russell M. Agne, David Conrad, and Robert J. Nash in *The Science Teacher*, 41 (November, 1974), 12-17.

34David F. Salisbury, "Engineer Fights to Turn 'Swords' into 'Plowshares.' " *The Christian Science Monitor*, June 25, 1974, p. F6.

35*Ibid.*

36Mumford, *Pentagon of Power*, p. 141.

37*Ibid.*, p. 186.

38*Ibid.*, p. 241.

39*Ibid.*

40*Ibid.*, p. 248.

41*Ibid.*, p. 250.

42*Ibid.*, pp. 260-68.

43*Ibid.*, p. 257.

44A helpful tool is a multi-media package called "Patterns of Human Conflict" developed by the Center for War/Peace Studies in cooperation with Warren Schloat Productions, hc.

45Mumford, *Pentagon of Power*, p. 300.

46Ben B. Seligman, *Most Notorious Victory: Man in an Age of Automation* (New York: The Free Press,), pp. xiii-xiv.

47*Ibid.*, p. xxiii.

48Robert L. Heilbroner, in foreword to *Most Notorious Victory*, p. x.

49Theodore Roszak, *The Making of a Counter Culture*. Anchor Books (Garden City: Doubleday and Company, 1969), p. 7.

50*Ibid.*

51Mumford, *The Pentagon of Power*, p. 373.

52*Ibid.*, p. 375.

53Theodore Roszak, "htroduction: The Human Whole and Justly Proportioned," in *Sources*, edited by Theodore Roszak. Harper Colophon Books (New York: Harper and Row, 1972), p. xxii.

[54]Mumford, *Pentagon of Power*, p. 433.

[55]Fromm, *The Revolution of Hope: Toward a Humanized Technology* (New York: Bantam Books, 1969), p. 30.

[56]*Ibid.*, pp. 33-34.

[57]Mumford, *Faith for Living*, p. 33.

[58]John Kenneth Galbraith, *The New Industrial State*, Signet Books (New York: New American Library, 1967), p. 19.

[59]Mumford, *In The Name of Sanity*, p. 53.

[60]Mumford, private interview, March 29, 1968.

[61]Mumford, "Authoritarian and Democratic Technics," *Technology and Culture*, V (Winter, 1964), 2-3.

[62]Mumford, private interview, March 29, 1968.

[63]Merle Curti, *The Growth of American Thought* 2nd ed. (New York: Harper, 1951), p. 708.

[64]Mumford, *The Myth of the Machine*, p. 233.

[65]William K. Stevens, "Bright Milwaukee Students Find School Dull and Form Their Own," *New York Times*, February 13, 1970, p. 38.

[66]"The New Craftsmen," *Newsweek*, February 16, 1970, p. 72. Mumford would well understand this man's feeling because he has long felt that the clock introduced mechanical routine into man's life. See Mumford, *Technics and Civilization*, pp. 14-15.

[67]Lewis Mumford, "Leisure to Replace Work?" *Science Digest*, February, 1942, p. 8.

[68]Mumford, *The Transformations of Man*, p. 177.

[69]Mumford, *Technics and Civilization*, p. 411.

[70]Mumford, "Leisure to Replace Work?" p. 8.

[71]Ashley Montagu, *Education and Human Relations*, (New York: Grove Press, 1958), p. 21.

[72]René Dubos, "Avoiding 'Future Shock,' " *Christian Science Monitor*, May 14, 1974, p. F8.

✌ chapter 4
organic architecture:
symbolic and functional

IN A well-documented article on environmental education in *Architectural Forum*, Ellen Perry Berkeley asserts that architecture may not follow Reading, 'Riting and 'Rithmetic as the fourth foundation stone of education, but she continues:

> . . . environmental studies are increasingly making their way into the formal education of children. Maps, models, constructions, games, trips, films, photographs, and television are the media for a message pointing to the importance of environment in its vital sense and in its social and political implications.[1]

This is a heartening development after many years of environmental neglect both inside and outside schools. The examples of environmental education Ellen Berkeley discusses are exciting attempts to focus attention on architecture and the total natural and man-created environment.

The "Design of Alternative Futures," begun at Berkeley, California, involves students in the design of a future community featuring space frames and space capsules. MATCH boxes (Materials and Activities for Teachers and Children), developed by the Children's Museum of Boston, feature travelling "City" and "Houses" kits that encourage learning by doing. "Planning for Change," a curriculum for fourth and fifth grades developed by C. Richard Hatch Associates and taught in Harlem, helps children see that the environment can be changed by human action. Students analyze their own neighborhood in terms of its people, housing and jobs; plan improvements; and use the entire city as a resource. "Our Man-Made Environment" being tried in Philadelphia, a course in "Urban Affairs" at Philadelphia's Mantua-Powelton Mini-School which operates in a warehouse and in the city at large, and the "Model City Project" also being attempted in Philadelphia are several other examples of exciting environmental programs.[2]

Mumford would grant that many of these experimental projects are not only worthwhile but point toward a more holistic, ecological approach to architecture and education. Innovative programs of this kind underline Mumford's contention that a building is not a self-sufficient structure, but part of a natural and civic environment. As the architect should understand the effects of sunlight, climate, soil, landscape, and local habits and interpret the social functions and needs of a community,[3] so too should children be encouraged to understand environmental limitations and potentialities as well as interpret social forces at work in their local community and communities around the world.

Mumford has always insisted that the community be treated as a major element in design, claiming that before architecture can produce more than isolated masterpieces, "our social skill must be pushed at least as far as our engineering skill, defining the several functions of a city and controlling the use of land for the benefit of the whole community."[4] For Mumford, architecture is a social art which combines form and function, the romantic and the utilitarian, means and ends. He criticizes Benedetto Croce and Geoffrey Scott (the author of The Architecture of Humanism) for seeking "to separate the esthetic moment from the practical, the ethical, and the meaningful attributes of the same activity."[5] But he praises Frank Lloyd Wright for pioneering with modern construction techniques while at the same time creatively grounding his work "in the permanent realities of birth, growth, reproduction, and the natural environment."[6]

More than any other modern architect, Wright fulfills Mumford's criteria for great architecture: Wright thinks "both scientifically, in terms of means, and imaginatively, in terms of the humanly desirable ends for which these means exist."[7] Mumford explains his affinity to architects in general by citing their professional ties not only to means and ends but also to openness and closedness, to extroversion and introversion, to flexibility with some permanence, to the subjective as well as the objective. A mature, modern architecture, if Mumford has his way, "will take into account the functions and purposes of the whole man and not try to whittle him down to the size and shape that will fit some less-than-man-size formula."[8] Wright accomplishes this to a remarkable extent in his organic architecture, although he sells out in his dehumanizing proposal for a mile-high skyscraper and in his plans for "Broadacre City." Henry Hobson Richardson as "the first architect of distinction in America who was ready to face the totality of modern life"[9] comes close to Mumford's high standards. And Louis Sullivan, in Mumford's words "the Whitman of American architecture," [10] understands the architect's responsibility to organize the forces of modern society, discipline them for humanistic ends, and express them in the plastic-utilitarian form of building. [11]

These great architects take a much more philosophical, organic view of architecture, like Mumford himself, than many who forfeit their professional, aesthetic and social responsibilities by designing what Mumford accurately calls "barracks architecture" or "picture-book architecture." In the first group are most modern factories, office buildings, schools, and high-rise apartments and in the second many homes, summer residences ("chalets"), gas stations, and restaurants. "Barracks architecture," Mumford notes, generally "arises out of a very narrow and imperfect idea of human needs: it is produced to fit a single purpose — land speculation or profit-making."[12] "Picture-book architecture" is oriented toward eye-catching novelty, dishonest copying or distortion of past forms, and easy profits for the builder-operator. Instead of designs which give increasing weight to biological, psychological, social, and personal criteria, as Mumford prefers,[13] a good many modern architects regard mechanical function and visual nostalgia as the most important design criteria. Perhaps Wolf Von Eckardt, architectural writer for *The Washington Post* and one of the country's more influential critics, is fully justified in accusing leaders of the architectural profession today of "arrogant social irresponsibility."[14]

The Total Environment

Mumford's view of architecture as "the complete synthesis of all the elements that are necessary for a life-sustaining social environment"[15] is far from narrow or limited; architecture, he writes, is concerned not only with the building itself, but "with the whole complex out of which architect, builder, and patron spring, and into which the finished building . . . is set."[16] To be honest, life-affirming and socially functional as well as aesthetically pleasing, modern architecture desperately needs a modern culture that encourages these qualities; architecture, in turn, can and should express the humanizing attributes of such a culture.

It is clear that Mumford cares deeply about the total environment in which architecture plays both a symbolic and functional part. While he never underestimates the importance of the building itself as a vital experience, commenting that one does not merely see a building with one's eye, "one feels it; one adjusts the muscles to it; one's nervous tonus is lowered or heightened by it,"[17] his chief interest lies in buildings "as a many-sided expression of the human mind: not just its intelligence and practical mastery, but its feelings, its prophetic aspirations, its transcendental purposes."[18] Every building performs work, even if it is only to shed the rain, but every building also makes a visual impression upon the beholder and modifies at least in some slight way the feeling or behavior of the viewer.[19]

Mumford has long been a scathing critic of architects, not simply those who build "barracks" or "picture-book" buildings, but those who properly reject antiquated symbols while also rejecting "human needs, interests, sentiments, values, that must be given full play in every complete structure."[20] The architects of the United Nations headquarters in New York, for example, failed to do justice to the symbolic and expressive functions of architecture by treating the skyscraper office building as a monument.[21] Of high-rise buildings generally, Mumford consistently condemns the notion that a skyscraper is "a proud and soaring thing:"

> This was giving the skyscraper a spiritual function to perform: whereas, in actuality, height in skyscrapers meant either a desire for centralized administration, a desire to increase ground rents, a desire for advertisement, or all three of these together — and none of these functions determines a 'proud and soaring thing.'[22]

Mumford's criticism of the United Nations tower neglects the fact that large amounts of office space were needed by various U.N. departments; ample space in New York City might not have been available otherwise without burrowing into the ground, an alternative Mumford would surely oppose. Nevertheless, he makes a valid point when observing that skyscrapers in general, and the U.N. tower in particular, symbolize impersonality, bureaucracy, congestion; values not worthy of promotion.

In a wider sense, skyscrapers are symbols of the machine with its typical reliance on quantity, automation, and the anti-organic. Because of its sameness, monotonous multiplication of spaces, immense size, and accent on financial status, the skyscraper symbolizes modern industrial culture's preoccupation with the mechanical or technical dimension of life rather than with the biological, the social, and the personal.

The United Nations building might symbolize man's unlimited creativity; his capacity for strong emotional attachment; his concern for every human being and all forms of life; his desire for fellowship within his own community, his region, and his world instead of the powerful and privileged realm of bankers, brokers, and corporation executives so close at hand. If architecture's key symbolic role is accepted, it would be difficult to deny that the United Nations tower symbolizes bigness and bureaucracy more than personal and cultural fulfillment in terms of man's unbounding creativity and desire for world peace and fellowship.

The most successful architecture combines form and function or, put another way, creative design and technical accuracy or, still another, symbolic meaning and functional integrity. Mumford's enthusiasm for Wright's engineering innovations is balanced by Wright's sensitivity to the land and to man's needs and purposes. Architecture fails, Mumford knows, if it does not express in symbolic form the function of a building as well as the aspirations of those who use it. Form may follow function, but function or mechanical efficiency should not prevail to the extent that symbolic meaning depends only upon machine values and not upon human values. To have functional integrity, a building cannot pretend to "do" something that it does not or cannot do; rather, it should be designed efficiently and in tune with its purpose. At the same time, it is neither honest nor successful if its symbolic role as an integral part of the natural, historical, and social environment is neglected.

Architecture and Education

The importance of architecture for education rests upon the synthesis of function and symbol. As a symbol of man's ideal self, architecture has the power to express a great range of human feelings, beliefs, attitudes, and visions of the future. As a functional art which relies upon mathematics, engineering, and various forms of technology, architecture contains numerous possibilities for exploring scientific-technical problems ranging from the strength and potential uses of materials to the making of blueprints for an experimental school or city center. Architecture can be an effective ingredient of environmental education by providing opportunities for students and teachers to visit, examine, and evaluate structures and architectural complexes that do and do not combine symbol and function. Students might construct models, perhaps even buildings themselves, which make provision for both important aspects.

In Otaniemi, Finland, students of the Technological Institute played a major role in planning and constructing a large student center-cafeteria-auditorium called Dipoli which ranks in the author's opinion as one of the most impressive and important buildings of the latter half of the twentieth century. Not only magnificent to behold, Dipoli is an eminently functional structure providing attractive spaces for student activities and recreation, flexible spaces for dining and dramatics which can be enlarged through flexible walls to seat many hundreds of people or made smaller to seat only thirty, and several unique restaurants open year-round to residents of nearby Helsinki as well as to students. The architects and student builders of Dipoli tried many innovative engineering techniques not only in the movable walls but in the undulating, poured concrete roof punctured by irregularly shaped skylights. The whole effect of light and shadows created by the roof, sky-lights, clerestories, and large windows is not only dramatic but expressive of man's highest creative potential. One can readily see why students are proud of this organic structure which took much time and great skill to build. With huge granite chunks blasted from the foundation piled around its base and sited on rising ground among majestic firs, Dipoli is convincingly a part of its environment. As a building that continuously demonstrates the unlimited imagination of human beings to the students and visitors who use it day and night, summer and winter, Dipoli is symbolic of our ability to build not only with technical precision and ingenuity but with feeling for beautiful form, color, and texture.

An important contemporary problem that American students and teachers might investigate concerns the monotony and what Ada Louise Huxtable, architectural critic of the *New York Times*, calls the "anti-street, anti-people"[23] attitude of much modern, monumental architecture. She speaks of "architectural pollution" that affronts us in our cities, of glass-encased skyscrapers designed by world-famous concerns like Skidmore, Owings and Merrill which grossly abuse the environment. "They are disdainfully anti-street," she insists, "excruciatingly awkward in their connections to their neighbors and, in the former case, [a new skyscraper in New York] belligerently disruptive of the skyline seen from Central Park".[24]

Added to this criticism might be the fact that most tall glass buildings are extremely wasteful of energy. Moreover, numerous individuals and organizations are now beginning to react negatively to the excessive formality and coldness of such buildings rising throughout the country and in many parts of the world. Environmentally-oriented groups are demanding a less severe architecture in their cities, a return to more natural materials appropriate to the region, and a smaller, less monumental scale for all new construction. One group in Burlington, Vermont, for instance, has organized to try to influence the design of the city's urban renewal project. Called "Save Our City," this citizen's group hopes to convince authorities that community people should be included in planning and designing the architectural environment they will inhabit for many years. The group is focusing on potential energy waste resulting from a planned glass-encased hotel perched on a hill overlooking Lake Champlain. The inappropriateness of a large poured concrete underground shopping mall for a small, intimate city like Burlington is also being questioned.

Citizen's groups like "Save Our City" function effectively in an educational capacity, alerting people to problems in their community, helping them work together toward common ends, encouraging them to dig further into old newspaper files and interview formidable officials. Sharing newly-acquired knowledge and working out constructive strategies in group meetings are important parts of this experience which Mumford would find valuable for all community people, young and old. School children and youth could become involved through concerned parents, administrators, and teachers who realize that the architectural environment of their city or town affects their lives and, above all, that the process of citizen involvement is vital in a democratic society.

In Cambridge, Massachusetts, architects from The Architects Collaborative (TAC) regularly visit fourth grade classrooms in the Harrington School and architects from other firms visit most of the city's fifteen elementary schools. Sponsored by the Boston Society of Architects' "Urban Awareness Program" and the Cambridge school system, this project helps young children look more closely at their city and its architecture. Dr. Elizabeth Boyce, who developed the curriculum, sees great value in the program: "We want the youngster to become sensitive to his surroundings — and also to know how he can change them . . . The architects . . . help explain what's beautiful in life: color, form. Their expertise adds the dimension of seeing."[25] Architects, teachers and students engage in some fascinating activities: they map their classroom and nearby Hardwick Street, which includes the "furniture" of the street like trees, telephone poles, trash baskets and so on, and they build several three-dimensional models of the street from blueprints of architectural elevations showing the street as it actually looks and as it might look with imaginative changes.[26]

As a model for other schools, the Cambridge program sounds outstanding. Mumford knows that architects have seldom brought their talents into public schools, so he would be encouraged by this group of architects who are helping children see and experience their environment. On the other hand, he might find it ironic that the architects visiting the Harrington School come from the architectural firm founded by the late Walter Gropius, since Gropius was an early leader in the international style which has overrun our cities with tiresome high-rise structures and turned its back on the organic needs of people. Nevertheless, it is fitting that members of Gropius' firm are involved in education since the master himself was deeply concerned with architectural education all his life and the German Bauhaus which he directed was a beehive of creative learning activity. Hopefully, architects who become involved in school curriculum in the future will pay greater attention to the organic, life-affirming, social dimensions of architecture which Mumford writes about and less to the anti-social, economic-dominated aspects that prevail in most of our cities and towns. The Cambridge experiment seems to emphasize the former and thus sets the pace for constructive involvement of architects in the public schools.

Another focus for studying organic architecture in educational institutions is the area of housing. Trends in housing, alternative housing styles, land-use planning in relation to housing, the social nature of housing, biological and psychological need-fulfillment in housing would be worthy of close examination. Mumford has had a lasting interest in housing from the experience of living in an experimental cluster community in the 1920's to the present. Lately, his notion of housing to maximize personal growth and social interaction has been echoed by a number of critics. Ada Louise Huxtable, for example, reports that low-rise housing is back in fashion as a healthy reaction to the impersonal, crime-infested high-rise apartments that were thrown together for many years. The official destruction of parts of Pruitt Igoe, a gigantic public housing complex in St. Louis, admitted the failure of what Huxtable calls, "the high-rise housing dream of the tower in the park,"[27] a dream that Mumford always considered a nightmare.

Teachers and students might investigate various public housing or low-income housing designs in various parts of the country. Which ones seem more livable? What services should be included in new housing schemes? What are the advantages and disadvantages of low-rise, high-rise, and medium-rise buildings? In what ways are prefabricated or factory built units superior or inferior to built-on-site units? Why is housing important to good physical and psychological health? How can housing be made more ecologically sound? What are the possibilities of building "post-industrial" houses or homes that use no external energy like the prototype structures being built in Maine and Vermont? Why do some families own two or more comfortable homes in our affluent society and others live in two or three rooms they can barely afford? Why is it difficult for poor rural people to find housing other than a trailer? Should decent housing be a right guaranteed every citizen rather than a privilege granted to some and denied to others? These and other questions would provoke serious exploration of this issue.

Of the many housing experiments in recent years, Habitat in Montreal is one of the more exciting. Partly constructed for Expo '67 and completed in 1971, Habitat has enjoyed a 100% occupancy rate and boasts a waiting list of over one hundred names. Habitat is certainly not low-income housing, but as a model of a "total environment," of industrialized housing that provides privacy, a garden, a sense of identity, nearby shops, fresh air and sunlight, it is unsurpassed.[28] Other "Habitats" are being planned by Moshe Safdie, the architect, in Baltimore, Rochester, Puerto Rico, and

Israel. But even in the case of Habitat, successful as it is, some reservations have been expressed about the practicality of building such complex, unconventional structures on a wide scale.[29] For his part, Mumford would be pleased with the multiplying Habitat-inspired experiments in attractively designed, organically-sensitive housing. But he would also remain skeptical about the industrialization of housing, fearing that housing produced on an assembly line may lose human scale and fall short of fulfilling human needs. All of the many problems and possibilities of housing could be grist for analysis and speculation in schools and other settings.

Educationally, architecture might also be used as a concrete way of approaching history, Mumford suggests.[30] The history of a people and their way of life over a period of centuries might be traced in their architectural accomplishments. Tied into such a study would be factors like climate, geography, occupations, and cultural development in other areas. Students could analyze a building or a group of buildings from the point of view of historical continuity and relationships to surrounding buildings, natural forms, and spaces. If possible, the visual impact of the structure, inside and out, might be assessed and the total work evaluated with well-defined criteria in mind.

Many questions might be asked and then investigated: What is appealing and not so appealing about a specific building? Does the building function properly or does it fall short of the hopes of the architect and/or users? What mistakes were made? How can they be corrected? Could the architect have used better materials? Did he take into account the whole environment out of which the building emerged? Were siting and landscaping treated as integral parts of the whole? Is the work as it stands both symbolic and functional? Does it symbolize imperialism, like many government buildings in Washington and some old storehouse-like museums (much to Mumford's disgust),[31] or does it symbolize openness and a willingness to experiment with new forms and radical ideas? Does a particular architectural work have anything to say about the society in which it functions? What do skyscrapers, rotting slums, monotonous housing projects, sleek high-rise apartments tell about the priorities of a society? Does the architecture of an area reveal knowledge about the economy, climate, population density, or cultural concerns of that area and its people?

After probing these and other questions, students and teachers might design new architectural forms to create a more aesthetically pleasing, more humane, or simply more interesting physical environment. They might become actively involved not only in analyzing architecture in natural, social, technological, and aesthetic perspective but in solving some of the problems they encounter. In this way observation and careful investigation would be combined with work in the field to plan and build a future environment for humankind.

Aesthetics, Morality and Function

In carrying on this demanding task of helping to create the future, teachers and students should keep in mind three pivotal qualities which Mumford mentioned in an address at the University of Rome: "esthetic form, moral character, and practical function."[32] The union of these three in his philosophy is such that the absence of one or another in a work of architecture turns it for Mumford "into a hollow shell, a mere piece of scene-painting or technological exhibitionism, like Buckminster Fuller's tetrahedral domes — not a fully-dimensioned building that does justice to all the varied demands of life."[33] From the point of view of aesthetic form, students and teachers might consider ways that buildings can be designed imaginatively with greater pleasure for the eye and the mind. For moral character, they might investigate ways to convey better the function of a building and more adequately express symbolically what Mumford has called "the essential character of our humanity."[34] In terms of practical function, the actual and projected uses of a building might be studied to see if efficiency can be improved or if fewer materials might be used to achieve the same desired result or if new substances might be substituted for conventional ones that are more limited in their applications.

Mumford predictably concludes the Rome address by urging that "the organic and human components that are now missing in our compulsively dynamic and over-mechanized culture"[35] be restored and elevated to a higher place than ever before: "The time has come for architecture to come back to earth and to make a new home for man."[36] Tired of the stress on disposable containers and space capsules by some experimentalists, Mumford seeks a reorientation to earth problems and earth architecture.

Though students and teachers may derive a great deal of

enjoyment from experimenting with every conceivable kind of structure and planned environment, and should be encouraged in these endeavors, Mumford shows great wisdom in stating that earth-oriented environmental problems need first priority. Architecture can help to create a new home for humankind, but this new home should be suitable for a multi-dimensioned, not a one-dimensioned person. Many solutions to housing and other problems offered by Buckminster Fuller and his ardent followers depend too much upon crowding people together in megabuildings or in far-out projects that may strip us of our biological and spiritual need for fresh air, open spaces, freedom of movement, privacy, and diversity. In the final analysis, Mumford's concern for a full-bodied contemporary architecture of humanism makes much more sense than the technologist's concern for novel architecture that tends to forget our organic nature.

Students and teachers can explore many approaches to coping with the problems of a truly fulfilling, aesthetically significant environment for human beings. Such an undertaking could lead to some basic assumptions about men and women, but the effort can only be rewarding if the most important needs of human beings and the kind of environment that is most likely to nourish those needs are doggedly examined. In doing this, architecture will become intimately related to philosophy; one's concept of architecture and one's world view will become inseparable. Architecture will have grown from a parochial interest in buildings to an outlook, a way of looking at humanity — our past attainments, our present preoccupations, and our future aspirations.

[1]Ellen Perry Berkeley, "Environmental Education from Kindergarten Up," *Architectural Forum*, CXXX (June, 1969), 46.

[2]*Ibid.*, pp. 46-50.

[3]Lewis Mumford, "Reflections on Modern Architecture," *Twice A Year*, II (Spring-Summer, 1939), 140-41.

[4]Lewis Mumford, "The Arts," in *Whither Mankind: A Panorama of Modern Civilization*, ed. by Charles A. Beard (New York: Longmans, Green and Company, 1928), p. 308.

[5]Mumford, *The Human Prospect*, Edited by Harry T. Moore and Karl W. Deutsch (Carbondale: Southern Illinois University Press, 1965), p. 216.

[6]Mumford, *The Brown Decades*, 2nd Rev. Ed. (New York: Dover, 1955), p. 169.

[7]Mumford, "The Pragmatic Acquiescence: A Reply," in *Pragmatism and American Culture*, ed. by Gail Kennedy (Boston: D.C. Heath, 1950), p. 56.

[8]Lewis Mumford, "Monumentalism, Symbolism, and Style (Part Two)," *Magazine of Art*, November 1949, p. 260.

[9]Mumford, *The Brown Decades*, p. 118.

[10]*Ibid.*, p. 143.

[11]Lewis Mumford, ed., *Roots of Contemporary American Architecture* (New York: Reinhold Publishing Corporation, 1952), p. 163.

[12]Lewis Mumford, *Architecture* (Chicago: American Library Association, 1926), p. 28.

[13] Mumford, "Monumentalism, Symbolism, and Style (Part Two)," p. 259.

[14]Wolf Von Eckardt, *A Place to Live: The Crisis of the Cities* (New York: Delacorte Press, 1967), p. 380.

[15]Mumford, "Reflections on Modern Architecture," p. 141.

[16]Mumford, *Sticks and Stones*, p. 199.

[17]Mumford, *Architecture* (Chicago: American Library Association, 1926), p. 23.

[18]Mumford, "Architecture as a Home for Man," *Architectural Record*, CXXXXIII (February, 1968), 114.

[19]Mumford, "Function and Expression in Architecture," *Architectural Record*, CX (November, 1951), 106.

[20]*Ibid.*, p. 107.

[21]*Ibid.*, pp. 106-7.

[22]Mumford, *The Brown Decades*, p. 153.

[23]Ada Louise Huxtable, "Anti-Street, Anti-People," *New York Times*, June 10, 1973, p. 24.

[24]*Ibid.*

[25]Quoted in "Getting An Architect's View of the City" by Frederick Hunter, *Christian Science Monitor*, April 12, 1974, p. F3.

[26]Hunter, "Getting An Architect's View," p. F3.

[27]Ada Louise Huxtable, "Another Chance for Housing," *New York Times*, June 24, 1973, p. 23.

[28]Peter Tonge, "The Hanging Gardens of Montreal and Seattle," *Christian Science Monitor*, Aug. 24, 1973, p. 15.

[29]Ada Louise Huxtable, "Some Handsome Architectural Mythology," *New York Times*, January 13, 1974, p. 8.

[30]Lewis Mumford, "The Builder's Art," *New Republic*, November 16, 1927, p. 361.

[31]Mumford, *Sticks and Stones*, p. 150.

[32]Mumford, "Architecture as a Home for Man," p. 114.

[33]*Ibid.*

[34]Mumford, ed., *Roots of Contemporary American Architecture*, p. 169.

[35]Mumford, "Architecture as a Home for Man," p. 116.

[36]*Ibid.*

✌ chapter 5
the city:
urban realities and
utopian dreams

LEWIS MUMFORD is one of the foremost living historians and critics of the city. His biting attacks on contemporary urban forms and institutions, intensive studies of the city in history, and recent collection of essays on urban issues have not always met with accolades, however. Mumford's critics have ranged from caustic *Time* journalists to the respected Harvard professors Morton and Lucia White who tie him to a long American tradition of anti-urbanism.[1]

Mumford is not anti-urban, as the Whites charge, even though he respects small town or village values more than one might expect from a devoted urbanist. Rather, Mumford is deeply concerned about the city and its growing depersonalization and anti-organicism. Instead of hating or romanticizing the city, he visualizes possibilities of making urban areas appealing, healthful, and social-self-renewing places in which to live. Certainly his vision is not confined to the city as it exists today or as it existed in the past; certainly, too, his concept of the city "as an essential organ for expressing and actualizing the new human personality — that of 'One World Man' "[2] is not only radical but worthy of much more intensive investigation than the Whites provide. Mumford explains his conception of the city of man:

> The old separation of man and nature, of townsman
> and countryman, of Greek and barbarian, of citizen and

foreigner, can no longer be maintained: for communication, the entire planet is becoming a village; and as a result, the smallest neighborhood or precinct must be planned as a working model of the larger world.[3]

The city for Mumford should be a microcosm of the world with all of the cultural diversity and personal differences which that implies. It should be a meeting place, as it has been historically;[4] it should foster dialogue;[5] and it should welcome conflict and tension as positive community values just as they were welcome in ancient Greek cities.[6] As a geographic fact, the city expresses regional individuality with perhaps a river as unifying agent of the region; the natural environment, Mumford suggests, takes on a social form in the city.[7] The essential task of the city is:

> . . . to provide the maximum number of favorable opportunities for large populations to intermingle, to interact, to interchange their human facilities and aptitudes as well as their economic goods and services, to stimulate and intensify by frequent contact and collaboration, many common interests that would otherwise languish.[8]

This is the ideal function of cities, but today they fall far short of the ideal as the social-physical-natural environment rapidly deteriorates. For a century the drift to suburbia by people cherishing suburban values has continued, contributing to urban woes. The exodus in search of space, natural beauty, and clean air, ingredients of every premechanized city, has been helped by the real enemies of the city, Mumford asserts: expressway builders, automobile manufacturers, city political machines, and soaring taxes.[9]

Rather than being anti-city himself, Mumford is distressed about anti-urban trends today. One such trend is proliferation of standardized high-rise structures and another the "complementary but opposite image of urban scatter and romantic seclusion often called suburban."[10] If Morton and Lucia White are right in believing that Mumford gives considerable, perhaps too much, attention to the flaws and disintegration of modern cities, they are wrong not to recognize that Mumford makes many constructive proposals to rehabilitate old cities and build integrated new ones to relieve the old. The need is great to renew old neighborhoods, not by indiscriminate wholesale destruction practiced in the nineteen-fifties and sixties, but by citizen-community participation in the planning, construction, and reconstruction of homes, schools, medical and recreational facilities, and shopping areas. Also needed will be a plan for decentralization into new towns and cities which will be economically, racially, and socially balanced as well as attractively designed. Sociologist Michael Harrington echoes Mumford's proposals for combatting urban decay:

> To achieve human scale, there must be new towns and rehabilitated old neighborhoods, large enough to provide diversity of people and economic function, but small enough to encourage sociability and a politics of participation. [11]

Mumford's Precursor: Patrick Geddes

Mumford credits his Scot mentor, Patrick Geddes, with being "perhaps the first modern sociologist to appreciate the role of the city in the development and continuation of the social heritage." [12] Geddes' book, *Cities in Evolution*, was a landmark in urban studies and Geddes' role as civic educator, though not fully appreciated in the early twentieth century or even today, was appreciated by his enthusiastic followers including Paul Goodman, Philip Boardman, and of course Lewis Mumford. Geddes' approach to cities was undoubtedly influenced by his training as a biologist — he worked with the great T.H. Huxley — but Geddes, like Mumford, refused to be pigeonholed into any single discipline whether it be biology, ecology, sociology, botany, zoology, or philosophy.

Comparisons between Geddes and Mumford do not stop at their common rejection of compartmentalization. In describing the older man's qualities, Mumford sounds like he is describing himself. He observes that Geddes was a philosopher of life in its fullness and unity; Geddes passionately believed in insurgence, the capacity to overcome threats to the organism by human power, plans, and dreams. [13] Like Geddes, who paid heavily for his refusal to be pigeonholed, [14] Mumford has been criticized for spreading himself too thin and for creating "grandiose metaphysical" plans for urban and cultural renewal. [15] Nevertheless, both have been concerned about over-specialization and, most significantly, both have been a remarkable combination of artist and scientist, practical man and idealist, rural mind and urban mind.[16]

Geddes carried on a systematic study of the city from Edinburgh's Outlook Tower which he established in 1892 as a civic and regional museum and sociological laboratory. As one of the first innovations in his work to improve the congested slums of Edinburgh, Geddes made a small park or garden from every patch of unusable or unused land, not unlike New York's efforts in recent years to create "vest pocket parks" or efforts by Boston residents to construct small but imaginative playgrounds with colorful murals painted on the ends of overshadowing brownstones. Geddes practiced what he called "conservative surgery," a process which respected and preserved the best qualities of native life while improving conditions and relieving the strain of congestion wherever possible.[17]

As a technique for modern-day urban renewal, Geddes' method is far superior to those obsolete techniques which destroy neighborhoods for urban expressways, bulldoze inner-city communities like Boston's once-vibrant West End, or prepare the way for what Paul Goodman calls "neo-technical slums."[18] "By a melancholy irony," Goodman writes, "some of us followers of Geddes wryly praise the hideous old slums over the neo-technological slums, for they had more human scale and pullulation of life."[19] Mumford might not go that far, but he joins Goodman in attacking the anti-humanism and sterility of brick high-rise apartments and housing projects in New York and other cities.

Geddes was more concerned explicitly with education than Mumford, and he was no less critical of traditional educational methods and curriculum. His explosive definition of "mis-education" so impressed one student, Philip Boardman, that Boardman, in trying to bring Geddes' ideas to the attention of American progressive educators in the thirties, quotes it verbatim. Since it was the kind of inspirational response which attracted Mumford to Geddes, not to mention Paul Goodman who years later wrote *Compulsory Mis-Education*, it seems appropriate to quote Geddes at length. Education, or rather mis-education, bellowed Geddes to his students:

> . . . is verbalistic empaperment incrusted in student's minds by a bureaucratic examination machine! And as for those who run the machine, with their hundreds of

subjects all unrelated one to the other and all divorced from life, I call them blithering, doddering, unspeakable fools who cheat youth of its heritage. My friends, there is only one salvation from this betrayal — Life! I have preached life for over fifty years, I have tried to put it in city slums, in halls of residence, into my plans for the University of Jerusalem. And now, with my span of days near its end, I can tell you more certainly than ever that life is the only subject in my curriculum, that life itself is the only justification for any study.[20]

Mumford could not describe his own philosophy of education more succinctly: the study and experience of Life in all its dimensions.

At a later date Geddes admitted to Boardman that his fiery remarks about mis-education were simply meant to shake students from complacency, but the truth and wisdom of his response remained indelible to Boardman. The "bureaucratic examination machine" of which he spoke is still very prominent and those "blithering, doddering, unspeakable fools" can still be found hovering about the classrooms and offices of many an educational institution. One need only sample Diane Divoky's collection of articles in *How Old Will You Be in 1984? Expressions of Student Outrage From the High School Free Press* to realize how much mis-education, irrelevance, and repression are featured in contemporary American schools.[21] Not a small number of students in high schools as well as in colleges and universities are rightfully demanding, like Geddes and Mumford, that Life — its meaning and lack of meaning, its quality and lack of quality, its humanizing aspects and its dehumanizing aspects — become the central focus for curriculum and teaching-learning in every educational setting.

One concrete way educators could work toward Geddes' Life-centered concept of education would be to heed his plea to students: "Get out and explore the world for yourself!"[22] Educators could, and should, give increased attention to student-teacher exploration outside the confines of school buildings. Because both Geddes and Mumford stress the significance of direct, first-hand experience as a vital ingredient of education, it might be instructive to review Geddes' pioneering work in urban education which profoundly influenced Mumford.

In accordance with Aristotle, Geddes believed that one's vision of the city must be "synoptic;" that is, one should see the whole of it. To survey the city in a way that reveals interrelated functions, one should look at it as a geographer, biologist, psychologist, economist, religionist:

> We thus distinguish half-a-dozen main groups of specialisms, each of which tends to exclude the others to far too great an extent; hence it becomes necessary for us as students of sociology to try to avoid the limitations of their cultivators by uniting all of the city into a single living whole.[23]

The city should also be glimpsed as a whole in terms of the past, the present, and the future; past history can be related to present development and the present to future possibilities. Most important, active steps can be taken to create the future, thus making the survey "no longer purely speculative, no longer utopian in the vague dreamland sense, but Eutopian in the definite sense — that is making the best of the place here."[24] This concept of utopia, or "eutopia" by Geddes' definition, is carried over by Mumford even as far as the spelling is concerned. For both men "eutopian," in contrast to perfection and escapism implied by utopian, always stands for the better world which human beings can build if they apply their intelligence and energy to the task.

Geddes wanted educationists (a term he used himself)[25] to look at every aspect of the city and encouraged students to do likewise, but only in light of a "widening series of geographical relations from our immediate neighborhood to the world."[26] As world citizen and educationist, he began studying a small park or garden and suddenly widened out into patterns of the whole community. Or he started with a practical urban planning project which emerged into a regional plan or a plan for world food production.[27] A great proponent of travel, particularly on foot, Geddes observed cities in the context of their region and culture. He also organized "City Exhibitions" using photographs for comparative purposes at a time when photography was still a young art.

Mumford reports that students have carried on the kind of survey and replanning of neighborhoods in Philadelphia that Geddes suggested a half-century earlier.[28] There is no reason why students and teachers in cities around the world could not undertake similar surveys to diagnose and then treat some of the diseases that plague urban centers. One interesting federally-funded environmental education project in California, for example, includes an urban excursion to acquaint students with life in San Francisco's seamy Tenderloin District. Suburban high school youth in the program interview prostitutes, commuters rushing to catch trains home, and North Beach nude dancers. Each student at some point is required to stop a person on the street; provide false information about himself; and ask for help in finding a place to stay overnight, a bite to eat, and a job.[29]

The "urban awareness" program in Cambridge, Massachusetts involves elementary age children in an exploration of their city. Children use aerial maps to locate their own homes, compare housing density in poorer neighborhoods with that in affluent ones, and identify photographs of various urban landmarks. The High School Geography Project in Cambridge and elsewhere asks students to focus on problems dealing with city planning, hunger, water resources, and religion, among others. Methodology includes role-playing and simulation games, group activities, model building; tools include aerial photos, records, filmstrips, and a plastic map on which to "build" cities. The educational affairs director of the Association of American Geographers, designers of this curriculum, reports that it has been adopted in over 350 school districts across the United States.[30] Mumford and Geddes would be heartened by some of the new curriculum projects like the above, but they would be disappointed by the resistance of some teachers, administrators, and parents to innovative, non-textbook oriented approaches which may require more time and effort but may also guarantee more satisfying results.

Urban Historian and Critic:
Praise and Criticism

"There is nothing new in the present urban situation," Mumford claims, "except that these evils are still with us, on a vaster scale, in a more difficult and desperate form, than ever before."[31] As an historian of the city, he has traced the development of urban forms from their beginnings and for many years has been critical of twentieth century "metropolitan civilization" for failing to distribute equitably the benefits, both social and material, that it controls through technology and physical organization.[32] Two of the biggest problems which concern Mumford are the large size and great density of cities and the poor quality of housing occupied chiefly by minority group members. Though neither of these is new, both are more critical and "desperate" today than ever before, as Mumford admits.

In one of his books written over a half-century ago, Mumford explains that a city "does not exist by the accretion of houses, but by the association of human beings."[33] Continuing to explain that a place ceases to be a city when congestion or expansion reaches the point at which human association becomes difficult, he contends that schools, clubs, libraries, gynmasia, theaters, churches and so forth which compose a city "can be traced in one form or another back to the primitive community: they function on the basis of immediate intercourse, and they can serve through their individual units only a limited number of people."[34] Reiterating this assumption a year later, he warns that cities are growing too big, are falling behind in the "barest decencies of housing," and are getting more expensive to operate, more trouble to police, and more impossible to escape from in leisure hours.[35]

Mumford sees no need to change this assessment today. Nor is he dismayed by vehement critics like Jane Jacobs, author of *The Death and Life of Great American Cities*, who proclaims: "To limit the size of great cities, because of the acute problems that arise in them, is profoundly reactionary."[36] Still clinging to Ebenezer Howard's original ideas elaborated in *Garden Cities of To-Morrow*, Mumford firmly believes there are natural limits to urban growth "inherent in the very nature of city life, and that beyond these limits malformation, disorganization, and deterioration" result. [37] Returning to the never-distant organic metaphor, he asserts:

> In every biological species there is a limit to size . .. So with the constitution of cities . . . If it overpasses the bounds of growth, absorbing more people than it can properly house, feed, govern, or educate, then it is no longer a city; for its ensuing disorganization keeps it from carrying on a city's function.[38]

One of the basic assumptions that Mumford challenges is the idea that the largest, the greatest or the most is automatically the best, the finest or the most desirable for human beings. Bigness does not necessarily mean best; if anything, the bigger the city the more mechanical facilities, the more roads and sewers, the more dumps and skyscrapers are needed. He bitterly comments as a young man: "no matter what the Rotary Clubs and Chambers of Commerce may think of them, these mechanical ingenuities are not the indices of a civilization."[39]

Mumford suggests that the crisis in the city really stems, at least in large part, from overcrowding and the consequences of congestion: poor recreational opportunities, shrinking open space, lack of privacy, foul air, gigantic schools, solid and liquid waste disposal problems, extraordinarily high prices of land that forces higher buildings, crowded and inadequate public transportation, and a ludicrous amount of space devoted to streets and parking lots. Many of these can be alleviated by banning automobiles from inner cities, by improving maintenance of parks, by using technology more creatively to make public transportation both comfortable and convenient, and by turning solid wastes into reusable raw materials. But at base, the congestion in housing, compounded by inferior quality of much housing construction and the heavy concentration of low income people in deteriorating downtown areas, should be seriously questioned as a way of city life.

"If the places where we live and work were really fit for human habitation," Mumford asks incisively, "why should we spend so much of our time getting away from them?"[40] The sad fact is that biologically, psychologically, and spiritually, large American cities are today what Mumford accurately said they were in 1938: "life-inimical or life-destructive environments."[41] He wants the city to become a life-nourishing human environment with much greater provision for sunlight, fresh air, free movement; for the sight and smell of grass, flowers, and trees.

Like the primeval environment, the city as a human environment has been exploited and raped during the last century. Yet, contrary to those who believe Mumford's bias is essentially anti-urban because of his displeasure with modern city development, he affirms: ". . . it is in and through the city, with all the resources it offers for the mind, that man has created a symbolic counterpart to nature's creativity, variety, and exuberance."[42]

The great urbanologists, Mumford contends, are men like Frederick Law Olmsted who "naturalized the city" by "using the landscape creatively"[43] and Patrick Geddes and Ebenezer Howard. Progressive urbanologists are not people who simply use the city to further business ends or politicians who dump millions of dollars into pet projects but quickly forget the miserable living conditions of poor people. The displacement of nature in cities, notes Mumford in a characteristically philosophical way, rests partly upon illusions about the nature of man and his institutions: "the illusions of self-sufficiency and of the possibility of physical continuity without conscious renewal."[44] Man is not and cannot be self-sufficient; he depends on other selves not only for survival but for enrichment of his own self through person-to-person contact. He is no more self-sufficient from other organic forms — nature in all its forms — than he is from his fellow-man. Neither can man function as a continually creative, feeling entity if he does not, like nature itself, undergo the process of renewal — renewal of his energies, his thoughts, his relationships. Clearly, Mumford believes that nature as a part of city existence is an important prerequisite of renewal.

Mumford has been criticized for clinging to a "romantic" conception of the city, for trying to make the city into something which it neither is nor can become: a kind of expanded New England village which provides a healthful, pleasant, cooperative environment for all. He has been criticized for not understanding the complexity of large cities, for stressing congestion too much, and for trying to create an urban utopia which has little or no chance of success today because government and corporate trends point in the opposite direction. Though each of these criticisms is worth considering, it can also be argued that Mumford's concern for a more human, natural, and less crowded environment in cities is not only worthy of praise, but should be given top priority by planners, government officials, and city residents, not to mention educational leaders.

It is unfair to label Mumford a romantic dreamer with little or no idea of the practical realities of modern urbanism. A more accurate assessment would consider him an urban utopian (or "eutopian" by his definition) who understands the whole dilemma of urban life and is not hesitant to make radical proposals based on historical evidence and visionary thinking. He knows that the suburb or traditional suburban life is not the answer to urban woes, pointing out the "problem of the archetypal suburb today is to trade some of its excessive biological space (gardens) for social space (meeting places)."[45] A major problem of the congested city is just the opposite: to introduce more open spaces, squares, and pedestrian malls to both fulfill the social functions of the city and make it a favorable place for establishing a home and bringing up children. [46] Mumford knows that the creation of a better balance between city and country is the future task of urbanization.

As opposed to suburban sprawl as much as any architect, planner, or environmentalist, Mumford desires a much more expansive, creative style of life than suburbs traditionally provide. The current trend toward neglect of the cities by state and federal governments and unplanned, one-sided development of suburban areas is wrong, he believes. As an alternative to current policies he proposes greater attention to the needs, both material and spiritual, of urban residents and to the establishment of new communities within the region for those who wish to leave the city proper.

Both parts of Mumford's alternative intimately involve the black populations of inner cities, but unfortunately he does not seem as sensitive to the plight of black Americans as he might be. Perhaps because Mumford believes so strongly in the common humanity of all people, he has not focused on racial attitudes and prejudices that divide one person from another. Of course, very few sociologists or anthropologists before the mid-nineteen sixties recognized the extent of racial injustice in urban ghettoes or sensed the implications in vast Negro migrations to large northern cities. But this is no excuse for Mumford's failure to deal more specifically and more compassionately with black problems, or what is called often "the white problem" of racism.

Mumford deplores slums and slum living, even accusing the "upper classes" of building damp, sunless, airless "slums of their own, with as little concern for their own hygiene as they showed in their tenement properties."[47] But he never thinks in terms of distinctive black problems which make it much more difficult for blacks to become equal members of American society than for ethnic whites. He never looks closely at the question of prejudice or at segregationist policies which discriminate against blacks. In his latest writing, he admits that civil disturbances in cities are at least partly understandable as long-delayed reactions to poverty, slums, unemployment, discrimination, segregation, and police animosity. But he sounds patronizing when stating his conviction that the underlying causes "for the recurrent outbreaks of violence among the disturbed minorities" are not to be found solely in the rotting physical condition of cities.[48]

Efforts to make the city a life-affirming environment must be made, of course, but it is not just the city but rather the "whole body politic" [49] which demands attention. Violent outbreaks are simply local examples of widespread collective violence that mark the last half century, he continues, reverting in a much too literal way to the biological-organic metaphor:

> Constant indoctrination in violence is the main office of our ubiquitous agents of mass communication and mass education. To believe that a single organ of the body politic, the city, can be cured of this disease while the same deadly cells flow through the entire bloodstream is to betray an ignorance of elementary physiology.[50]

Few would deny that the film and television industries thrive on violence and that violence is a mainstay of American culture, but Mumford seems to forget that urban suffering can be greatly alleviated without the whole "body politic" being completely cured of violence. Black residents can be guaranteed a living wage, a diversity of job opportunities, decent housing, and a warm welcome by white people living in the cities and the suburbs.

Mumford does not reject the possibility of curing many city ills through large injections of money and talent, but he does urge a "go slow" approach to urban renewal until past mistakes have been corrected and new procedures, plans, and regional agencies are created. Do not immediately pour billions into a program for the cities, but eventually spend as much on urban redevelopment as on annual military expenditures, he exhorted the Ribicoff Committee on governmental expenditures in 1967.[51]

Unfortunately, Mumford's "go slow" approach to the cities can be used by reactionary politicians to stall desperately needed aid to bleeding cities, aid for everything from experimental urban education to public transportation. Recent administrations have agreed with Mumford that billions ought not to be poured into cities and they certainly have no intention of eventually equalling the amount spent by the military. Aid to cities is withering as conditions worsen. Some past mistakes in urban renewal have already been corrected: at least a few renewal agencies are less arrogant, more receptive to community views, and more willing to grant the community a key role in planning. But the Model Cities Program, one hopeful way to involve citizens in urban reconstruction, has been emasculated by the federal government. And this has happened after the Report of the National Advisory Commission on Civil Disorders, that document promising in theory but almost forgotten in practice, called for a greatly expanded rather than reduced Model Cities Program.

In his "Postscript: The Choices Ahead" concluding *The Urban Prospect* (1968), Mumford seems at last to appreciate some of the problems of black and Puerto Rican citizens in large American cities. He still speaks of upper-class ghettoes (high-rise apartments with every conceivable amenity) and lower-class ghettoes (row housing infested with rats and sometimes hardly fit for living) in the same breath and takes pains to observe that most urban problems today were visible a half century ago. But this can hardly give much comfort to suffering blacks and Puerto Ricans still trapped in decaying structures, many of which adjoin fire-gutted tenements. Mumford is right to be cautious in his approach to revitalizing the cities, but only up to a point: he is right to urge that the early mistakes of urban renewal continue to be analyzed and corrected when necessary, but he is wrong in not fully appreciating the desperate situation in American cities today.

By being over-cautious, Mumford plays into the hands of his enemies who are all too ready to find reasons based on racism (explicit or implicit) or "economics" to postpone, perhaps to stall indefinitely, massive assistance. By suggesting that city problems are part of a much larger contemporary crisis he makes a correct though often forgotten assessment. But all the same he opens himself to charges of conservatism, obstructionism, and unrealistic idealism . . . which are partly justified. Even if one agrees that all of society needs overhauling, the very real crises of the cities demand huge financial-moral support and drastic political reform immediately.

Mumford might strongly endorse the Model Cities Program as a small but significant step in the right direction, but he does not. He might show enthusiasm for black self-help programs in ghettoes or for effective community organizing in cities like Chicago, but he does not. In his studies of cities, and especially of American arts and culture, he might have given blacks a larger, more accurate role, but he did not.

Mumford seems threatened by any hint of separatism which he fears may hinder the ideal of an integrated society and this threat blinds him to realities of black existence in a largely white society.

Even the fact that he consistently, stubbornly uses the term Negro and refuses ever to use the term black or Afro-American which a good many blacks prefer is indicative of his refusal to see blacks in a different light than he did in the past. Regrettably, too, Mumford pays very little attention in his writing to the civil rights movement and its greatest leader, Martin Luther King, Jr., when this historic movement jolted the national and world conscience during the nineteen-sixties. W.E.B. DuBois, Malcolm X and other black leaders are never even mentioned.

We might agree in part with Mumford that "there is no Negro problem and no Puerto Rican problem: there is only a human problem"[52] when it comes to urban renewal or world peace, but we should be more aware than he that at present Negroes and Puerto Ricans do face serious problems that white people and rich people do not face. It is much too easy for Mumford to talk of human problems in broad, general terms and not come to grips with the "black revolution" in the United States and in the "Third World."

Mumford is so convinced that the neighborhood unit is all-important for healthy growth that he opposes busing out of the neighborhood to achieve racial balance in schools. His reasons for rejecting busing differ from those who want to keep white children from mingling with black children and those in the black community who favor control of their own predominantly black neighborhood schools. Mumford considers it a mistake to think that segregation can be alleviated through busing, even as a temporary expedient, though his reasoning on this point seems a bit fuzzy. He believes it most unfortunate that individuals he does not respect (like Boston's long-time champion of de facto segregation, Louise Day Hicks) maintain the same position he does.[53]

The recent violent disturbances in Boston must be upsetting to Mumford, but he might claim that the widespread opposition to busing among white ethnics tends to confirm his view that busing is not a satisfactory solution to the problem of segregation and never will be.

Mumford's hard-line against busing is representative of an occasional intransigence — an unwillingness to accept short-range achievement even when long-range solutions are difficult to attain. His opposition to busing as a means of integrating schools is short-sighted if one believes that integration is a worthwhile educational policy and an effective means of creating a truly open, integrated society in the future. Surely, busing is not a final answer for the future, but it may be a necessary expedient at the present time.

At the base of Mumford's opposition to busing is an ever-present faith in mixed housing and mixed communities as a counter to the current system of segregated, homogeneous housing and communities. The neighborhood is the key element in his scheme; an important assumption is that small units must be rebuilt and revitalized in order to succeed in dealing with the complex problems of large units.[54] He has even stated that "there is not a difficulty faced by the United Nations, seeking to achieve a balance between tribalism and cosmopolitanism, that will not have to be worked out in the smallest neighborhood."[55]

Mumford assumes that neighborhoods should be integrated not only racially but by ethnic, age, and economic groups. That neighborhoods are not integrated today and, indeed, are becoming increasingly polarized in great cities as blacks fight for community control and whites protect their domain with vigilante organizations does not deter Mumford from emphasizing what might and, to his way of thinking, very definitely should be happening in urban neighborhoods in spite of current trends.

Mumford's stress on integrated neighborhoods, though largely unfulfilled at present and a distant prospect at best in large cities, deserves careful consideration. His desire to build neighborhoods into active political units on a scale small enough to encourage wide participation[56] and his suggestion that the core of any neighborhood housing program "should be, above all, the provision for the health, security, education and adult care of young children"[57] make a great deal of sense. Crediting his antagonist Jane Jacobs with pointing out a fact to which many planners and administrators have been indifferent — "that a neighborhood is not just a collection of buildings but a tissue of social relations and a cluster of warm personal sentiments"[58] — Mumford envisions the neighborhood as a humanizing organ of urban life and a base for constructive participation in regional, national, and world affairs.

With Mumford's undiminished enthusiasm for integrated, balanced communities, perhaps it is not astonishing that he asks blacks and Puerto Ricans if "they are willing to move out of their present neighborhoods, even if this means scattering widely in a mixed community, and losing some of their present identity and cohesion."[59] He knows this is a difficult question to answer in the affirmative, but he sees no other alternative to continued urban segregation and congestion. If the decision is made to disperse, and Mumford rightly grants that this decision rests in the hands of those immediately concerned, he proposes that minority individuals move to "New Towns, suburbs, or growing rural communities" where good housing, new job opportunities and "stable neighborhood facilities"[60] can be supplied.

Aware that many blacks would resist such a move, particularly more militant ones, Mumford also recognizes that an exodus would undermine black sub-cultures in the inner cities. But he cannot accept the high density of population in ghetto areas, even if ghettoes were completely rehabilitated and integrated; in order to provide housing for all of the present population, super-slums (high-rise slabs like those prominent in the Bronx, New York or grim housing projects planted in asphalt like Boston's Columbia Point) would have to be erected on a large scale in every big city. Mumford does not want to abandon the city as a viable home for human beings, nor oust minority individuals from their homes and neighborhoods without their approval. But he does want everyone alarmed about urban realities to face a basic reality themselves: it will be impossible to provide healthy, well-designed, comfortable housing and attendant community facilities for every present and anticipated resident of core cities. New technology may help to lessen the crisis, he asserts, but only decentralization will prove to be effective in the long run.

If some city residents are willing to move out of over-crowded quarters, their own situation may be improved and the possibility of improving the area they leave behind may be greater. With fewer people crowded into tight, limited space within the city, greater opportunities for establishing "a life-centered environment from the moment of birth"[61] would exist. With fewer residents, widespread demolition could be undertaken "in order to restore, in a century or so, some of the basic natural ingredients for a full and rich human life."[62] This last proposal is somewhat far-fetched at the present time, although the demolition of an unlivable, high-rise public housing project in St. Louis is already a reality. Mumford's proposal would not seem improbable if national and world priorities were directed to the welfare of people rather than to armaments and extravagant space exploration.

The biggest snag in Mumford's otherwise promising decentralization idea is that blacks and Puerto Ricans, even if they chose, would have very few decent places to move. He fails to consider whether or not residents in suburbs and rural areas would welcome minority members and make possible their move by providing adequate low and middle income housing. There is considerable evidence to doubt the welcome in terms of racial attitudes; in several Boston suburbs, probably not as conservative as those surrounding many American cities, suburban residents have fought vigorously to block reasonably priced apartment units. In Chicago in the late sixties, hordes of white racists spilled their venom when Martin Luther King and his followers marched through the white community.[63] The choice of moving out or not moving out actually depends more upon the white majority than the black minority; blacks, for the most part, do not have a real choice.

Blacks cannot move to totally new communities or New Towns either because, at least at present, they do not exist in the United States. In a few ways, Reston, Virginia and Columbia, Maryland satisfy Mumford's criteria for New Towns, but essentially they are glorified suburbs; Reston is now owned by Gulf Oil Corporation and one wonders, as Mumford would, how the profit motive can be reconciled with the human needs of residents.[64] Columbia has built some low income housing with federal aid, but no New Towns in the United States are really balanced with a variety of jobs for a variety of people.[65] None satisfy Mumford's criteria for dynamic urban communities in a regional context.

What Mumford would like are new communities which draw their population from present low, middle, and upper class whites and present low, middle and upper class minority members. But until such communities are planned on a regional basis, until state and federal governments pave the way by helping to finance and break down obsolete political barriers, blacks have little or no choice except to stay in their own urban neighborhoods and continue to work and organize for a better way of life. And this is already being done in a variety of ways: "urban homesteading" which involves rehabilitation of rundown housing has taken firm hold in Philadelphia, Baltimore, and Boston;[66] a community music center has joined other centers for the performing arts in downtown Boston;[67] and neighborhood men and women in Harlem have restored northern Central Park, once a neglected crime-ridden area which now boasts a rehabilitated boat house for daytime lunchers, boats and bicycles for rent, and fixed-up park benches.[68]

Whites can and should turn their attention to problems of suburban segregation: in short, to racism in all its ugly forms. Self-analysis is urgently needed in predominantly white communities, an analysis that closely examines quality and style of life, alienation, bigotry, and complacency. Human rights groups, active for some time in a few suburbs, should be organized in every community to invite blacks and Puerto Ricans of different persuasions to confront whites in schools, churches, and homes. Open housing could be made a reality, not a nice liberal notion; tastefully-designed low and middle income housing sponsored by non-profit organizations could be favored over plans for upper income development by private speculators.

Encounter groups might be formed to share experiences and anxieties, with any ensuing conflict seen as contributing to mutual growth and understanding rather than to destructive divisiveness. Parents, teachers, and students could follow the example of Wellesley, Massachusetts high school teachers and introduce black theater like LeRoi Jones' *The Slave* which profoundly stirred that community out of lethargy. Awareness, understanding, compassion, love — and action based on these feelings — is urgently needed. Toleration, a passive and acquiescent notion, is not satisfactory. Only robust effort and a sincere desire to join with minority individuals in solving mutual problems will suffice.

Though Mumford foresees no miraculous recovery from current urban dilemmas, and in fact undervalues the efforts being made by city residents themselves to better their condition, he does hope for one miracle, a miracle dashed many times during his life but a remote possibility still:

> ... the one conceivable miracle that might yet occur is that a sufficient number of people should recognize that every part of our life must be overhauled, including the technology of Megalopolis and the supporting ideology of an affluent society under an ever-expanding economy.[69]

Mumford is realistic enough to know this miracle is far from probable, but as long as there is a chance he will fight for it.

Mumford considers his contemporaries who "conceive the new forms of the city solely in terms favorable to the machine, and to an even larger exploitation of the machine's capability"[70] old-fashioned, rather than avant-garde. Those who think of new forms primarily in terms of unique materials and mechanics — hygienically weather-proofed steel and plastic geodesic domes over whole cities, underground cities buried in cavernous vaults and undersea cities in waterproof graves, ever-higher skyscraper cities and endless linear cities — are on the wrong track, he feels. They are particularly foolish when speaking glibly and joyfully of mammoth cities or, like the planner Constantin Doxiadis, of world cities forming one giant, amorphous, dehumanized megalopolis.[71]

City in the School: School in the City

A city, Mumford writes in *The Culture of Cities*, "is a concentrated socialized environment, where administrators and energizers, assimilators and creators, may react upon each other in a common sphere."[72] Every community should provide the necessary structures for a dynamic social environment. In the medieval city, the church was the essential social nucleus; in the baroque city, the palace with its theatre, concert hall, and art gallery were at the center; and in the industrial age, factories, offices, and stores sprawled along traffic arteries. In a biotechnic order, however, the home and school constitute the hub of the community. Neighborhoods, determined by the "convenient walking distance for children between the farthest house and the school and playground in which a major part of their activities are focused"[73] or based upon "the needs of families . . . the needs of all age groups for having access to certain cultural facilities: the school, the library, the meeting hall, the cinema, the church,"[74] are a central feature of biotechnic communities.

In a neighborhood, the pre-adolescent child should have daily contact with light industries, markets and various other activities which serve the community; the child's walk to school should provide a chance to explore natural forms and to observe men and women at work. One of the many faults of present suburban schooling "is the blank dullness of the ride to school . . . there is nothing like a trim, orderly, defensively respectable suburban environment to discourage a child's imagination — or, for that matter an adult's."[75] The walk to school as an educative activity has been largely neglected by educators, Mumford rightly contends, although at least one small suburban town, Lincoln, Massachusetts, has recognized the problem by constructing simple walking-bicycle paths through the woods and across private property for elementary children to take to school.[76]

If the school is the basic social nucleus of the biotechnic community, community resources from libraries to laboratories, from museums to churches, are absolutely vital. The community or city itself becomes the chief instrument of education, with schools and universities reaching out beyond the restrictive walls of buildings to include involvement in the activities of political committees, neighborhood action groups, and other civic organizations. No aspect of the city — how it is structured, how it functions, why it is a favorable or unfavorable home for man, how it can be made more compatible with an ideal vision — would be left out when the city becomes an instrument of education.

The main interest of education from Rousseau to Dewey in Mumford's view has been "to effectuate, through collective means and processes, a better political society."[77] He therefore rejects the tenaciously held notion that the chief purpose of education is to mold individuals into fixed patterns. Instead, Mumford insists that education develop flexible and many-sided personalities who are vocationally prepared but not narrow-minded specialists. He would much prefer that education concentrate on an open-minded though skillful amateur than on an all too rigid professional specialist. As he sees it, the process of education includes transmissive training of the young, but even more important, experimentation and innovation in light of humanistic goals. The aim of education is the development of a questioning, risk-taking, compassionate human being living in a society which respects uniqueness but which encourages cooperation with others.

Mumford never wants it forgotten that the school is but one aspect of education, that education of the child at home among family members and friends and the ongoing process of socialization no matter where it occurs are very important. Nevertheless, he concedes that the school is "the main symbol of the educational process"[78] and, as such: " . . . may be defined as an environment modified for biological and social development: an environment especially concerned with growth, which no longer treats the processes of growth as accidental intrusions on an ideal pattern.[79] Personal and social growth in the direction of fullness and purposefulness represents Mumford's most earnest hope for schools. But what kind of a school does this require and what kind of program for the schools?

One thing is certain: Mumford does not want the brand of education peddled in the schools of Megalopolis, the fourth state of city development suggested by Geddes, which concentrates on bigness and power:

> Education becomes quantitative: domination of the cram-machine and encyclopedia, and domination of mega-lopolis as concrete encyclopedia: all-containing. Know-ledge divorced from life: industry divorced from life-utility: life itself compartmentalized, dis-specialized, finally disorganized and enfeebled.[80]

Rather than this kind of school dedicated to knowledge stuffing and the socio-political status quo, Mumford pleads for schools that challenge giantism and knowledge divorced from life. Decentraliza-tion means the introduction of small units in schools and in every part of the city: small neighborhood and community groups, small classes and small communities which take the place of mass regulations, mass decisions, and mass actions imposed by remote leaders and administrators.[81] The possibilities for direct participa-tion in learning are considerably greater in small units than in large, thus increasing the personalization and humanization of education.

Though he is not explicit on this point, Mumford would favor more experimental, interdisciplinary courses and programs in colleges and universities. He would enthusiastically endorse seminars and independent study projects in junior and senior high schools which cross traditional subject lines to explore city and suburban conflicts. Grass roots organizations working to restore a neighborhood, cut down crime or offer medical advice to drug users would be examples of small units in urban areas combatting bigness and attendant impersonality. How to humanize a school and humanize a city: that is Mumford's overarching concern. Size and numbers, though apparently superficial on first inspection, are far more significant in the operation of a school or a city along humanistic lines than many other factors.

Mumford's point is well taken that the density, bulk, and sheer quantitative numbers of megalopolitan civilization block or at least hinder self and social actualization by making small units and individual attention less and less possible. Decentralization of school districts and decentralization of city governments, with some central authority for practical and coordinative purposes, is necessary if all citizens, young and old, are to receive a share in their own destiny. As long as cities and suburbs grow octopus-like and schools consolidate as they continue to deteriorate physically, quality education that depends heavily on small group interaction and individual attention will suffer. Out of necessity, schools will become more automated, more programmed to accommodate overcrowding and, in so doing, may revert to the traditional right-or-wrong answer approach or to cramming which Mumford finds despicable.

More individualized study, small group work, involvement with clusters of community people, and emphasis upon teacher-student and student-student relationships is needed. Less mass testing; confinement to the school building proper; formality and hierarchical distance between teachers, administrators and students; and passive lecturing is called for. Mumford outlines eloquently the steps that he believes lead to a modern and much superior education:

> From the drill school to the organic school: from the child school to the child-adult school: from a desiccated environment to a living environment: from closed issues and mechanical indoctrination to open inquiry and cooperative discipline as a normal process of living . . .
> From the part-time school, confined to a *building*, to the full-time school taking stock of and taking part in the whole life of the neighborhood, the city, the region: from an education whose truths and values are in good part denied by the actual environment and the social practice of the community to an education that is integral with the demands and possibilities of life and that shirks no needed effort to make over reality in conformity with purpose and ideal . . . [82]

The implications in Mumford's reorientation of education to life-fulfillment are far-reaching. His organic school would center on life itself, following Geddes, and approach all problems ecologically. Man and nature, the biological, social, and physical environments, would all be interrelated. The quality of life in cities, in suburbs, and in rural areas would gain attention; urban planning, for instance, would become appropriate as a field of study, but not urban planning in any narrow professional sense. Schools would no longer be limited primarily to children; as community centers, children and adults, the very young and the elderly, the married and the single, would have meeting places for talking, debating, exercising, making crafts, eating, and drinking. As Mumford wisely observes, the possibility of varied age groups being visibly together in centers outside the home — whether they be storefront churches, health clinics, or community schools — helps to form a real community. [83]

"Open inquiry" and "cooperative discipline" would be hallmarks of the new education. Honest, straightforward inquiry into personal and social difficulties affecting one's self, one's community, and humankind, with no fear of controversial subjects like population control, democratic socialism or the military-industrial complex, would be encouraged. Indoctrination from government, military, industrial and any other power group would be discouraged. That is not to say, however, that any power or special interest group from the American Legion to the National Association of Manufacturers to the Democratic Socialist Organizing Committee would be denied the right to present its case in the schools. On the contrary, "open inquiry" would mean that any organization or individual, no matter how reactionary or radical, would be welcome. The teacher's role would become one of helping students analyze, clarify and evaluate the arguments expressed, the presuppositions made. No line of questioning would be considered off bounds as students and teachers come to grips with social-political philosophies and perspectives which may seem strange or threatening. Value clarification would be an especially valuable tool and teachers would exercise every opportunity to help students come to personal terms with the value content of each issue and problem studied.

The school would become a full-time partner and facilitator in the community with staff, students, and residents working toward the maximum development of individual potential and social partnership. Education of this sort would freely experiment with ideas and programs while continuously sorting out and assessing on the basis of a broad humanistic framework. Effort would consciously and shamelessly be made to "make over reality," as Mumford puts it, or to work for change in present conditions when necessary to increase compatibility with human ideals and purposes. As always, the open goal of self and social realization would determine the rightness or wrongness, the strength or weakness, of a potential course of action.

John H. Fischer, former president of Teachers College, Columbia University, and chairman of the board of trustees of the Center for Urban Education, has called for "bold programs of systematic inquiry, experimentation, and evaluation" for urban education and urban planning that includes analysis of interrelationships between schools and the city.[84] Fischer realistically concludes:

> To be sure, we cannot marshall all these resources without altering existing political and administrative mechanisms. We shall need new laws, new agencies, and new money; but most of all, we need a new vision, newly shared, of what city life at its best might be, and do, and give.[85]

Mumford could not be more in agreement not only with the need for new mechanisms and new agencies to restructure schools and the community itself, but with the need for looking beyond current urban practices and urban misery to the city which might "become" if education, government, and individual citizens dedicated themselves to a more complete urban life. Perhaps, then, it is not astonishing that Fischer chooses to quote Mumford at length:

> Lewis Mumford put it well: 'We must now conceive the city not primarily as a place of business or government but as an essential organ for expressing and actualizing the new personality . . . Not industry but education will be the center of [activity] and every process and function will be approved . . . to the extent that it furthers human development . . . For the city should be an organ of love; and the best economy of cities is the care and culture of men.'[86]

The city as a means of education and education for a better city go hand-in-hand. Mumford understands what John Fischer, Paul Goodman, and others articulate in terms of education: the city as material for curriculum and background for teaching contains vast, largely unmined resources for educational theory and practice. [87]

The Parkway School in Philadelphia, Community Quest in Honolulu, and a handful of other experiments using the city's institutions and people as resources are a good beginning. Now it is time for educators in every metropolitan area of the country to utilize the city as a fertile source of information and ideas, of artistic creativity, and of knowledge about people and their subcultures. Urban realities in some ways are grim, but urban possibilities are promising. Educators could brighten urban prospects by committing themselves to renewal of the city as an exciting and life-asserting place to live.

---

[1]Morton and Lucia White, *The Intellectual Versus the City* (New York: The New American Library, 1962), p. 204.

[2]Mumford, *The City in History* (New York: Harcourt, Brace and World, 1961), p. 573.

[3]*Ibid.*

[4]Lewis Mumford, "Concluding Address," in *City Invincible: A Symposium on Urbanization and Cultural Development in the Ancient Near East* (Chicago: Chicago University Press, 1960), p. 227.

[5]Mumford, "University City," Introductory Address in *City Invincible*, pp. 10-11.

[6]Mumford, *The City in History*, p. 178.

[7]Mumford, *The Culture of Cities*, p. 319.

[8]Mumford, *The Urban Prospect*, p. 128.

[9]*Ibid.*, p. 203.

[10]*Ibid.*, p. 115.

[11]Michael Harrington, "Cities to Live In," review of *The Urban Prospect*, by Lewis Mumford, *New Republic*, May 25, 1968, p. 23.

[12]Mumford, "Patrick Geddes, Victor Branford, and Applied Sociology in England: The Social Survey, Regionalism and Urban Planning," in *An Introduction to the History of Sociology*, ed. by Harry Elmer Barnes (Chicago: University of Chicago Press, 1948), p. 680.

[13]Mumford, "Mumford on Geddes," *Architectural Review*, CVIII (August, 1950), p. 82.

[14]*Ibid.*, p. 81.

[15]White, *The Intellectual Versus the City*, p. 236.

[16]Mumford, "Mumford on Geddes," p. 87.

[17]*Ibid.*, p. 86.

[18]Paul Goodman, "The Human Uses of Science," *Commentary,* XXX (December, 1960), p. 465.

[19]*Ibid.*

[20]Patrick Geddes, quoted in "An Adventure in Education," by Philip Boardman, *Progressive Education,* XXI (February, 1935), 81.

[21]Diane Divoky, *How Old Will You Be in 1984? Expressions of Student Outrage From the High School Free Press.* Discus Books (New York: Avon Books, 1969).

[22]Boardman, "An Adventure in Education," p. 78.

[23]Patrick Geddes, "A Suggested Plan for a Civic Museum (or Civic Exhibition) and Its Associated Studies," in *Sociological Papers,* Vol. III (London: Macmillan and Company, 1907), p. 204.

[24]Patrick Geddes, "A Suggested Plan for a Civic Museum," p. 199.

[25]*Ibid.,* pp. 209-10.

[26]*Ibid.,* p. 209.

[27]Sir William Holford, foreword to *Pioneer of Sociology: The Life and Letters of Patrick Geddes,* by Philip Mairet (London: Lund Humphries, 1957), p. xv.

[28]Mumford, "Mumford on Geddes," p. 86.

[29]"Students Prowl the Streets to Learn About Cities," *New York Times,* Dec. 10, 1972, p. 109.

[30]Robert Reinhold, "Where, But Also Why, How," *New York Times,* June 17, 1973, Sect. 4, p. 9.

[31]Mumford, *The Urban Prospect,* p. 233.

[32]Mumford, *The Culture of Cities,* p. 300.

[33]Mumford, *Sticks and Stones,* p. 229.

[34]*Ibid.*

[35]Lewis Mumford, "Regions — To Live In," *The Survey: Graphic Number,* May 1, 1925, p. 151.

[36]Jane Jacobs, quoted in "Jane Jacobs: Against Urban Renewal, For Urban Life," by Leticia Kent, *The New York Times Magazine,* May 25, 1969, p. 35.

[37]Lewis Mumford, "Introduction" to *The New Towns: The Answer to Megalopolis,* by Frederick J. Osborn and Arnold Whittick (New York: McGraw-Hill Company, 1963), p. 2.

[38]Mumford, *The City in History,* p. 184.

39Lewis Mumford, "The City," in *Civilization in the United States*, ed. by Harold E. Stearns (New York: Harcourt, Brace and Company, 1922), p. 14.

40Mumford, *The Urban Prospect*, p. 9.

41Mumford, *The Culture of Cities*, p. 422.

42Mumford, "Closing Statement," p. 729.

43Mumford, *The Brown Decades*, p. 88.

44Lewis Mumford, "The Natural History of Urbanization" in *Man's Role in Changing the Face of the Earth*, ed. by William L. Thomas, Jr. (Chicago: University of Chicago Press, 1956), p. 387.

45Mumford, *The Urban Prospect*, p. 89.

46*Ibid.*

47Mumford, *The Brown Decades*, p. 110.

48Mumford, *The Urban Prospect*, p. 238.

49*Ibid.*, p. 239.

50*Ibid.*, p. 240.

51*Ibid.*, pp. 241-42.

52Mumford, *The Urban Prospect*, p. 254.

53Mumford, private interview, March 29, 1968.

54Mumford, *The Urban Prospect*, p. 18.

55*Ibid.*, p. 247.

56*Ibid.*, p. 20.

57*Ibid.*, p. 250.

58*Ibid.*, p. 185.

59*Ibid.*, p. 248.

60*Ibid.*, p. 249.

61*Ibid.*, p. 18.

62Mumford, *The Transformations of Man*, p. 153.

63*King: Montgomery to Memphis*, a filmed documentary of the civil rights movement shown in theaters across the nation on March 23, 1970, made this abundantly clear.

64Michael Harrington has written in this regard: "Last year when Gulf Oil replaced the innovators at the Reston 'New Town' in Virginia with conventional managers, it was announced that the new directors would pay attention to the market rather than social and aesthetic ideals." Harrington, "Cities to Live In," p. 24.

[65]"Cosmopolis," A.B.C. telecast, May 12, 1969.

[66]Jeannye Thornton, "Homesteading in Boston," *Christian Science Monitor*, Jan. 8, 1974, p. 4A.

[67]Nora E. Taylor, "Community Music Center Celebrates Its New Home," *Christian Science Monitor*, Oct. 31, 1973, p. 5.

[68]David Winder, "Harlem Restores Park," *Christian Science Monitor*, Sept. 1, 1973, p. 6.

[69]Mumford, *The Urban Prospect*, p. 241.

[70]Mumford, "Introduction" to *The New Towns*, p. 1.

[71]Lewis Mumford, "Trend is Not Destiny," *Architectural Record*, CXXXXII (December, 1967), 132.

[72]Mumford, *The Culture of Cities*, p. 471.

[73]*Ibid.*, p. 472.

[74]Mumford, *The Urban Prospect*, p. 69.

[75]*Ibid.*, p. 28.

[76]See "Landscaping Lincoln-Style," in *Space for Survival: Blocking the Bulldozer in Urban America*, edited by Charles E. Little and John G. Mitchell, (Richmond Hill, Ontario: Simon and Schuster of Canada, 1971), pp. 50-55.

[77]Mumford, *The Culture of Cities*, p. 475.

[76]*Ibid.*, p. 472.

[79]*Ibid.*, p. 476.

[80]*Ibid.*, pp. 289-90.

[81]*Ibid.*, p. 475.

[82]*Ibid.*, pp. 476-77.

[83]Mumford, *The Urban Prospect*, p. 35.

[84]John H. Fischer, "Schools for Equal Opportunity," in *The Schoolhouse in the City*, ed. by Alvin Toffler (New York: Frederick A. Praeger, 1968), p. 152.

[85]*Ibid.*, pp. 152-53.

[86]Lewis Mumford, quoted by Fischer in "Schools for Equal Opportunity," pp. 152-53 in *The Schoolhouse in the City*, ed. by Alvin Toffler (New York: Praeger Publishers), ©1968.

[87]See Paul Goodman, *Utopian Essays and Practical Proposals* (New York: Vintage Books, 1962).

❧ chapter 6
education and the
new town movement

WALTER L. CREESE, an authority on human environments, believes that the great value of Lewis Mumford's work lies in the combination of urban and rural values in his writings on architecture and city-regional planning.[1] Nowhere is this combination more apparent than in Mumford's life-long concern for the garden city or New Town movement. As early as the 1920s, Mumford asserted that the essential elements in garden cities — the common holding of land by the community and the cooperative operation and direction of the community itself by all the people — were neither distinctive nor completely new to America. The New England village up to the mid-1700's "was a garden-city in every sense that we now apply to that term, and happily its gardens and its harmonious framework have frequently lingered on, even though the economic foundations have long been overthrown."[2] The Puritans set up regulations to limit growth and apportion land, Mumford observes, continuing to remark rather devilishly:

> A friend of mine has called this system "Yankee commu-nism," and I cheerfully bring the institution to the attention of those who do not realize upon what sub-versive principles Americanism, historically, rests.[3]

Contemporary critics of New Towns, like William H. Whyte, might take note of these historical foundations when they argue that Americans cherish private ownership and mobility too much to ever accept or live in "utopian"[4] communities. Perhaps it is Whyte's misunderstanding of New Towns, or at least Mumford's conception of them, that leads him to conclude: "mobility does breed problems, but it is also a dynamic and in the oversight of this the self-contained community is irrelevant if not contradictory to the main sweep of American life."[5]

Certainly Mumford is interested in a dynamic community, but that does not mean he favors the present high rate of transiency which breeds rootlessness and alienation. Moreover, no community is or can be self-contained, as Whyte labels New Towns; Mumford, with his regional and global perspective, is well aware of this fact. Though defending the garden city as a distinct entity, Mumford sees it as part of a regional network of towns and cities:

> The point is that the garden-city is useful only as a concrete objective in a complete scheme of regional cities . . . Saltaire, Pullman, Port Sunlight, Letchworth [early experiments] are drops in the bucket . . . the aim of a garden-city movement must be to change the shape of the bucket itself; that is to say, the frame of our civilization.[6]

If New Towns are "contradictory to the main sweep of American life," as Whyte maintains, then so much the better. Mumford, in 1927, was trying to get to the roots of this "sweep" or direction and reorient America to an organic, cooperative economy rather than the competitive, money-centered system which Whyte apparently assumes is best.

New Town History

But what of the New Town movement itself: What preceded this movement in the nineteenth century and along what lines did it develop? Robert Owen's proposal to build small balanced communities in the open country and Fourier's scheme for phalansteries contributed to the idea of a rational civic economy, according to Mumford. Communities inspired by Owen and Fourier differed from middle-class suburban settlements in that integral relationships to industry were achieved, provision was made for the social life of workers, and a small civic whole was formed. A major weakness was their frequent dependence upon the initiative of an "enlightened employer" who sometimes happened to be tyrannical.[7]

Mumford credits Ebenezer Howard, author of *Garden Cities of To-Morrow* (1902), with fusing the ideas of Owen, Fourier, James Buckingham, and Henry George into the original conception of the garden city or balanced urban development.[8] Actually it was a utopian novel, *Looking Backward*, by the American, Edward Bellamy, that inspired Howard to conceive an ideal town as essentially a socialist community.[9] Howard wanted a city small enough to be manageable but large enough to insure variety and diversity; he hoped to relieve urban congestion by establishing new urban centers limited in area and population. Mumford explains that Greek cities, notably Miletus, followed this form of growth between the sixth and fourth centuries B.C., and while this kind of development lasted "it not merely prevented congestion, but maintained a balance between town and country that may have been one of the conditions that fostered the extraordinary creativity of Hellenic culture up to the Hellenistic age."[10] Not only did Howard wish to unite town and country by emphasizing their interdependence and complementarity, he also wished, in Mumford's words, "to utilize the facilities of modern technology without sacrificing the social advantages of the historic city."[11]

Howard knew, as Mumford does, that a single garden city or even a scattering of mini-cities would not be adequate. Therefore, he insisted on the creation of a regional unit to develop at least ten cities with a total population of a third of a million. These "town clusters" would be interconnected by a public rapid transit system enabling them to operate as a single unit when necessary.[12] Most important, the cluster of small cities would offer social and cultural advantages that no single town or small city could provide — a greater number of options for work, education, and leisure time.

Many of Howard's ideas were translated into New Towns built in Britain and America during the early part of this century. New Towns blossomed all over Britain after World War II when the New Towns Act went into effect, but until recently in America very little attention has been focused on the kind of city and regional authority Howard conceived. In the late twenties, however, Clarence Stein and Henry Wright, with Mumford's strong encouragement, adapted the garden city idea to the automobile age with pedestrian traffic well separated from auto traffic. Architectural critic Wolf Von Eckardt cites Radburn, New Jersey, which Stein and Wright planned, as the first "to reconcile the demands of livability with mobility."[13] Mumford especially likes Radburn's concept of neighborhood calculated roughly in terms of the number of families needed to support an elementary school.[14]

By 1938 the term "garden city" had been appropriated by various interest groups and soon became distorted and perverted. Sometimes it was considered synonymous with an ordinary bedroom suburb and used derisively; sometimes it was cause for a good belly laugh.[15] Mumford found it necessary to correct the often distorted image of garden cities by reiterating their characteristics: land must be held by a common authority; growth and population must be controlled; a functional balance must be achieved between town and country, and between housing, industries, markets, schools, recreation, and all the other needs of a genuinely balanced community.[16]

Contemporary New Towns

The New Towns movement in Britain, Sweden, and Finland in the second half of the twentieth century has been generally successful although, quite naturally, a number of problems arose as the experimental towns began functioning. Unfortunately, clusters of balanced towns, as Howard and Mumford proposed, have not been constructed. The result is complaints from inhabitants about isolation, lack of varied activity, and too much sameness. Farsta, Sweden, is more a suburb of Stockholm than a New Town even though it contains many characteristics of the latter. Cumbernauld, near Glasgow, Scotland, is approved by both Mumford and Von Eckardt, even though of higher density than many New Towns. Both men oppose too much open space or greenery, just as they oppose too little, because getting around on foot becomes difficult, and creative urban design may be sacrificed for excessive concern with greenery.[17]

Reston, Virginia is one of the best known planned communities in the United States. Unfortunately, Reston developer Robert E. Simons ran into financial difficulties and the community quickly became restricted to upper middle-class residents. Today Reston does not satisfy the need for socio-economic balance even though the town is progressive in terms of its respect for the natural environment.

Columbia, Maryland has been more successful than Reston in providing government subsidized housing for middle and low income families. A number of light industries have been attracted to Columbia and social-cultural-recreational services are available in the community. Most important, Columbia is racially integrated: about seventeen percent of the present population is black and adult residents are generally pleased that their city is mixed. Nevertheless, some problems have resulted from integration; new residents bring old prejudices with them and the rich-poor problem generates tensions in Columbia as elsewhere. The youth director for the village of Harper's Choice, Samuel F. Prentice, Jr., points to one of the difficulties for young people:

> Here there are no roots, no structure. Everything is new, everything is creative . . . The open community and the experimental open high school are in a way disorienting . . . Teens are constantly being asked, 'What do you want?' and they are not sure.[18]

One black youth experienced a number of problems when his family moved to the new city from an all-black neighborhood, but he has considerable faith in Columbia as an integrated community. He would like to see more blacks in top management positions in the city and has other constructive suggestions to make. But he also affirms:

> To me . . . what is incredible in Columbia is to go around the elementary schools, or look out in the back of my yard and see all kinds of kids playing together and getting along . . . Columbia has a potential to make this a community that cares about each other — not just tolerates each other. It will take work.[19]

This young man, Douglas Toomer, has an attitude that other New Town residents and future residents might emulate. The potential he talks about is the personal-social potential Mumford envisions in New Towns. It is a potential that easily justifies the study and designing of new communities in schools, colleges, and community education centers; it is nothing less than the potential for greater humanness through interaction with others.

Tapiola, Finland is a relatively low density town which conserves a great deal of countryside, but, at the same time, is a balanced community which makes it possible for children to walk to school, to enjoy recreation at a centrally located indoor swimming pool, and to visit small factories nearby. A central shopping area, free from cars, is reached quite easily by foot, bicycle, or bus from any part of town; it contains stores, offices, restaurants, and a discotheque. A concert hall and art center are planned, light industries are in operation, and a variety of housing, ranging from several attractive apartment towers and low-rise apartments to row houses and single family homes, is available.

In the early nineteen-fifties, Heikki von Hertzen, the guiding spirit behind Tapiola, helped to organize the non-profit Housing Foundation Asuntosäätiö composed of the Family Welfare League, the Confederation of Finnish Trade Unions, the Federation of Civil Servants, the Central Association of Tenants, the Mannerheim League, and the Association of the Disabled. The Housing Foundation has since created a town in which different social groups work and live in harmony with each other. "We do not want to build houses or dwellings but socially correct surroundings for modern man and his family," writes the author of a colorful brochure about Tapiola.[20]

New communities where people of all backgrounds and interests can find housing and work, recreational-educational-cultural resources, and a genuine spirit of community are sorely needed today. Up to the present time in the United States and in many other affluent countries, few alternatives to congested, antiquated cities have been offered. Individuals either have had to embrace suburbia with its long commutes and possible social deficiencies — snobbery, segregation, status seeking, political irresponsibility[21] — or settle for cramped housing, sparse greenery, heavily polluted air, poor public services, and rising crime rates. New housing, with few exceptions, has been confined to dismal housing projects, fancy apartments for the well-to-do, or developments in suburbs where most industry has moved.[22]

Certainly much attention should be directed to suburban housing; restrictive zoning ordinances, building codes, and construction regulations should be investigated, and fair housing and civil rights legislation implemented. Federally subsidized, non-profit, low- and middle-income housing should be built in suburbs where "snob-zoning" presently excludes the less fortunate. Appealing urban housing, like that in the Washington Park redevelopment area of Roxbury, Boston's black community, should be expanded.

But another alternative for integrated living ought now be brought to the fore: New Towns and cities defined, as Howard and Mumford saw them, not as suburbs, but as the antithesis of suburbs: "not a more rural retreat, but a more integrated foundation for an effective life."[23] Urban residents, now tightly packed together in substandard dwellings, should at least be offered the choice of living in a dynamic community which promises breathing space, excellent community schools, and pleasant surroundings. Not the least appealing quality of this alternative would be an opportunity for every citizen to participate in personal and social decision-making, to become actively involved in planning and running his/her own community.

A recent study sponsored by Laurence S. Rockefeller recommends that New Towns be built as laboratories for making the nation's cities more livable. The study, known as "Man and His Urban Environment," proposes that "New Towns be financed by public corporations and that they have a controlled pattern of growth. Housing for varying economic levels would be included and services such as power, water, sewage and waste disposal utilizing new technologies would be centralized. Land would be permanently leased to users rather than owned by them. Mumford would agree with Rockefeller's assertion that:

> The future of our country may depend upon our succeeding in an effort to plan and manage our constantly growing urban areas in such a way as to make living in them rewarding rather than frustrating.[24]

An especially promising proposal for two New Towns within an urban area was announced in the late 1960's. Development of two communities on Welfare Island in New York City would provide housing for low, middle, and high income groups; open spaces in the form of five parks, new schools, and a day care center; a promenade around the island to take advantage of the waterfront setting; shops; a community swimming pool; subway connections with Manhattan; and a twenty-five acre "ecological park" sponsored by the state and city. Automobiles would be left in garages upon arrival on the island.[25]

Since the Welfare Island proposal, a number of other New Town developments have been announced. Franklin Town will be built on a fifty acre site near the center of downtown Philadelphia. A privately sponsored development, Franklin Town will provide three to four million square feet of office space, housing for 4,000 families, over a thousand hotel rooms, and recreational facilities. One of the most important features of this town within the city is the City Council ruling that all homeowners displaced by the development must be relocated in the new community.

In Minneapolis, Cedar-Riverside will have five residential neighborhoods, each with its own support facilities, schools, day care centers, and health centers. By 1992 the population of Cedar-Riverside is expected to reach 30,000. Flower Mound New Town in Texas will cover about one-third of the area of the present town of Flower Mound and eventually have a population of 65,000. Almost half of the development will be residential with homes varying widely in price.[26]

One of the more unique new cities is being built in North Carolina by McKissick Enterprises, headed by lawyer and civil rights leader Floyd McKissick. Soul City will include mixed-income, multi-racial housing; industrial parks providing jobs for many of the 50,000 future residents; open spaces and recreational areas; schools; shopping plazas; a public transportation network; and an Afro-American Cultural and Trade Center. Only a dream for five years, Soul City has finally gained not only federal and state support but also encouragement from once-skeptical local leaders and citizens. Black capitalism will play a large role in this huge project which is being supported financially by a number of banks and insurance companies. Whether or not residents will play a planning and governing role in Soul City is not clear at this time, but it is definite that Soul City, as McKissick proudly states, is "the largest economic venture undertaken by a black man."[27]

Implications for Education

What are the implications for education in the New Town movement? Because towns and cities are being planned at the present time, educators are offered magnificent opportunities to involve students in research, planning, analysis, design, and even execution of new cities. From far-reaching philosophical problems like the nature of man and his purpose in life to social problems dealing with the degree of flexibility possible in New Towns, from political problems of participation by all prospective residents in policy-making to technical problems revolving around the need for simultaneous building of housing and services for an entire community, a study of new cities would make for exciting and relevant learning. An especially critical problem to be confronted in New Town planning concerns implications of such a development on the human and natural environment of a selected area. The disciplines involved in studying New Towns could range from sociology (What problems may minority members encounter in an entirely new setting?), to economics (How can New Towns be financed? What are the implications in private development of New Towns?), to art (How can New Towns create an atmosphere that artists would find appealing?), to history (Will, or should, New Towns have historical roots? Can history be constructed from day to day events? Can and should traditions be fostered?).

At least one college, Goddard, includes a "course" or project concerned with the design of new cities in which economic and institutional forms serve human purposes and the inhabitants serve as planners. Dividing time between the Goddard campus in Vermont and work in Cambridge, Massachusetts, students and teachers carry on planning and research, study present legislation, look at current examples of town development, interview individuals for their opinions, and analyze past mistakes. In Cambridge, they work closely with professional planners.[28]

Furthermore, study of New Towns need not be limited to experimental colleges or colleges in general. Elementary and high school students, and adults as well, could work fruitfully on new city projects crossing virtually all subjects and fields of interest. One extremely important first step would involve learning the desires of inner city residents for housing, services, and community life. With this information, gained through personal interviews, neighborhood gatherings, and questionnaires, students would have a much better idea of what kind of living conditions people actually want, thus eliminating arbitrary decisions based on hypotheses.

The planning of and subsequent living in a New Town or community can be a valuable educational experience for all involved. A California community group known as the Pahana Town Forum, "Pahana" meaning "lost brother" in the Hopi Indian language, has decided to build a New Town where people can grow and relate to each other in a warm, trusting environment. The town will have a maximum of 3,000 inhabitants and combine some initial planning with slow growth over a number of years. Individuals in the Pahana Town Forum have agreed on a number of basics for their community: cars will not be permitted but walking, bicycling, horseback riding and possibly a quiet bus service will be encouraged; recycling and alternate energy sources will be promoted; a small experimental college and a school system centered on community resources will be organized; and town meetings rather than a city council will be set up. [29] Community education programs in other parts of the country might follow the example of the Pahana Town Forum and give attention to the designing and building of alternative communities.

A very different kind of New Town is being planned in Southern New Jersey. Called Seabrook Farmington, it will be managed by the re-entry and environmental systems division of the General Electric Corporation. About half of the six thousand acres will be zoned for farms and open space and the rest will house most of the 45,000 projected residents. Undoubtedly, Mumford would be skeptical about involvement of the GE re-entry and environmental systems division in this huge project; what will result from the space-oriented megamachine being put to work on New Towns, he might inquire? The vice president of the division would not allay his fears when he boasts:

> Having been a major participant in our Government's space program . . . General Electric has assembled a team of scientists and managers with project capabilities never before dreamed . . . It is only fitting that we harness some of the talent that helped propel us to the moon and focus it on building a better environment here on earth. [30]

Perhaps we can learn some things about building from the space program, but if Mumford is right about the organic and aesthetic needs of men and women, children and youth, then we will have to be wary of modelling a human community on a megamechanical enterprise. The super-planning of Seabrook Farmington in contrast to the informal, almost casual planning of the Pahana Town Forum would provide an excellent point of departure for educational study. What are the advantages and disadvantages of each? Which project seems to offer more opportunities for citizen participation? What effect might the profit motive have on one of them? How can alternative New Towns compete with industry-managed New Towns which obtain funds from a Florida-based real estate investment trust, as the Seabrook owners did?

At the center of the new community planning process is a conflict between the planner and the planned for, a conflict worthy of vigorous educational debate. Mumford wants to plan *with* people, but much of his effort in New Town planning deals with planning a balanced community *for* people. He seems to fear that giving individuals too much freedom to define the kind of community they want will lead only to a psychological-sociological-aesthetic mediocrity because people have not been adequately educated to make such decisions. If Mumford is right, it might be best at present for imaginative planners and ecologists, after learning needs and desires, to plan the sort of New Town which they believe will not only satisfy future residents, but also provide features which may or may not be considered by non-professionals. Just what role untrained individuals would play would always be open to discussion.

Ideally, however, the important qualities and features of a desirable community would become a focus of education at all levels so that individuals themselves — with professional assistance when needed — could plan new cities from conception as well as plan the social and physical rehabilitation of neighborhoods and whole sections of present cities. This educational program might incorporate debate on the problems of urban congestion and deterioration, the meaning of community, the need for privacy, the advantages and disadvantages of decentralization, the functional as well as aesthetically pleasing design of housing and public buildings, and the role of automobiles now and in the future. How low-income families can be educated to help plan and live in new cities, if that is where they choose to live, and even more fundamentally, how to educate families to the potential opportunities available in this new kind of community might be considered. Ways to persuade state and federal governments to support balanced New Town development could be included.

Until the time when individuals become sufficiently aware of New Town possibilities, perhaps it is necessary for planners and other professionals to play a large part in planning and design. But great responsibility rests with educators whose job it is to introduce this subject to students and then, in joint effort, to experiment with imaginative new means of decentralization and alternative life-styles.

As the idea of new communities catches hold, planners and educators must increasingly give greater authority to the people who live or plan to live in these new areas. As planners become consultants and educators become resource people, they must cease, as the socio-economist Robert Theobald asserts, to tell people in the ghettoes or in New Towns "what they ought to value and instead, in consort with them, design environments which will provide them with the capacity to develop their humanness." [31]

In every deliberation and action educators have an obligation to include all parties involved; educators must increasingly work with professional planners, ecologists, anthropologists, sociologists, and architects but especially with community groups who rightly demand self-determination.

Population Control

Mumford alleges that New Towns cannot be successful without coming to grips with the problem of population growth, an issue which should become an integral part of the school and college curriculum:

> Each growing institution, be it a factory, a hospital, a library, a university, a department store, must handle the problems of quantitative growth, and seek to establish a dynamic equilibrium and a controlled method of growth . . . Only on such terms will it further its own development and harmonize it with the larger regional pattern necessary for the orderly growth of urban communities. [32]

Quantitative growth must indeed be the concern of every institution if New Towns, based on controlled growth, have a chance for success. But the problem is a much deeper one that goes to the roots not only of New Town, urban, and regional development but also affects the survival of every person on earth. The problem reaches out to all people who need comfortable housing no matter what local cultural style it may incorporate, adequate and nourishing food, work to perform which is not drudgery, and as much education in the broadest possible sense as desired.

In order for these most basic needs to be satisfied, must limits be placed on the earth's population? Even with new sources of food from the oceans, which have yet to be developed on a large scale, is there a maximum number of human beings and other animals which the earth can harmoniously support? Aside from basic needs, can privacy be assured in housing or when taking a walk in the woods if the population is allowed to grow uncontrolled? Can a sense of community with mutual respect ever be achieved in gigantic, still growing cities like New York and Tokyo where people are crowded together in subways, slums, and sterile apartment projects? What are the effects of overcrowding and congestion on human behavior?[33] Can New Towns be built along the lines described by Howard and Mumford without planning carefully for population growth? And most important, if control is necessary, how can it be accomplished without intimations of or actual practice of discrimination, bias, favoritism?

The latter problem suggests fundamental questions concerning the nature of racism, the psychological insecurity of minority groups, and the basis of authority for making critical decisions. One question leads to another and another. In studying the New Town movement and solutions for urban dilemmas, all of these and a multitude of other questions should be considered, not only in theory but in actual contact with those who have a particularly large stake in matters of population control, in moving to New Towns from ghetto areas, and generally in receiving their due share after many years of indignities. Possibilities for exploring the most demanding urban problems, rectifying mistakes of the past, and designing communities of the future are almost unlimited. It is imperative that educators at all levels follow Mumford's leadership and focus on these rich possibilities.

---

[1]Walter L. Creese, telephone conversation with the author, July 21, 1969.

[2]Mumford. *Sticks and Stones,* p. 30.

[3]*Ibid.,* p. 18.

[4]Meaning idealistic and self-contained in a derogatory sense. See William H. Whyte, *The Last Landscape* (Garden City, N.Y.: Doubleday, 1968), p. 240.

[5]*Ibid.*, p. 228.

[6]Lewis Mumford, "The Fate of Garden Cities," *Journal of the American Institute of Architects*, XV (February 1927), p. 38, quoted in Walter L. Creese, *The Search for Environment — The Garden City: Before and After* (New Haven, Conn.: Yale University Press, 1966), p. 306.

[7]Mumford. *The Culture of Cities*, pp. 391-93.

[8]Mumford. *The Urban Prospect*, p. 145.

[9]F.J. Osborn, "Preface," to Ebenezer Howard, *Garden Cities of To-Morrow* (Cambridge, Mass.: M.I.T. Press, 1965), pp. 20-21.

[10]Lewis Mumford, "Introduction," to Frederick J. Osborn and Arnold Whittick, *The New Towns: The Answer to Megalopolis* (New York: McGraw-Hill, 1963), p. 3.

[11]*Ibid.*, p. 2.

[12]*Ibid.*, p. 5.

[13]Von Eckardt, *A Place to Live: The Crisis of the Cities*, p. 364.

[14]Mumford, *The Urban Prospect*, p. 68.

[15]Mumford, *The Culture of Cities*, p. 396.

[16]*Ibid.*, p. 397.

[17]Von Eckardt, *A Place to Live*, p. 366; Mumford, *The Urban Prospect*, p. 74.

[18]Quoted in Jo Ann Levine, " 'Integration is Caring, Not Just Tolerating,' " *Christian Science Monitor*, May 5, 1973, p. 11.

[19]Quoted in Jo Ann Levine, " 'Integration is Caring, Not Just Tolerating,' " p. 11. Reprinted by permission from The Christian Science Monitor © 1973. The Christian Science Publishing Society. All rights reserved.

[20]See *Tapiola Garden City*, a brochure published by The Housing Foundation Asuntosäätiö, Tapiola, Finland. For an excellent first-hand account of a visit to Tapiola, see Wolf Von Eckardt, *A Place to Live*, pp. 347-59.

[21]Lewis Mumford, *The City in History*, p. 502.

[22]The co-executive director of the National Committee Against Discrimination in Housing, Inc. states: "73% of the nation's industry

has moved to the suburban areas in the last decade." *Boston Herald Traveler*, May 13, 1969, p. 3.

23Lewis Mumford, "The Garden City Idea and Modern Planning," introductory essay in Howard, *Garden Cities of To-Morrow*, p. 35.

24Quoted in "Towns Envisioned as Labs for Cities," by Murray Illson, *New York Times*, Nov. 19, 1972, p. 59.

25Ada Louise Huxtable, "A Plan for Welfare Island is Unveiled," *New York Times*, October 10, 1969, p. 45.

26Jean Christensen, "Planned Towns as Big Business," *New York Times*, Aug. 5, 1973, Sect. 3, p. 13.

27Quoted in John Robinson, "Soul City: A Dream Buttressed by Black Capitalism," *Boston Sunday Globe*, May 26, 1974, p. A-3.

28"New Cities Project," Course listing in "Greatwood Courses," Goddard College, Fall, 1969, pp. 7-9.

29David Holmstrom, "Do-It-Yourselfers Plan to Build New Small Town Without Cars," *Christian Science Monitor*, July 5, 1973, p. 5.

30Quoted in Donald Janson, "New City Planned in South Jersey," *New York Times*, June 17, 1973, p. 23. © 1973 by The New York Times Company. Reprinted by permission.

31Robert Theobald, "Planning *with* People," in William R. Ewald, ed. *Environment and Change: The Next Fifty Years* (Bloomington, Indiana: Indiana University Press, 1968), p. 185.

32Mumford, "Introduction," *The New Towns*, p. 5.

33*New York Times* feature article, "Delays on Subway Infuriate Riders," January 21, 1970, p. 39, documents the frustration and depression which prevails among New Yorkers supposedly conditioned to crowded situations. One man makes this perceptive comment: "I've taken the subway all my life . . . Why, even when I was a kid we were pushing people out of the way, behaving like a stampede of cattle. That's life, or anyway, that's life in New York. But these delays are something else. Why, you have no time any more. You have time for nothing, time for nobody." © 1970 by The New York Times Company. Reprinted by permission.

❧ chapter 7
regional survey and planning: toward educational synthesis

THE REGION as a cultural, geographic, and economic unit has been one of Mumford's prime concerns since the nineteen-twenties. Like Geddes' interest in the region, Mumford's centers on the constant interpenetration of rural and urban values, natural open spaces and man-made containers for space, simplicity of outdoor life and sophistication of cultural customs. For Mumford the region is a whole, with the city, its environs and the countryside as integral parts.[1]

"With our modern means of communication," Mumford observed as early as 1928, "the region is now the locus of activity, not the single unit of a city."[2] The regionalism he espouses does not deny the conveniences of modern life but rather sees telephones an and radios, highways and airplanes bringing many advantages of the city to the entire region:

> Regionalism as a modern social reality . . . is, essentially, the effort to provide for the continuous cultivation and development of all the resources of the earth and man; an effort which recognizes the existence of real groups and social configurations and geographic relationships that are ignored by the abstract culture of the metropolis and which opposes to the aimless nomadism of modern commercial enterprise the conception of a stable and settled and balanced and cultivated life.[3]

Because regionalism recognizes differences that arise out of geographical-historical backgrounds and emphasizes regional and cultural variation of all kinds, regionalism can be interpreted as a counter-movement to dehumanizing specialization and homogenization. In conceiving a regional culture, Mumford notes, " . . . one should think of an orchestra with each piece and each musician distinct in its functions and capacities, yet supplementing the others, rather than as a massing of mechanical drums, each drum monotonously thumping out the same beat."[4]

Of the basically two kinds of unity in regionalism — unity by suppression in which a single uniform pattern is maintained and unity by inclusion in which a multitude of different patterns find common elements or become elements in a complex configuration — Mumford clearly opts for the latter.[5] Local dialects, foods, occupations, customs, architecture, and clothing should be encouraged because they represent better adaptations to the actual conditions of life in the region than do their standardized counterparts. The emphasis in regionalism, in sum, must not be upon the area or the place "but upon what the place fosters, upon the quality of its life."[6]

Mumford's desire for individualized, well-integrated regions is not based on a nostalgia for past times and past ways. He attacks vigorously the kind of wistful regionalism expressed in Uncle Remus stories; in the stories of Howells, Garland, and Bret Harte; and in Mark Twain's *Life on the Mississippi*,[7] but praises the vitality of New England embodied in murals painted by the distinguished Mexican artist, Orozco, at Dartmouth College.[8]

The delusion of attempting to return to a past that no longer exists, expressed today in pseudo-colonial gas stations in New England and in non-functional columned architecture virtually everywhere, is a serious problem for regionalism. No one is more repulsed by this fakery than Mumford who fears over-contentment with dreams of archaic revival rather than genuine regional renewal in terms of man's accumulating discoveries, desires, and humanistic purposes.[9] What Mumford considers sentimental regionalism attempts to perpetuate an obsolete image while it conveniently forgets achievements of integrity in the past (like the New England libraries and railroad stations of Henry Hobson Richardson neglected for so long) and honest contemporary achievements (like the recent Boston City Hall denounced angrily by aroused traditionalists).

Regionalism should certainly not be confused with nationalism or national states in Mumford's scheme. Regionalism has a more local and concentrated objective, except where national and regional boundaries happen to coincide.[10] To him, nationalism "is an attempt to make the laws and customs and beliefs of a single region or city do duty for the varied expressions of a multitude of other regions"[11] and to do so through indoctrination in the schools, propaganda in the press, restrictive laws, and the suppression of minority opinions.[12] Distrusting nationalism as militaristic at heart, Mumford downplays the national state in much of his writing and accents the region with its intimate social ties and the world with its wider human fellowship. Stressing the equally important need for world interchange and for roots in the region, not one before the other but both together, he never wavers from the conviction that real patriotism comes not from right-wing nationalistic fervor but from immersion in the everyday life and hopes of the region.

Contemporary so-called "patriots" with their flag-waving and ostentatious parading might well accept Mumford's view and turn to constructive involvement in their own regions, whether this entails feeding the hungry, rehabilitating prisoners, or revitalizing the environment. With a vigorous regional culture they would be much better prepared to deal with problems and prospects in the region at large — the entire globe — and thereby become patriots of the world itself rather than myopic "patriots" of a single state. Doing so they would join the quintessential patriots of today: those young people and adults who place human needs first by opposing militarism and racism and ugliness wherever they occur.

Regional Planning

"The grasp of the region as a dynamic social reality is a first step toward a constructive policy of planning, housing, and urban renewal," Mumford writes in The Culture of Cities.[13] A feel for and understanding of the region comes through intensive, ongoing exploration of natural, economic, political, and human resources; a thorough grasp of the region prepares the way for regional planning which is concerned with the broad development and renewal of the area and its culture.

Regional planning recognizes the close relationship between congested cities and the relatively unpopulated countryside.

Regional planning was called "the New Conservation — the conservation of human values hand in hand with natural resources"[14] almost half a century before the "New Conservation" of the 1960's and 1970's changed the meaning of conservation from the simple preservation of an unspoiled area here or there to a more inclusive ecological exploration of the impact of human beings on the natural environment of earth.

For Mumford, a central question of regional planning is:

> . . . how the population and civic facilities can be distributed so as to promote and stimulate a vivid, creative life throughout a whole region . . . The regionalist attempts to plan such an area so that . . . the population will be distributed so as to utilize, rather than to nullify or destroy, its natural advantages.[15]

Mumford has not fundamentally altered this early interpretation. If anything, he feels the regional approach is more necessary today than ever; in 1961, for instance, he speaks of the need to turn the whole regional landscape into a collective park,[16] and four years later urges that regional authorities be established to curb land speculation and restrict uses of land that do not conform with public policy.[17]

Back in the nineteen-twenties regional planning was one of the big issues in American planning, according to Walter Creese, and Lewis Mumford was one of the most active in fostering this concept.[18] In 1925, Mumford contrasted two different regional plans of New York State in a speech before the American Institute of Architects. The first plan included the area within a fifty mile radius of New York City and was, in Mumford's words, "an attempt to promote better living conditions by costly plans for more traffic, higher buildings, increasing land-values, more intensive congestion."[19]

The other plan, Henry Wright's, included the whole state and maintained that "technical ability can achieve little that is fundamentally worth the effort until we reshape our institutions in such a way as to subordinate financial and property values to those of human welfare."[20] The second plan was highly preferable to Mumford in 1925, as it is today, even though history has shown that planning — or the lack of it — followed the first route and only now are Americans awakening to the vital need for thinking along the lines of the second plan.

In May 1925, an entire issue of *The Survey:Graphic Number* was devoted to regional planning. Mumford's article, "The Fourth Migration," introduced the issue and the editors commented: "A brilliant review of the trend of folk-movement in America, and a forecast of the new migration, already stirring into motion, that may turn the drift of population from the cities to the land."[21]

To underline its relevance many years later, Mumford deliberately chose "The Fourth Migration" as a preface to *The Urban Prospect*. It is regrettable that the fourth migration — a decentralization and redistribution of population throughout the region — has been taking place as a flight to the suburbs rather than in a way Mumford favors. Regarding the fourth migration, he commented in 1925: " . . . we may either permit it to crystallize in a formation quite as bad as those of our earlier migrations, or we may turn it to better account by leading it into new channels."[22]

In the past four decades the migration to the suburbs has followed the bad examples of past migrations, particularly the first; clearing the continent and exploiting the land has been ruthlessly copied in the proliferation of subdivisions and the contempt for community values. The black migration from the rural South to the ghettoes of large Northern cities has followed still other migrations, like the second, from the countryside and other nations into factory towns and cities that were considered solely as places of work, not as healthy places to live and bring up a family. The fourth migration has not yet led into new channels, although hopeful signs are beginning to appear. They range from a renewed interest in New Town development to the New York State Plan of the mid 1960's which emphasizes that regional planning lies beyond the scope of municipal action alone.

Regionalism and regional planning are more alive in the world today than ever before. Stuart Chase notes that regional interest is growing in Europe with the Common Market and in Latin America for a common market; in Africa where about fifty states have become "sovereign nations" the need for effective regional development and planning is very great.[23] The Scandinavian countries continue to work closely together and regional planning in England and Scotland is widespread.

But in the United States regional planning has been slow to take hold. One major reason has been the large number of overlapping, separate units of government that effectively obstruct regional cooperation; in the Chicago area alone there are over one thousand units of government.[24] Mumford recognized this problem in a 1925 speech when he urged a more satisfactory administrative unit than either state or city had proved to be — the political region.[25]

Michael Harrington, one of America's most observant social critics, agrees with Mumford and others that regional governments capable of coordinating revitalized cities, New Towns, rural areas, and open spaces are necessary. Metropolitan units are too small to be effective since they concentrate only on urban or built up areas and are hostile toward a regional mixture of land uses. Harrington believes that regional legislatures for democratic decision-making are needed; like Theobald, and to a lesser extent Mumford, he is concerned about *who* does the planning and strongly insists that citizens play a vital part in the planning and governing process.[26]

Harrington is correct to view problems of the poor and powerless in regional perspective. *The Report of the National Advisory Commission on Civil Disorders* confirms both Harrington's and Mumford's faith in regional thinking, emphasizing that the crises confronting cities today cannot be met without the cooperation of both suburbs and cities. The regional cooperation favored by the Commission may take various forms — metropolitan government, regional planning, joint endeavors — though, unfortunately, it relies exclusively on state leadership.[27]

Harrington and Mumford would not simply look to the state or even to the federal government to mediate between cities and suburbs, but would look to the regions themselves to organize and operate as balanced, integrated, largely self-governing units. Though Mumford thinks of regions as autonomous to a considerable extent, he never forgets the important need to work out areas for inter-regional cooperation and super-regional authority.[28] His brand of regionalism does not aim at either economic or cultural self-sufficiency, but it does aim at a more even development of local resources; industries would be varied and locally suitable while extra-regional production and consumption would reach beyond national borders to the world at large.[29]

An example of regional planning in action which hopefully promises to spread to other parts of the country is the Minneapolis-St. Paul area where a planning authority that crosses city, town, and county boundaries is operating. The authority has the power to act upon problems that mutually affect the one hundred or so communities in the region, problems like public transportation, sewage disposal, incineration, air pollution, and so forth.[30]

In Massachusetts, the Metropolitan Area Planning Council, composed of dozens of cities and towns around Boston, has conducted studies on open space needs among various other activities. One M.A.P.C. recommendation for open space near the urban center, a peninsula in Hingham Harbor called World's End, has been saved from the eager hands of developers by the efforts of citizens who purchased it for public parkland. Mumford would be pleased with this citizen victory for many reasons, not the least that World's End was originally landscaped by Frederick Law Olmsted and is accessible to hundreds of thousands of people in high density areas not far away. The potential in natural areas like World's End for school visits — for the study of ecology, geology, and landscape design, for example — is vast. Certainly the possibilities extend beyond field trips made for years by students in Harvard's Graduate School of Design to this once privately-owned peninsula.

Several years ago, Boston's mayor met with officials of surrounding cities and towns to discuss ways of tackling regional problems and later proposed a metropolitan government for Boston and its bedroom communities. And a former Polaroid executive has been devoting most of his time recently to the creation of "Norumbega," a regional cluster of eighteen suburbs west of Boston which would become an "integral city."[31] Ian MacHarg at the University of Pennsylvania has been making regional ecological studies in Maryland and other states; the New England Regional Commission has been considering railroad difficulties and recreational needs in New England; and Toronto, Ontario has been dealing with various municipal problems on a regional basis. Significant though these recent steps are, they barely scratch the surface. Regional planning must eventually be understood by people in cities, in suburbs, and in rural areas for what it is: an intelligent way to plan growth and development in order to assure a life-affirming environment for all.

Urban dwellers would benefit from regional planning by receiving greater financial assistance and expanded transportation-communication-recreation links with the rest of the region. Suburbanites would benefit by increased contacts with inner city residents representing various ethnic traditions — especially if a region-wide school system were established — and by cultural resources of the city. Rural dwellers would benefit through diminished isolation and greater access to innovative schools, regional libraries, theater groups, workshops, entertainment, and jobs. Urban, suburban, and rural residents would enrich the cultural life of each other while maintaining the distinctive characteristics of each. Mutuality would become the key of regionality.

Regional planning could make use of environmental techniques like scenic easements to encourage landscape preservation; tax reductions to encourage farming; and land-use planning to specify areas best suitable for homes, factories, schools, roads, recreation, and open space. A new conception of zoning would guarantee that families in different socio-economic groups or individuals who happen to have different skin colors would not be zoned out, as much "snob zoning" in the suburbs does today. Schools would become balanced socially and racially because housing eventually would be integrated. Until neighborhoods are balanced, however, children would be bused to neighboring parts of the region in order to share experiences with children from a different milieu. The Supreme Court recently has dealt this possibility a serious blow, but region-wide school systems will have to become a reality if the national commitment to integration is honest.

A stubborn regional planning problem appearing in the New York State plan of the mid-1960's centers on the treatment of statistical probabilities as firm, almost pre-determined predictions. Mumford is troubled by this tendency and criticizes the plan's taking for granted that the number of people in New York State will rise from sixteen to thirty million by the year 2020. Arguing that many unpredictable factors may nullify this estimate, he deplores the tendency "to treat the technological forces and institutional practices now in operation as if they were immortal."[32]

The same fatalistic tendency can be seen among educators who predict that schools will inevitably grow larger in physical size and among highway engineers who assume that automobiles will always multiply and therefore require many more miles of asphalt. Perhaps the greatest perpetrators of this faulty creed are corporate executives in many parts of the world who joyously predict steady economic growth that will guarantee bigger and safer profits for years to come. Seldom stopping to consider the implications of expansion of multinational corporations in terms of natural ecology or the quality of life generally, these narrow-visioned individuals are content, even delighted, to accept statistical projections as inevitable truth.

For regional planning to succeed, this tendency must be overcome. Individuals must become aware, as Mumford observes, that *trend* is not *destiny*. Men and women can and must be in creative control of their destiny;[33] unlimited expansion is not an absolute. The present crisis in our cities, the segregation of our suburbs, the deterioration of our environment are not final and irrevocable. Regional planning may help us out of our present dilemmas although, with Mumford, we cannot say with absolute certitude that it will. We *can* say with assurance, however, that human energy and imagination can be applied much more than at present to experiments centering on regional planning and cooperation.

Surveying the Region: A Different Approach to Education

Mumford demonstrates keen interest in regional survey as the basis of a radically different educational approach in which all of the arts and sciences are ecologically related to each other and to the student's experience in his community and region.[34] Regional survey as a movement toward synthesis in education paralleled movements in other fields like plant ecology in science, the concept of the region in geography, the concept of community in sociology, and the concept of the person in psychology, Mumford explains. Developing from Patrick Geddes' work at Edinburgh in the 1890's, it was continued by his student Victor Branford and in this country tried on the elementary level by Caroline Pratt and Lucy Sprague Mitchell in the nineteen-twenties and thirties.[35]

Regional survey can be distinguished from other attempts at educational synthesis in several notable ways, in Mumford's view. First, orderly knowledge comes not from prescribed verbal or pictorial presentations but rather "comes directly from the student's observation of, and participation in, the activities of man and nature."[36] Other approaches, like one proposed by H.G. Wells which seeks unity through encyclopedic gathering of contributions by numerous specialists, have serious defects because they proceed from results already given:

. . . results wholly external to the student's experience, whereas what is needed is a unified *approach*, in terms of the *process* of study, rather than a unified *result* through the more systematic massing of already formulated knowledge.[37]

Revealing his affinity to progressive education, Mumford argues that a unified approach to knowledge comes from the active process of regional survey, not from the more passive accumulation of ideas and facts. The use of scientific method and empirical evidence are strongly endorsed, although he is characteristically careful not to embrace any single method or system of education. Mumford's survey begins with an infant's exploration of his own yard and neighborhood and continues to expand and deepen as the discovering child-student perceives and integrates more and more separate parts of his environment.

The second distinguishing feature of regional survey as educational synthesis is its deep respect for history. Each part of the environment, notes Mumford, is correlated with every other part not only in space but in time. Historical survey complements regional survey, acting as a necessary corrective to unilateral or unitemporal thinking.[38]

Since Mumford always writes from an historical viewpoint, it is not surprising that survey as a spatial concept is balanced by survey in time perspective. The continually evolving natural and man-created environment — both in space and in time — is the core of Mumford's course of study, of which the structure of society and the dynamic processes of personality and culture are integral parts. "The knowledge of where people live, what they do, how they feel and express themselves, what types of association they form, in what realm their fantasies play,"[39] are all vital elements of regional survey, he explains.

As students involve themselves in the active process of survey, they begin to evaluate their social, physical and natural environments, eventually formulating policies, plans and projects to change the existing order.[40] Though this idea may not seem new, it is just as relevant as it was almost forty years ago. Fortunately, today it is falling on much more receptive ears in schools and universities.

Regional survey cannot begin too early in a person's life or extend too long. In every sense it is life-time education not confined to schools, colleges or university extension courses, though taking a more formal role in these institutions. Regional survey is environmental education in the most inclusive sense, beginning with the child's home environment, reaching into his immediate neighborhood, his community, his region, and the entire earth. A mother's love and family's affection are the foundation of this education that continually demonstrates deep respect for all organic life; heightens awareness and understanding of one's conscious and unconscious fears, compulsions, desires; encourages fellowship and cooperation with one's brother and sister no matter where he/she may live; and provides tools of action for the reconstruction of society. Regional survey demands participation in the educational process at every stage and denies that certain individuals whether they be professors, religious leaders, or presidents have a monopoly on wisdom, truth, and power. "Power to the people" is as appropriate a slogan for regional survey as it is for citizens of the Third World struggling for freedom and equality.

Mumford emphasizes that self-knowledge and social-knowledge must begin at home; that is, both within the individual in the form of discipline and insight and within the confines of a closely-knit family and small neighborhood. If one's self is not developed or actualized to the fullest extent possible, he believes, one cannot make a positive impact on society which toughly resists change. Home and neighborhood offer security to the individual, enabling the child-adult to interact freely with others on a personal scale. Mumford's stress on family, home, and neighborhood reveals a traditionalist streak, but he is never ashamed of traditionalism rooted in the fundamental human need for intimacy, love, and mutual sharing.

If education begins in the home and neighborhood, it very soon reaches into the community and region which Mumford still considers "at home" in the sense that customs, traditions, and perhaps geography are distinctive or characteristic of the particular area. He wants education to create regional citizens with humanistic, cooperative attitudes:

> These people will know in detail where they live and how they live:they will be united by a common feeling for their landscape, their literature and language, their local ways, and out of their own self-respect they will have a sympathetic understanding with other regions and different local peculiarities.[41]

Educational institutions, he correctly realizes, have barely begun to use regional resources and develop regional citizens.

No region is or can hope to be self-contained or isolated from other regions, especially in the modern world. Strong roots in the region, Mumford asserts, will facilitate relationships with distant regions — with the global region, so to speak. His assumption is justified if regional appreciation does in fact lead to a more encompassing appreciation of all cultures and peoples, but sturdy roots in the region could also lead to blind worship of one's own region and prejudice toward others. Mumford seems at least partly cognizant of this danger in his attacks on sentimental regionalism.

In the 1930's, America was not nearly as mobile a society as it is now. Today, many people do not have a feel for the region in which they live and, if current industrial trends continue, most Americans will not be afforded an opportunity to "grow" roots in a region. A "sense of place" has become a "sense of placelessness" for many. These realities, however, do not belittle Mumford's conviction that intimate contact and interaction with one's own region can and should prepare the way for inter-regional cooperation. If people feel secure that their own basic needs, as well as their needs for education, recreation, freedom, and participation will be satisfied, perhaps they will be more willing to see that others receive similar benefits.

Mumford would like a world-wide regional survey to explore and assess the potential of every region — "geologic, climactic, vegetative, zoological, historic, cultural, psychological, aesthetic." [42] The kind of intensive study of the local environment done by Thoreau needs to be done throughout the world: "For a survey of the possibilities of human existence, in a new ecological pattern, region by region, is the necessary basis for the resettlement and recultivation of the planet." [43]

Such a survey would do more than survey in the conventional sense of listing, cataloging or simply reviewing. The regional-world survey would examine all resources, human and natural, and from the data gathered make recommendations and specific proposals for radical improvement in the living standard of all peoples. More than fact-gathering or descriptive, this would be a normative survey with the end in view the reconstruction of regional and world culture.

Survey as Educational Process

Mumford suggests that a world survey can become "an instrument of education in which every member of the community may be enlisted, not least school children."[44] Regional survey can be conducted in every region of the planet, perhaps loosely supervised by a World Education Commission. Part of the experience of every student might include a year or two of active involvement in the survey of a distant region. Just as school children in Great Britain cooperated on a land utilization survey in the 1930's, students could carry on systematic local surveys of soil, geology, climate, industries, social institutions, and history. This would be a process, explains Mumford, "of grasping in detail and as a whole what has hitherto been taken in through passive observation in city and countryside."[45]

Regional survey as an instrument of education has far-reaching implications. In 1940 Mumford criticized what many young people today are criticizing: the lack of vital educational opportunities in the community and the plethora of drill, cramming, and joylessness in traditional classrooms. Is it any wonder, Mumford asked in a derisive tone at the time, that young people are so fascinated by speed and radio?[46] Is it any wonder, we might ask in a more charitable way, that drugs and violent acts are prevalent in the last quarter of the twentieth century or that runaways and dropouts are a major social problem?

Surely schooling is not the sole culprit for a steadily growing dissatisfaction with American society; present national priorities have generated disgust and disillusionment among young and old alike. But schools and colleges must share part of the blame since most have not responded to the needs of young people for constructive involvement in social problems facing their community, region, and world. Regional survey is one potentially effective way of responding to a generation that demands a new culture based on respect for the earth and respect for humankind, rather than exploitation of the earth and oppression of the poor.

It should be clear that by regional survey Mumford does not mean the kind of survey that one finds prominently in liberal arts colleges, teacher training institutions and, increasingly, junior and community colleges. In most cases such fragmented courses using the lecture method and assorted readings are presumed by faculty and administrators to satisfy the need for general education. This, of course, they do not do. All too often survey courses are superficial, haphazard reviews, and almost never do they incorporate intensive group experiences or field experiences which involve students in community or regional revitalization programs. Mumford means much more than survey in its traditional sense: for example, he identifies four stages of regional planning which can be applied to regional survey as an educational process that incorporates work toward a more livable world as well as conventional survey and study.

The first stage is a literal survey of the region, accumulating data and interpreting it through maps, charts, photographs. From this diagnosis, an outline of needs and activities in terms of social ideals and purposes is drawn up; philosophers, artists, and educators are especially needed in this stage, Mumford affirms. Then comes imaginative reconstruction and projection of the plan proper, and finally readaptation of the plan as it encounters traditions, resistances, and sometimes unexpected opportunities.[47]

The influence of Geddes and sociologist Victor Branford is great in Mumford's four stages, as well as in his whole concept of regional thinking. Because they were specifically concerned with regional survey as an educational tool, even more than Mumford, it might be fruitful to take a brief look at their foundational work in this area.

Mumford credits Geddes and Branford with a great achievement during their lifetime: the method of civic and regional survey which exerted a positive influence on the teaching of history, civics, geography, and nature study in the primary and secondary schools of Britain. "The incomparable city-development reports of Sir Patrick Abercrombie and his school," Mumford adds, "have their source in Geddes' teaching and example."[48]

Unfortunately, Geddes' contributions to regional survey have not been appreciated by modern teachers and educators, partly because his most important teaching was person-to-person and partly because his writing was difficult to comprehend. Geddes authority Philip Boardman declares that "not only was Geddes one of the most significant teachers of the past fifty years, but he is potentially one of our greatest educational leaders."[49] Boardman's enthusiastic estimate of Geddes may be exaggerated, but it would be hard to deny that Geddes' life and teachings have important implications today.

Geddes, Boardman tells us, approached learning through first-hand experience, not through textbooks or formal schooling. Extremely versatile, he travelled throughout Europe, Asia, and America and into a dozen sciences and professions including biology, sociology, civics, and town planning. His Outlook Tower has been called the world's first sociological laboratory. The tower was an observatory overlooking the whole region between the Highlands and the North Sea, but it was also a symbol of synthesis in thought and action (or "synergy".) Of the Outlook Tower, out of which grew Geddes' regional survey, G. Stanley Hall commented that it offered every man and woman truly interested in education "a departure filled with infinite possibilities."[50] Boardman eloquently summarizes Geddes' educational philosophy in the following words which apply as much to Mumford as they do to Geddes:

> [Geddes] measured every method, course, teacher and institution by its value in terms of human life, by its relation to what was really vital . . . From the post-mortems and chaotic specialization of ordinary education, to the bio-centric concept of regional survey for regional service — such was the transition Geddes sought to make in every stage of education from kindergarten to graduate school.[51]

Mumford points out that Geddes relied very little upon books unless they were personally verified by observation and experience.[52] Geddes himself makes this clear in an essay, "Civics: As Concrete and Applied Sociology," when he insists upon "the same itinerant field methods of notebook and camera . . . as those of the natural sciences" and sharply criticizes the "dreary manuals" used so long in schools.[53]

Mumford's skepticism about books and verbalizing when not coupled with direct observation and involvement is similar to Geddes'. For Mumford, as for Geddes, educational institutions should make use of charts, photographs, reading material, and various media in connection with more active experiences. Vicarious tools like films and tapes may be used to augment, to clarify, or to balance what to some extent has already been or will be directly perceived or experienced through the eyes, ears, and hands. Though aptly utilized to introduce an issue, stimulate discussion, or present a problem, they should never claim exclusive power in the school. Geddes and Mumford are correct to call for a balance between watching, reading, talking, observing, experimenting, and doing. To Mumford's credit, he praises Dewey and instrumentalism for reacting to the essentially leisure-class notion of thinking as:

> ... the reflection of what one reads in a book or gets by hearsay from other people: the great achievement of the scientific method was to supplant the scholar's chair — which does in fact peculiarly serve one phase of the thinking process — by the work of the field and the laboratory, by exploration, observation, mechanical contrivance, exact measurement, and co-operative intercourse. [54]

If Mumford seems to place excessive emphasis on activities, it is only because he feels the need to balance a long tradition of overemphasis on verbal skills with a new attention to making, doing, and participating in non-verbal ways.

Victor Branford sees regional survey growing out of interaction between field biologists and sociologists, historians, and teachers. Their aim is a mode of observation and research "that unites the naturalist's outlook with the humanist's inlook."[55] Regional survey, Branford believes, should investigate the partnership between man and nature not through print and picture, but in the open air. Nevertheless, he grants the need for books and illustrations as aids to full enjoyment and understanding. Very much in tune with Geddes' and Mumford's balanced approach, Branford calls for "an alteration of rambles in the open with studies in the closet. To get fixed on one or the other habit, is the common error."[56]

The Natural Environment As Focus

Geddes and Branford in Great Britain and Mumford in America have always emphasized the relationships between man's natural home and man's psycho-social well-being. What better focus for regional studies in schools and colleges than the land itself, than ecological relationships and the natural environment? Mumford challenges educators directly, asserting: "laboring on the land, laboring for the land, should be the first initiation of every boy and girl in their duties toward the whole community."[57]

Like Pestalozzi many years before, Mumford believes that manual labor whether in a garden, park, field, orchard, or forest should be an integral part of every child's education. To insure a program of outdoor education for all, Mumford suggested over thirty years ago a youth conservation corps, an expanded Civilian Conservation Corps, requiring every boy and girl to serve at least a year working on environmental projects. Organized regionally, the corps also would provide opportunities for the most adventurous to work in other parts of the country and world.[58]

Conceiving the corps as backbone of a new democracy, mixing races and socio-economic classes, Mumford hoped that prejudice and snobbery could be undermined. Not limiting its activities to the land or to conservation in any narrow sense of the word, such activities as fighting insect pests; planting trees along roadsides; fixing up slums; and introducing different kinds of art, crafts, music, and theater to other parts of the country would be included. "Such regional experiences — and inter-regional experiences," Mumford submits,

> . . . are the very basis of communal health. They begin
> and end with a loving awareness of one's environment,
> comradely intercourse with and participation in the lives
> of one's fellows: a role in the regional drama, and a part
> . . . in regional history.[59]

Mumford's idea of a youth conservation corps could be greatly expanded today to include rallying public opinion against the use of toxic defoliants by power companies and highway departments, clearing debris from city alleys, protecting endangered species, studying the consequences of oil spills and thermal pollution on animals and fish, investigating the effects of airplane noise on residents living near jetports, and a host of other environmental projects. Most of these activities represent ways of dealing with critical regional problems plaguing virtually all highly industrialized and developing countries.

The Regional Environmental Corps, a more inclusive name, could become an integral part of secondary education. Students would work in their own region with teachers who have a sound grasp of the humanistic-cultural-biological-political implications of environmental education. Humanistically, students and teachers might explore the philosophy of conservation: the value of wilderness, natural scenery, and recreation space to mental and physical health. Culturally, they might investigate the effects of congestion and dilapidated housing on ghetto dwellers, of increasing alienation resulting from government bureaucracy, of urban and suburban sprawl without adequate safe-guards for community values. Biologically, the possible genetic changes caused by pesticide build-up in animals and foods, the danger of radioactive wastes from nuclear power plants, and the ecological imbalance caused by excessive nitrogen in water and sulfur dioxide in air could be examined. Politically, students and teachers might explore the hurdles facing tough land-use legislation, survey the attitudes of elected representatives toward environmental issues, and enlighten the public about pending environmental bills.

Though the environment has become a popular rallying point for educators during the last few years, Mumford's interest in and sensitivity toward the natural environment has remained consistent for over half a century. In the mid nineteen-twenties, long before others, Mumford recognized Henry David Thoreau's genius, contrasting the Concord philosopher-naturalist with the exploitative pioneer:

> In short, Thoreau lived in his desires; in rational and beautiful things that he imagined worth doing and did. The pioneer lived only in extraneous necessities; and he vanished with their satisfaction: filling all the conditions of his environment, he never fulfilled himself . . . What Thoreau left behind is still precious; men may still go out and make over America in the image of Thoreau. What the pioneer left behind, alas! was only the burden of a vacant life.[60]

In 1931 Mumford wrote of the need for a new philosophy of nature, based on Goethe and Thoreau,[61] and continued to criticize America's destruction of her natural environment. Citing an example of hypocrisy, Mumford comments bitterly: "It was in vain that the American proclaimed to the heavens that he loved his rocks and rills, his woods and templed hills: his actions were a derisive commentary on those pious words."[62] Almost forth years later, young people and ecology-conscious older people are pointing with bitterness to the very same American hypocrisy.

In *The Culture of Cities* Mumford writes much about the
desecration of the natural environment and the perversions of
democracy regarding nature. Destruction of the land in the act of
making nature accessible destoys what is valuable in wilderness
areas, a fact many are just beginning to realize. When will we begin
to understand that "man cannot achieve a high level of economic
life or culture in an environment whose resources he has plundered
and defaced,"[63] and live and teach accordingly? Mumford's
observation that "Civilizations have risen and fallen without
apparently perceiving the full impact of their relations with the
earth,"[64] may have fallen on deaf ears in 1938, but it should not
today if civilization is to survive. The earth is our home; if we do not
maintain it with care and respect, our home will become a putrid
prison or deadly trap.

Mumford contends in *The Condition of Man* that a new sense of
our relation to nature and nature's relation to us came from
Rousseau, Chateaubriand, Hugo, Cooper, Melville, and of course
Thoreau. "Without this upsurge of romanticism," he adds, "the
forces of life might have been routed."[65] He has always found
romanticism a necessary check for excessive industrialization and its
attendant ugliness. This may best be demonstrated by Mumford's
high regard for landscape architecture.

As the Western world became mechanized, landscape
architecture had a compensatory part to play. The "deliberate
culture of the whole landscape," of metropolitan parks and
parkways, of riversides and mountain trails, modified "our whole
picture of the 'machine age' and its future."[66] It is not surprising that
one of Mumford's most respected Americans is Frederick Law
Olmsted, the creative designer of Central Park in New York and the
metropolitan park system in Boston. Nor is it surprising that he
greatly admires Benton MacKaye, the father of the Appalachian
Trail, whose philosophy of "outdoor culture" is a quest for harmony
between natural and man-made environments.[67]

Perhaps Mumford's strongest rationale for his interest in the
conservation movement is expressed at a conference on "Future
Environments of North America." In the "Closing Statement" of the
conference, he asserts:

> . . . our conservation movement with its broad founda-
> tions, ever since George Perkins Marsh, in both natural

and human history . . . demonstrates the irrationality of allowing any single factor to dominate the rest of the environment. Our technology has overemphasized the factor of power, of mass production and standardization; it seeks to decrease variety in order to provide quantity. Our aim rather should be to promote variety in order to curb this monotonous quantification.[68]

Just as Thoreau's chief mission was to introduce "civilized" men to the natural possibilities of the environment, Mumford notes,[69] his own mission has been to alert twentieth century man to the perils of destroying nature and to the human values worth preserving in its conservation.

Socio-Political Problems As Focus

Regional survey need not confine itself to problems or issues of the natural environment, though these may serve as a central theme. Whatever its thrust at the time, education for individual growth and community-regional-world improvement — the prime purpose of regional survey — should always keep the following in mind: study and diagnosis of problems is only half the job of teachers and students. The other half necessitates working to change detrimental conditions; in short, working for a more equitable, attractive, and livable environment. Regional survey is education that welcomes a diversity of viewpoints, that strives for fairness, that looks at every conceivable side of an issue and ecologically attempts to relate parts to the whole. But regional survey does not pretend to be completely "objective," something which no institution or person can possibly be, as historian Howard Zinn eloquently observes.[70]

Regional survey does not remain neutral to the critical problems facing people since its orientation is normative. Regional survey maintains that the residents of the planet should control all resources of the planet and not forfeit this right to dictators, bureaucrats, or corporate potentates. It holds that poverty and the resulting human suffering can be eliminated. It is committed to health care, literacy, and basic freedoms like freedom of speech and assembly for all. Rather than sidestepping controversial issues and community involvement, as much education does today, regional survey becomes immersed in social and political action.

Specifically, what kinds of problems, besides those dealing with the natural environment, might regional survey include? What methodology should it follow and who should control it? Urban problems such as the extent and consequences of unemployment among minority group members, provision of medical and dental care for young and old, difficulties encountered with welfare, tension between races, and monopoly of power by a handful of politicians would be worthy problems for study in an intensive or not so intensive way depending upon the interests or readiness of students and teachers.

Suburban problems that might be explored include availability of space (or unavailability of it) for community gatherings, adequacy of public transportation to the city, job or career opportunities, extent of school and housing segregation, and accessibility of stores, churches, and theaters. Rural issues like declining farm production and its regional implications in terms of fresh food supplies, steady disappearance of open spaces,[71] condition of rural housing, difficulties in finding employment, and provision for creative leisure time activities nearby could be included.

Students and teachers throughout the region might investigate problems and issues that affect all three areas of the region — urban, suburban, and rural — though in the early years the local milieu of the child might be stressed. To see most of these issues as primarily regional, not as exclusively urban, suburban or rural problems, would be an ongoing curriculum goal. From this regional perspective the following constructive questions that cross urban-suburban-rural lines might arise: How can the city and the suburbs work together for integrated communities, balanced racially, socially, economically, and by age groups? How can environmental problems like air and water pollution, which defy political boundaries, be attacked on a regional basis? How can recreational and leisure time activities be enriched and broadened through adult education?[72] How can law enforcement and treatment of arrested persons focus on social rehabilitation rather than on punitive measures? How can highway planning be carried out with the cooperation of all citizens of the region rather than be decided upon by state highway engineers who pay little or no cognizance to the upsetting effects of their plans on personal and communal values? None of these questions lies beyond the realm of possibility for serious consideration.

Regional survey as a process implies continual interaction between and among students, teachers, and other residents of the region. It can stimulate deeper I-thou relationships in groups small enough to encourage sensitivity to the feelings, needs, motives of others. Active participation in group projects encourages cooperation, a vital feature of this education. Time for reading and thinking by oneself is balanced by time for group diagnosis, group planning, and group action to alleviate the problems encountered.

The region itself would serve as a giant laboratory for participants in regional survey. "Field work" would be given top priority, though reading of all kinds (factual, fictional, and technical), group discussions, role playing, simulation games, laboratory work, and audiovisual presentations would complement activities outside the formal school building. Drawing and painting, music and dance, crafts and dramatics, key elements of this education, would encourage self-development and self-expression. Aesthetic education is so important, in fact, that Mumford wisely comments: "Where such an environment is lacking, even the purely rational and signific processes are half-starved: verbal mastery cannot make up for sensory malnutrition."[73] Aesthetic education that stimulates keen perception and awareness, encourages transformation of the environment, and increases sensitivity to processes at work in artistic endeavor remains at the forefront of regional survey.

In the local community and in the larger region students might interview specialists in fields ranging from politics to physics, from manufacturing to religion; conduct opinion and attitude surveys among citizens of all backgrounds and ages; and go on walking excursions throughout city and country-side, as Geddes, Branford, MacKaye, and Mumford did so frequently. They could analyze the natural and man-made resources of a small area using techniques developed by Philip Lewis in his study of the entire state of Wisconsin.[74] Or they could measure the social benefits (or detriments) of a highway route using measures of "social value" suggested by ecologist Ian McHarg — urbanization; residential quality; historical, agricultural, recreational values; and the value of wildlife, water, and resistance of soil to erosion.[75] Other community-regional experiences might include purpose-oriented visits to industrial plants, mental hospitals, and prisons; living for a week or more with other families; regular recording of impressions and reactions on paper, tape, and film, in photographs, diagrams, and sketches; and a myriad of additional activities initiated by students to gain a deeper understanding of regional problems and prospects.

One of the goals of regional survey might be the development of regional museums to portray, in Mumford's words, "in compact and coherent form the actual environment from the infinitely remote stars to the infinitesimal particles of protoplasm or energy: the place: the work: the people in all their ecological relations."[76] Unlike the bigness, acquisitiveness, and stuffiness of many existing museums, the regional museum would grow out of the distinctive culture of the region itself and never be confined to a single building of whatever proportions. The "museum" might take the shape of a mobile unit with traveling exhibits prepared by students. Or it might consist of a storefront center for craft and photography lessons, or a roomful of architectural models suggesting ways to renew the community. Preferably, it could be all of these and more.

The regional "museum" would certainly take advantage of natural, historical, and literary resources of the region, much as the Thoreau Lyceum in Concord, Massachusetts does. Housed in a weathered house adjoining the site of Thoreau's family home, the Lyceum contains a library and bookstore of Thoreau's writing available to students of all ages. It also features historical artifacts and maps of the Concord area; changing exhibits of objects, woodcuts, photographs, and rare books dealing with Thoreau's life and impact; a small gift shop selling handicrafts made by regional residents; and even a reconstruction of Thoreau's small Walden Pond house in the backyard. The regional museum, always evolving and taking many forms from the Thoreau Lyceum to mobile displays and festivals in isolated areas, has great potential as a teaching-learning tool to enrich and reconstruct regional culture.

Prescriptive as well as descriptive, regional survey means planning change and working for change go hand-in-hand with studying present conditions and trends. When students and teachers gain a balanced picture of their region and the desires of its residents they will hopefully gain some idea of alterations necessary to revitalize the region. After developing means of bringing about needed reforms, they can then work cooperatively on these reforms.

Though these last steps may be the most difficult and frustrating, certainly the most controversial, they must be undertaken if regional survey is to become more than an interminable, frustrating study or an innocuous exercise. Teachers and students should be held accountable for fostering cultural renewal through education. Administrators, for their part, should do everything they can to ease the difficulties that occur when pressure groups put on the squeeze or when unconventional practices alienate more cautious members of the community. School board members, elected by the community, should be chosen on the basis of their commitment to educational quality and equality. Ideally, they should give the greatest leeway possible to students, teachers, and administrators in their pursuit of regional "truth"; they should support measures designed to combat weaknesses and defend actions taken to invigorate life in the region. Cooperation between all parties — students, teachers, administrators, school boards, and community people — is the key to success of regional renewal.

What measures might students and teachers adopt and toward what end? To suggest but one example, high school students might decide after thorough investigation that tutoring of young children from poor neighborhoods might give those children a psychological-intellectual boost and perhaps reveal previously unapparent talents in dramatics, ballet, engineering, or zoology. Working with neighborhood organizations and social agencies, students could present plans for a tutoring program and try to persuade community groups to cooperate. The idea then might be presented to parents and children in their homes, and, if favorably accepted, details could be worked out together. It might be arranged, for instance, that each student in the program "adopt" two or three children several after-noons a week; the meeting place could be a local school or church and the subject matter might be anything from reading, chemistry, or mathematics to nature study, architecture, or crafts. The latter three might be given special emphasis: nature study might lead to a search for animal homes in a nearby park or a close look at organic life in a distant pond; architecture might involve saunters around the city, watching construction in progress or drawing plans for an ideal house and town; crafts might entail whittling mythical creatures from balsa wood or planning and filming impressions of one's friends and surroundings.

This tutorial program would aim to motivate children of lower-class families, though it would be applicable to middle-class children as well. At the same time it would grant responsibility and leadership to high-school participants. Supervised by teachers in a democratic way, students would be able to develop their own interests as they work with younger children and also have a fine opportunity to experience the complementary process of teaching-learning. Evaluation by all parties involved might indicate that this action program not only broadened the horizons of inner city children but also broadened the attitudes and outlook of high school students engaged in the project.

If innovative programs like the preceding are to succeed, schools must devote more time and effort to interpersonal relations. Regional survey is to a large extent dependent upon individuals and groups working together toward common, if flexibly defined, ends. Disagreements, misunderstandings, disputes are bound to arise; conflict should be encouraged as long as it leads to some kind of constructive outcome. But conflict and disagreement will be positive only if individuals respect each other as individuals and learn to understand why and how suspicion, anxiety, and fear operating in a group or between persons can block or destroy the best-intentioned efforts.

In order for regional survey to succeed as a unified system of education, control will have to shift from authoritarian teachers, administrators, and school boards to the consumers of education and the community of which they are a part. Though this demands a radical democratic reorientation, professionals will still have a strategic role to play. Professional educators, no longer automatically considered possessors of superior knowledge, will be assessed by their depth of understanding, their sensitivity to personality development and social needs, their ability to act cooperatively with students and community people. Respect will grow from daily transactions, if it grows at all, not from forced awe, power, or prestige.

Students and teachers will arrive at many decisions through consensus, always remembering that individual dissent and differences should be respected. In situations where a person decides to agree with the group in order to arrive at consensus but retains doubts and disagreement, the person should later feel free to express his differences and seek to persuade others to his way of thinking. Others, in turn, owe it to him to listen to new evidence and arguments. In this way, both the group and individual members of the group will be strengthened.

In line with Mumford's belief that they should accept greater political responsibility, students and teachers participating in regional survey would educate the public on issues they believe are vital to their own education in the region and world. They may do so through door to door canvassing on behalf of progressive candidates; leafletting, petitioning, and picketing to muster support; and sponsoring evening programs at local schools for residents who want to learn about the issues and concerns.

In short, if teachers and students were not satisfied with the proposals of elected officials, they would be encouraged to remedy the situation. They might work to oust reactionary officials by educating voters to the great social problems and value conflicts of the day, as well as to local school programs which require stronger support. They would be free to alert voters to the urgent need for dynamic, visionary representatives of the people instead of hackneyed incumbents. Only if students, teachers, and others wield considerably more power and influence in the educational process than at present will regional survey live up to its promising potential.

From Region to Planet

Mumford stresses that movement toward regional organization must be balanced by equally active movement toward planetary organization: "The need of the new age is to create balanced regional communities, which will be capable of operating within a world-wide framework."[77] Both forces are necessary — a localizing, regionalizing process and a universalizing process.[78] Regionalism, though growing out of local landscape and customs, should never be identified with self-sufficiency or self-containment; every regional culture has a universal side to it:

> It is steadily open to influences which come from other parts of the world, and from other cultures, separated from the local region in space or time or both together. It would be useful if we formed the habit of never using the word regional without mentally adding to it the idea of the universal — remembering the constant contact and interchange between the local scene and the wide world that lies beyond it.[79]

Because Mumford ties the universal or global to the regional, he cannot be considered provincial or isolationist in any sense. Looking back to Emerson's day "when the American spirit was truly robust," he reflects, ". . . the leading minds were regional and cosmopolitan: closer to their own community and more at home in the great world."[80] Certainly this was true of Thoreau and his deep affection for both the Concord woods and the *Bhagavad Gita*. It was no less true of Emerson himself and of Bronson Alcott and Walt Whitman. Love of region and nation and love of the entire earth were perfectly compatible in America's "golden day." They are equally compatible today.

Roots in the region and roots in the world go hand-in-hand, but one without the other presents a grave danger. Regionalism that becomes an exclusive preoccupation among the populace or in the schools becomes ingrown and incestuous; the weeds of isolationism and nationalism thrive in such a withered environment. Universalism, the quest for world community, that attempts to bypass regional organization or denies cultural diversity and historical continuities becomes impersonal, bureaucratic, and possibly totalitarian. But working together, regionalism and globalism lead toward One World community that Mumford sees as the only hope of humankind.

[1]Mumford, "Regions — To Live In," p. 151.

[2]Mumford, "The Arts," in *Whither Mankind: A Panorama of Modern Civilization*, ed. by Charles A. Beard (New York: Longmans, Green, 1928), p. 310.

[3]Lewis Mumford,"Toward a New Regionalism," *New Republic*, March 25, 1931, pp. 157-58.

[4]Lewis Mumford, "The Theory and Practice of Regionalism," *Sociological Review*, XX (April, 1928), 136.

[5]Mumford, *The Culture of Cities*, p. 311.

[6]Mumford, "Toward A New Regionalism," p. 158.

[7]*Ibid.*, p. 157.

[8]Lewis Mumford, "Orozco in New England," *New Republic*, October 10, 1934, p. 235.

[9]Mumford, *Faith for Living*, p. 268.

[10]*Ibid.*, p. 265.

[11]Mumford, *The Culture of Cities*, p. 349.

[12]*Ibid.*

[13]Mumford, *The Culture of Cities*, p. 305.

[14]Mumford, "Regions — To Live In," p. 152.

[15]*Ibid.*, p. 151.

[16]Mumford, *The Urban Prospect*, p. 86.

[17]*Ibid.*, p. 178.

[18]Creese, *The Search for Environment*, p. 303.

[19]Lewis Mumford, "Realities versus Dreams," *Journal of American Institute of Architects* (June, 1925), 198. Quoted in Creese, *The Search for Environment*, p. 307.

[20]*Ibid.*

[21]The Editors, *The Survey: Graphic Number*, April 15, 1925.

[22]Mumford, *The Urban Prospect*, p. xx.

[23]Stuart Chase, *The Most Probable World* (Baltimore: Penguin Books, 1968), p. 173.

[24]"Cosmopolis," ABC-TV, May 12, 1969.

[25]Creese, *The Search for Environment*, p. 307.

[26]Harrington, "Cities to Live In," p. 24. See also Theobald, "Planning with People" in Ewald, ed., *Environment and Change: The Next Fifty Years.*

[27]*Report of the National Advisory Commission on Civil Disorders*, p. 299.

[28]Mumford, *The Culture of Cities*, p. 348.

[29]*Ibid.*, p. 345.

[30]Theodore Jones, "Editorial," Radio Station *WCRB*, Boston and Waltham, Massachusetts, September 23, 1969.

[31]Stephen Silha, "New Solution for Urban Problems?," *Christian Science Monitor*, May 15, 1973, p. 18.

[32]Mumford, *The Urban Prospect*, pp. 179-80.

[33]Mumford, "Trend is Not Destiny," pp. 131-34.

[34]Mumford, "The Social Responsibilities of Teachers," p. 487.

[35]*Ibid.*, p. 486.

[36]*Ibid.*

[37]*Ibid.*, p. 487.

[38]*Ibid.*

[39]*Ibid.*, p. 488.

[40]*Ibid.*, p. 489.

[41]Mumford, *The Culture of Cities*, p. 386.

[42]Mumford, *The Transformations of Man*, p. 152.

[43]*Ibid.*

[44]*Ibid.*

[45]Mumford, *The Culture of Cities*, p. 384.

[46]Mumford, *Faith for Living*, p. 272.

[47]Mumford, *The Culture of Cities*, pp. 376-80.

[48]Mumford, "Patrick Geddes, Victor Branford, and Applied Sociology in England," p. 687.

[49]Philip L. Boardman, "Sir Patrick Geddes," *Social Frontier*, III (June, 1937), 273.

[50]G. Stanley Hall, quoted in Boardman, "Sir Patrick Geddes," p. 274.

[51]*Ibid.*

[52]Mumford, "Patrick Geddes, Victor Branford, and Applied Sociology in England," p. 682.

[53]Patrick Geddes, "Civics: As Concrete and Applied Sociology," in *Sociological Papers*, Vol. II (London: Macmillan and Company, 1926), p. 63.

[54]Mumford, *The Golden Day*, 4th ed. (New York: Dover, 1968), p. 132.

[55]Victor Branford, *Science and Sanctity* (London: LePlay House and Williams and Norgate, 1923), p. 47.

[56]*Ibid.*, p. 48.

[57]Mumford, *Faith for Living*, pp. 276-77.

[58]*Ibid.*, pp. 273-76.

[59]*Ibid.*, pp. 272-74.

[60]Mumford, *The Golden Day*, p. 59.

[61]Mumford, *The Brown Decades*, p. 71.

[62]*Ibid.*, p. 65.

[63]Mumford, *The Culture of Cities*, p. 335.

[64]*Ibid.*, p. 322.

[65]Mumford, *The Condition of Man*, p. 278.

[66]Mumford, "The Arts," pp. 304-5.

[67]See Benton MacKaye, *From Geography to Geotechnics* (Urbana: University of Illinois Press, 1968).

68Mumford, "Closing Statement" pp. 727-28.

69Mumford, *The Brown Decades*, p. 67.

70Howard Zinn, "The Academic Revolution: The Case for Radical Change," *Saturday Review*, October 18, 1969, pp. 81-82, 94-95.

71Mumford has deplored this trend for 50 years, but only now is it even being noticed. The Sierra Club has pointed out that at the present time in the United States oxygen-producing greenery is being paved over at the rate of one million acres per year. See David Brower, "A Proposal for Earth National Park," *New York Times* (advertisement), January 14, 1969, p. 30.

72Mumford is forceful about life-long education: "the period of education, and the period of experiment, instead of being limited to youth, must now range over every phase of life: only the grave brings the process to an end." See *The Culture of Cities*, p. 474.

73Mumford, *The Culture of Cities*, p. 51.

74Whyte, *The Last Landscape*, pp. 191-93.

75*Ibid.*, pp. 188-89.

76Mumford, *The Culture of Cities*, p. 447.

77Mumford, "Looking Forward," p. 352.

78Mumford, *Faith for Living*, p. 177.

79Lewis Mumford, The South in Architecture (New York, Harcourt, Brace, 1941), pp. 30-31.

80Lewis Mumford, "The Menace to the American Promise." *New Republic*, November 8, 1939, p. 65.

✿ chapter 8
one world:
building world community
through education

MUMFORD TRACES a series of historical transformations of man from prehistoric times to the present in *The Transformations of Man*. From archaic man to civilized man, axial man, Old World man, New World man, and post-historic man, he reviews the characteristics and traditions passed on from each period and culture.

A threatening transformation that has become a reality in many ways today, post-historic man concentrates on manipulating the external world, continuing and accelerating practices originally introduced by capitalism, advanced technology, bureaucratic administration, and totalitarian government. Human purpose and values have no place in this machine-conditioned culture; scientific intelligence reigns supreme and behaviorism enjoys a field day. [1] H.G. Wells' *The Shape of Things to Come*, Orwell's *1984*, and Jules Verne's *Journey to the Moon* provide a preview of post-historic culture. Mumford shudders to think of a completely automated post-historic culture, but recognized an abundance of already present post-historic traits: the suicidal stockpiling of nuclear, chemical, and biological weapons; the increasing uniformity of our natural and man-made environment; the growing dependence upon data banks and assorted computers that increase man's feelings of powerlessness and alienation.

The alternative to post-historic man, a theoretic possibility not an historic probability, is One World man whose culture is organically unified not mechanically rigidified, open not closed, global not provincial. "Such a culture must be nourished," Mumford asserts, "not only by a new vision of the whole, but a new vision of a self capable of understanding and co-operating with the whole. In short, the moment for another great transformation has come."[2]

The emergence of a new world society would not result from a series of minor modifications but, rather, would be a radical leap from one plane to another. Historically, it would be similar to the decisive leap "from the neolithic tribal community to a centralized state organization focused in cities, capable of dominating and ordering a whole river valley."[3] As with any emergence, however, its results cannot be definitely predicted.

Elements of continuity, persistence, and renewal would also be present in One World culture. Mumford accounts for them by noting what he calls the fibrous structure of society: "the fact that parts of man's life send forth threads and strands that penetrate through all the strata of time, modifying each new stage with the fibres of both organic and social memory."[4] Emergence would account for necessary radical changes, like the leap from a money economy to an economy built on human welfare, while fibrous structure would account for continuity and permanence, like the maintenance of old communal units — the family and the neighborhood.

Mumford is well aware of problems that must be confronted before such a transformation becomes reality. He knows, for instance, that world unity can never be achieved immediately or once and for all times. But he also knows the potentially disastrous price of giving up the quest. The goal of a peaceful and just world community, though tentative like other goals, is visible. And the end in view directs and orders the sequence that helps to bring about its accomplishment. He is confident that nothing less than such a far-reaching goal for humankind will suffice.

In the transformation to One World, elements of past transformations would play a vital role by undergoing regeneration and entering into fresh integrations. The communal pattern of village and family group, a feature of archaic man, becomes strengthened and renewed in cooperatives and neighborhood organizations — not as isolated communal forms but as local units in a worldwide cooperative. The civilized age contributes technological standardization and the establishment of laws which serve One World man by freeing him from drudgery and guaranteeing basic human rights which, Mumford contends, "are the very anchors of world government."[5] Axial culture offers the concepts of universal fellowship, love, myth, and conversion as axial religions slowly give up special claims to revelation and demands for exclusive spiritual leadership. New World values found in representatives of the "golden day" are reinstated and "mechanization measured by human need and limited vital norms"[6] is made an integral part of One World culture.

One World may not become a reality overnight, but it can become a reality in time. Mumford traces the historic transformations of man in order to emphasize the temporal dimension of man's existence; One World man will need to draw strength and courage and knowledge from all ages of man. He must choose wisely, adopting and renewing those aspects which serve human interests and rejecting those which depersonalize or dehumanize.

Like Theodore Brameld, Mumford is clear which road humankind *should* take in the future, but not at all sure which road *will* be taken.[7] The goal of cooperation on a worldwide scale, shared by both, depends on the will of individuals and governments to agree upon the goal and then strive ceaselessly toward it. Brameld and Mumford know that the will to do the job may be flabby, or even nonexistent. But they are also aware of the likely alternative to an integrated, cooperative world: the probable extinction of the human race by lethal thermonuclear weapons, chemical and biological agents, environmental pollutants, endless famine, and racial-class wars.

Gunnar Myrdal, the eminent Swedish sociologist-economist, has done as much as anyone to document and increase awareness of the global crises facing us today. The income gap between rich and poor countries widens, population rapidly increases, the race issue becomes more critical as rich white nations oppress struggling non-white nations, and the so-called aid to developing countries decreases. Myrdal deplores the fact that planning is almost totally absent in international relations and argues that a genuine world government is needed.[8] In tune with Mumford's anti-isolationist conviction that "decisions of utmost importance to the human race as a whole have been made as though only the interests of a single country need be taken into account,"[9] Myrdal points out that neither the United States nor any other country will be spared slaughter and destruction, or at the very least intense suffering and slow death, if a third world war erupts.[10]

In an essay in *Alternatives to the H Bomb*, Mumford describes two options open to man: "countries that possess the present instruments of global genocide must either bring about an open world or perish within a closed world."[11] By open he means open to the public, in full view for all individuals and governments to inspect and control. In the midst of the "cold war" between Russia and the United States, he knew such openness would be difficult, if not virtually impossible to accomplish. But with characteristic faith in man he believed it was still within human scope. Intelligence, imagination, audacity "on an heroic scale but by no means on a superhuman order"[12] were required then, just as they are today, for the forces of life to prevail over the forces of death. The wish-dream of global unity, if once impractical or utopian in the negative sense, is now so urgent and real a necessity, as Mumford's fellow visionary Erich Kahler affirms, "that the survival of human civilization depends on its fulfillment."[13]

Just how great is the need for world unity in order to insure survival? Are Mumford, Kahler, Toynbee, Kluckhohn, Brameld, Wagar, Falk and a host of other scholars unduly alarmed by the horrors of our age? The answer is "no" if socio-economic, racial, ecological, and military problems are considered in global perspective, rather than from a nationalistic point of view. Stuart Chase, whose concerns have paralleled Mumford's for a half-century, is struck by the growing economic interdependence of the planet; Myrdal by increasing social, economic, and racial disparities; David Brower and Richard Falk by ecological threats; and George Wald and William Boyer, among others, by worldwide militarism. All human beings live on this isolated sphere which for some time to come, perhaps forever, will offer no means of escape to another habitable planet. For Mumford and for those who believe that human priorities take precedence over warfare, missile-building and fanciful space shots, the moon and sterile space platforms are not viable alternatives to life on this rich and variegated earth. Our focus can and should turn from private profit and national "prestige" to the physical and spiritual welfare of every individual in every culture on earth.

Stuart Chase notes that the classical concept of national sovereignty is being weakened today. International cooperation is observed in air flights around the world, live television and radio transmission via satellite, weather satellites and air and water pollution control. One particularly significant landmark in the direction of One World is the supra-national control of Antarctica. [14] Chase finds encouragement, too, in the 1,987 agencies that are presently operating to unite the world's peoples including: The World Court, The World Bank, The International Monetary Fund, The International Development Agency, The International Labor Organization (which won the 1969 Nobel Peace Prize), the World Meteorological Organization, and the International Atomic Energy Agency. [15]

If Chase is more optimistic than Mumford about the weakening of national sovereignty, both agree that international affiliations must deepen and a world union be established. As early as 1919, Mumford appreciated the power of international unions and consumer co-operatives to assist in the development of "a truly federal world-organization which shall begin with the local production unit and ramify outward in increasing disregard of formal national boundaries." [16] In the thirties he realized that airplanes laughed at border restrictions that could easily halt trains and ships; every nation, every region was vulnerable. If his perception was true then, it is ever so much truer now. Describing the need for world cooperation, his prophetic words of 1938 are even more appropriate today:

> The task of modern civilization is to live in a wall-less world . . . if we cannot create a wall-less world our civilization will die: it will die by inanition, through the terrified expenditure upon 'protection,' or it will die by common extermination, aggravated by neurotic fury, the first time an autarchic state attempts to overcome its self-imposed sense of enclosure by committing an aggression upon an equal. [17]

Design of World Community

"We now stand at the beginning of an age of cultural cross-fertilization . . . the first true age of man," [18] Mumford declares. The meeting of east and west, north and south; the planetary interchange of manufactured goods and raw materials; the sharing of ideals, values, scientific discoveries, and of great numbers of people define the new goals of man. But how can this new unity of mankind, this world culture, be achieved and what design for it does Mumford have in mind?

Though he refuses to predict the exact nature of the world community that may emerge, Mumford does indicate a number of ways that world community might take place and how it might look. Essential ingredients for world unity include a willingness to learn from others and a willingness to confront the very real problems faced in common by humanity. This means, he adds, that "we must have the courage to abandon our limited national goals and commit ourselves to universal goals: goals that will mean as much to the countries that now oppose us as to ourselves."[19]

That is indeed a big order, particularly for the United States government which demonstrates over and over its prime concern for national rather than transnational interests. Unfortunately, we have pursued our selfish objectives across the globe. The United States has supported corrupt, repressive regimes in South Vietnam, South Korea, Greece, and the Philippines among other countries and has alienated millions of world citizens disillusioned with American pieties. Though this discouraging situation has depressed Mumford, it has not squelched his utopian vision of global unity. If anything, as the world crisis has grown more severe, he has become more insistent than ever on world cooperation, in spite of the obstacles.

The problem of creating a moral atmosphere for the long-range planning of a world order was recognized by Mumford in 1951. At that time he suggested "mild and conciliatory manners in dealing with those who persistently balk us," public admission that the United States can learn much from the Russians, and establishment of reciprocal two-way intercourse between the countries.[20] Several years later he proposed that the United States and the Soviet Union take bold steps to make the United Nations into a working machine, leading to world government.[21] Warning that nothing would emerge from an all-out atomic war, Mumford writes:

> Every positive act of love — offering food to hungry peoples, medical aid to the sick, friendly appreciation to the creative gifts of other nations and respect to their individuality — erects a barrier against violence.[22]

To develop a just world order, Mumford proposes a graduated world income tax dependent upon the wealth, resources, and productivity of each nation. The World Equalization Fund thus created would be operated by the United Nations to provide aid for health care, education, social services, technical assistance, and food whenever and wherever needed.[23] He also favors a world executive, noting that one of the great weaknesses of the United Nations was the failure to provide an effective world leader who could plan and act on behalf of every world citizen.[24]

Before the United Nations was established, Mumford realized that the poor distribution of natural resources — partly due to geography and partly to monopolies — required the pooling and sharing of resources on a worldwide basis.[25] Later he underlined his belief that uranium and oil deposits are common possessions that should be distributed according to human need, not be handed out as profits to the fortunate rich.[26] One World economy, Mumford contends, will need to even out gross inequalities in soil, climate and natural resources of all kinds; most of all, One World will need to reverse the blind assault on nature. Wilderness areas will need protection and restoration just as cities will need to slow growth and expansion for the earth to remain a life-nourishing environment for all.

Though strongly in favor of disarmament and always critical of the development of atomic weapons which have "produced the maximum of insecurity with the minimum amount of control," [27] Mumford has also been a realist about the need for preparedness. Critical of those who favored eliminating war instruments after World War I, he claimed that they were too willing to sacrifice what had already been secured. Further toughness is revealed in the provision for a world police authority: "For who is so naïve to think there will come a time in international affairs when the powerful will not seek to exert power and the violent will not seek by violence to impose their will upon the timid?" [28] Mumford would prefer the creation of an open world culture in which every citizen could travel freely and poke around at will; not dependent upon a purely official system to inspect armaments, every citizen would become a "policeman" and take the world for his precinct in order to guarantee security against both private and collective criminality.[29]

Though he makes a number of provocative suggestions about One World, Mumford's strength rests not so much on the measures to be taken to achieve world unity as on the futuristic concept of One World itself. If his failure to elaborate the means toward worthy ends is a basic weakness in his philosophy, his radical and timely goals — like that of world culture — are themselves of great value to educationists who all too frequently pass over the ends and purposes of education and become mired in methodological detail.

Educating for World Community

In order to make Mumford's goals more useful for educational practitioners, his proposal for a world culture will be examined in terms of school curriculum, the teaching-learning process, and the control of education.

The concept of world community might well be the central focus of all curriculum, as Brameld suggests.[30] Nationalism as an important stage of development in an oppressed country, but as a stumbling block to world unity when fanatically worshipped elsewhere, would be an appropriate subject for study. Imperialism and militarism, their history, meaning, and contemporary relevance, could be explored in depth.

Curriculum in all schools and colleges might revolve around a series of questions which continually demand response: What serious problems do we face that cross national boundaries? Why do many people of the world have little or nothing to eat and others have plenty? Why do some suffer and die from diseases that could be cured if medical aid were available? How is it possible that some families live in rat-infested buildings or tar-paper shacks while other families own two or even three comfortable homes? Why are tens of billions of dollars being spent every year by the military in the United States alone when this huge sum could feed, clothe, shelter and educate millions of poor people?

Even more fundamental questions could be pursued: Why do countries war against each other? Why cannot creativity expressed in multitudinous ways, rather than destructiveness, become a central goal of every person and government? How can our lives be oriented toward love and away from violence of all sorts, violence of poverty and racism as well as violence of war and murder?

Environmental pollution as a world problem that threatens to destroy the quality of human life, if not life itself, would be an excellent focus for curriculum from nursery school through university and adult education. As Mumford frequently observes, all earth-dwellers are interdependent and no more dramatic example of their interdependence can be found than the natural environment. The United Nations in recent years has recognized this by sponsoring the famous Stockholm Conference on global environmental problems, the Law of the Seas Conference in Caracas, and conferences on overpopulation in Bucharest and food in Rome. The newly chartered United Nations University will also give considerable attention to world environmental concerns. Kenya plans to contribute a natural resources institute, Malta an oceanic institute, Canada a program in urbanization and arctic studies, and Turkey an environmental engineering program. Earthquake research and flood control are likely projects of the UN University.

Air pollution which mocks state and national borders is one potent threat to humanity which at last has been recognized for what it is: a deadly serious business that nations must work on together, sooner or later. Sulfur dioxide resulting from low-grade oil used for heating and electricity production, carbon monoxide as an effluent of the internal combustion engine, and particulate matter in the form of soot and fly-ash constantly invade our air supply, not only endangering our health but steadily eating away at art treasures, architectural landmarks and food sources. The oxygen we require is limited and whether or not we will have enough fresh air to survive will depend upon the world rate of population growth, the growth of factories and cities, the fallout from nuclear tests, reseeding our forests, and other factors. Even if we survive physically, what kind of life can we lead if required to wear a mask, live under an environmentally-controlled bubble, or gasp for oxygen at a street vending machine as some Tokyo residents must do?

A transnational problem like air pollution could and should bring nations together. To combat this common enemy, a world authority backed by citizen vigilance around the globe might supervise and control the air that belongs to all of us — and to generations yet unborn who may suffer the genetic consequences of poisoned air. What more leading subject for world curriculum than the air every person breathes?

Environmental problems that encompass the earth are clearly not confined to air pollution. The fouling of streams, rivers, and oceans continues on all continents; from the poisoning of fish in the Rhine to the killing of shore birds at Santa Barbara. Man's plunder of nature threatens not only fish and wildlife but his own water and food supplies. Pesticides like DDT still menace humans and other animals; traces even have been found in the fatty tissue of Antarctic penguins. Unfortunately, when man aims a pesticide at a particular pest no one knows which other organisms may be eliminated by ricochet. Environmentalist David Brower reveals this startling possibility:

> If some pesticide, herbicide, or defoliant should by inadvertance kill too many of the 'nitrogen-fixing' organisms — those organisms that enable living things *to make use of* the nitrogen in the atmosphere — *then life on Earth could end.*[31]

Critical environmental concerns like these cause Brower to propose an "Earth National Park": a kind of wildlife preserve where *we*, the earth's inhabitants, are the "wildlife" needing protection from environmental conditions that would either destroy us or make our life hardly worth living.[32] Schools should listen attentively to Brower, whose ecological philosophy is close to Mumford's, and adopt a curriculum based upon human interdependence and the environment which nurtures us. And individuals, following Mumford's example of self-education in cities and regions, should educate themselves to the natural and human ecology of their local region and their earth.

Additional curriculum ideas for world understanding include the study of distant societies and cultures (like *Man: A Course of Study* which provides a good model); cross-cultural study of education and the broader role of enculturation; concentrated study of both relative and universal values, with an emphasis on the latter, and the implications in trans-cultural values like love, compassion and cooperation for One World; and an analysis of divergent ideologies with stress on common elements that might bring humankind together. This is only a sampling of curricular ideas, but it should be obvious that the number and variety of ideas leading toward world consciousness is virtually unlimited. The most pressing need at the moment is for educators to commit themselves to the idea of global unity and then address themselves as creatively as possible to curriculum that moves toward that goal.

The teaching-learning process should concentrate on non-threatening personal and group sharing of thoughts, opinions and feelings. Each class or group must itself become a cooperative community in order for the notion of world community to have personal meaning. This will require openness and directness on the part of teachers and students. Though individual expression of views should always be encouraged, teachers and students alike would be free to challenge bias or prejudice as they hear it. Only in a forum that invites and respects divergent points of view, but at the same time seeks consensus on problems of world civilization and ways to solve these problems, will teaching-learning be effective.

Consensual validation as a continual search for ethical justification, as a bridge from what *is* the world situation to what *ought* to be the world situation, could become the chief instrument of education. Already at work to a large extent in the jury system, as Theodore Brameld observes,[33] consensual validation in the classroom could operate on a number of levels — psychological, interpersonal, sociological — and its aim would be social-self-realization.

The first step in the process, Brameld suggests,[34] is the need for evidence. If the problem concerns developing countries and their immediate needs, evidence might be gathered through films and video tapes; United Nations and government publications; well-known and little known newspapers; magazines and journals ranging from *Ramparts* on the left to *American Opinion* on the right; discussions with university students and other visitors from developing nations; and if possible, a visit to a developing country arranged by the Experiment in International Living or a similar organization for first-hand evidence.

The need to maximize communication, a second step, is an on-going process. It involves sifting evidence and the use of persuasion, but on a deeper level a gradual sharing with others of one's feelings and attitudes, both conscious and preconscious. Maximizing communication implies putting oneself in another's shoes and trying to relate in as honest a way as possible. A great variety of reactions to the evidence of developing countries may be expressed and hostilities may arise; the teacher, as a group member, should encourage maximum communication but not interfere with the democratic process. He may challenge, provoke and question, but he must never use the role of teacher to command automatic respect or belittle student groping.

Stronger leadership by the teacher may be needed in the third stage of the continuum, reaching maximum agreement, but he should never attempt to manipulate the group. Rather, his role might be to cite some overlooked evidence and to comment upon observed interaction. It is important that he respect, and encourage others to respect, those members who hold fast to a particular viewpoint, realizing that consensus may hope for unanimity but rarely achieve it.

The final step, retesting the evidence, is necessary in order to decide whether or not the consensus is justified and therefore valid. The group reviews all evidence and the interactive process to see if the decision is appropriate. For example, suppose it is agreed that developing countries need large amounts of technological aid in order to raise their living standards. It is furthermore agreed that the group should take appropriate action by writing letters to the President, members of Congress, and the Secretary General of the United Nations, asking what steps they would propose to alleviate this problem and what they would suggest the group do to arouse interest in it.

To validate the consensus on this issue, members might question the sources of evidence received, and perhaps the speed at which consensus was achieved. Was intimidation or manipulation used to sway people? If so, to what extent would it invalidate the decision? Did members communicate freely? Was the decision made because it was popular or because it was morally right? What values were accepted as good and which rejected as bad or wrong? Was the consensus consistent with the larger needs of humankind? Through empirical retesting and thorough probing the consensus could become validated, or invalidated, as the case may be. The use of the Delphi Technique might prove useful to test the validity of the consensus.

In terms of control, a genuine world community will require a body of supra-national law, a system of world courts to apply the law, a well-financed world development fund and, of course, a world education authority — as proposed by Brameld[35] — to oversee education across the globe. The authority would carry out and sponsor educational research; set up guidelines for teacher education, school accreditation, and curriculum; and see to it that every man, woman, and child is accorded an equal educational opportunity. Through direct grants to poor regions for schools and colleges and through full scholarships to needy students for study and work in different parts of the world, the authority would help eliminate illiteracy and provincialism, improve occupational skills, sponsor retraining projects, and increase options for the use of leisure time. Local districts would retain considerable control over their own institutions, taking advantage of regional history, geography, and customs, but not separating themselves from the wider world community.

Local schools and colleges would be run by a community of professional educators, students, and other residents of the area. A graduated income tax, without loopholes, would provide financial support. Whenever feasible, policy decisions would be made by consensual validation with representatives of all groups involved. Within the educational institution — with or without walls — teachers and students would be given freedom to experiment within the broad limits of curriculum suggested by the world education authority and the local community. With this freedom, individuality and variety could be encouraged without sacrificing the ongoing goal of universal understanding and cooperation.

In the utopian system of control we have outlined, no pressure group like the John Birch Society could block the introduction of sex education into the school curriculum if the world authority decides that sex education is a vital necessity for world population control and full human development. But the local community and region would decide, within an established framework, what sort of sex education it wants for its children and how the subject of human sexuality should be presented in school. Local control within a larger centralized structure is the key to this approach which, if followed, could provide a solution to the sometimes agonizing dilemma between autonomous local control and bureaucratic, centralized control. Decentralization of control and limited centralization of authority can be compatible.

Relative and Universal Cultural Values

A debate between cultural relativism and cultural universalism has engaged many anthropologists and promises to involve more as world crises continue to threaten civilization. Philosophical anthropologists like Clyde Kluckhohn, David Bidney, and S.F. Nadel, confirming many of Mumford's and Brameld's views, believe there is hope for a peaceful, cooperative world in the study of cultural universals; that is, in trans-cultural patterns, attitudes and values. But other anthropologists like Melville Herskovits have a different perspective:

... the need for a cultural relativistic point of view has become apparent because of the realization that there is no way to play the game of making judgments across cultures except with loaded dice.[36]

In spite of their differing points of view, most anthropologists would agree that the twentieth century marks the rise of cultural relativism and the decline of the popular nineteenth century view of primitive cultures and peoples as immoral or savage. If their specialty was to become a respected science, anthropologists had to shake off the shackles of ethnocentrism. So cultural relativism became an obsession among early twentieth century anthropologists; the pendulum swung from emphasis on similarities and narrow moralistic judgments in the previous century to the highest respect for differences among peoples and cultures in this century. Such an extreme swing caused them, in Kluckhohn's words, to neglect the "equally real similarities upon which the 'universal culture pattern' as well as the psychological uniformities are clearly built."[37]

Though cultural relativism developed as a reaction on the part of Franz Boas and others to the ethnocentric bias of nineteenth century evolutionism, ethnocentrism has had a long history, Felix Keesing points out: states, nations, empires, and religious faiths have been marked by it whenever one or more peoples felt they had a right, a duty, or a mission to consolidate, even by conquest if necessary. [38] In Herskovits' view, extensive field work and better ethnological techniques have made it possible in this century to evaluate cultures in terms of their own context of values rather than in the ethnocentric terms of the evaluator. [39] Herskovits insists that "evaluations are relative to the cultural background out of which they arise" and "judgments are based on experience and experience is interpreted by each individual in terms of his own enculturation."[40]

David Bidney, a cultural anthropologist, acknowledges the evils of ethnocentrism; he is alert to the forcing of alien customs and institutions on native societies and of the punishments meted out for failure to conform. But Bidney disagrees with Herskovits' insistence that cultural values cannot be evaluated comparatively because any effort to do so presupposes an ethnocentric perspective. This is precisely what Herskovits maintains in his *Statement on Human*

Rights drafted in 1947 on behalf of the executive board of the American Anthropological Association and submitted to the United Nations Commission on Human Rights.[41]

Cultural relativists raise some complex and penetrating questions that have serious implications for the search for world order. Perhaps the most fundamental questions revolve around the concept of cultural laissez-faire suggested by Herskovits or of ethical neutralism suggested by Robert Redfield.[42] Is the "hands-off" policy suggested by strict cultural relativism adequate for the crisis age in which we live? Can anthropologists and educational philosophers afford *not* to search for and earnestly promote cross-cultural values which may lead to world unity? For Mumford, for Brameld, and for a growing number of anthropologists, their response is that cultural relativism, though essential as an antidote to ethnocentrism, is deficient. They maintain that scientific study of cultural universals is also needed in order for anthropologists to attain the stage, as Bidney puts it, "of making significant generalities concerning the conditions of the cultural process and the value of civilization."[43]

In an article entitled "The Common Denominator of Cultures," anthropologist George Peter Murdock argues that cultural differences have been studied especially closely, but universal similarities in cultures have been given relatively little attention.[44] As he sees it, universals of culture are not identities in habit or definable behavior, but similarities in definable behavior. Great behavioral diversity exists in all cultures, as Mumford would agree, but all cultures are built according to a basic plan — the "universal culture pattern" as Wissler calls it.[45] Murdock proceeds to list universal characteristics of cultures, including the fundamental nuclear family of father, mother, and children and the presence of incest taboos.

Clyde Kluckhohn also credits Wissler with observing that men everywhere are faced with problems which cannot be avoided because they arise out of the situation "given" by nature. As a result, the broad outlines of all cultures have to be the same everywhere. Cross-cultural comparison, Kluckhohn asserts, "can escape from the bias of any distinct culture by taking as its frame of reference natural limits, conditions, clues, and pressures."[46] In other words, the biological and psychological "givens" of human life make cross-cultural comparison and communication possible.

Kluckhohn is more interested in the similarities between and among cultures, in possible universal values, than most anthropologists. For this reason, among others, Brameld has been attracted to his ideas, but Mumford, surprisingly, has not been drawn to Kluckhohn in particular.[47] Kluckhohn maintains that conceptions of the "mentally normal" person have common elements in all human cultures; for example, the similarity of treatment given a person who threatens the lives of his neighbors without socially approved justification is striking. Even "truth" and "beauty" are universal values in human life, no matter how differently defined or expressed.[48] No culture can be found where the fact of death is not ceremonialized in some way.[49] Nor has a society ever approved suffering as a good thing in itself; suffering as means to an end or as punishment, yes, but for its own sake, no.[50]

Kluckhohn believes that "in principle, a scientific basis for value is discoverable"[51] because of the fundamental biological similarities of all human beings and because of the fact that human existence is invariably a social existence.[52] Like all scientific judgments, however, propositions about values are subject to revision; new knowledge or radically changed circumstances may alter universal values, he readily admits.[53]

Like Kluckhohn and Bidney, one of the more outspoken champions of cultural similarities, Mumford takes great interest in cultural universals while respecting cultural diversity and many relative cultural values. Today, he feels it is especially important to emphasize the universal:

> The fate of the human race . . . depends largely upon our moral decision to place torture, war, and genocide under the same inviolable rule. Relativism, by its indifference to the universal, by its insistence that all goods are equally valuable expressions of local taste or ephemeral impulse, actually places itself on the side of the tribal, the static, the unprogressive: processes and states that obstruct growth.[54]

Earlier forms of universalism like the spread of Christian missionaries (religious), imperialist exploitation (political), and standardization and uniformity (technical) had very serious defects, Mumford acknowledges, but universalism still lies "at the very center of a new integration of life."[55]

The task of the coming age is to work toward a universal morality based on friendly interchange, a world government with power to resolve conflicts and world citizenship for all. To accompany the breaking down of physical barriers in time and space, Mumford proposes the creation of a universalism "based on the spiritual wealth and variety of men: their unity in diversity achieved by working together for common ends. Out of that may come, in the fullness of time, a truly universal religion."[56]

Mumford grants that all men and women are biologically and socially members of a single species and that "humanity" as an open group that embraces all groups is an idea not yet realized. But he also takes pains to recognize differences in national and regional types as well as in language, accent, gestures and feelings between people living within a region. Unity and differentiation go hand in hand: "Unity does not annul difference, and difference does not undermine a dynamic unity."[57]

Always favoring the largest possible variety of opportunities and choices, Mumford affirms that variety in natural and physical environments and variety in personal and cultural perspectives widens the range of human choice. Variety should be nourished and uniformity starved to make life truly interesting. Why not create a single climate, he asks, or level all land, build up wilderness areas, and in other technologically feasible ways make men as uniform and efficient as possible? Only one problem remains with such a scheme, Mumford adds sarcastically: "Why should anyone, even a machine, bother to keep this kind of creature alive?"[58]

Mumford's love of variety and cultural individuality is clearly apparent in a message sent to guests at the *Menorah Journal* Anniversary Dinner in 1939. Noting that America had never been a land of totalitarian uniformity, he writes:

> The pattern of our culture has gained in richness and subtlety by the wide range of peoples, nationalities, cultural interests and religious traditions that have gone into it. If this was always at least partly true in the past, it will be even more true in the future.[59]

He even sees efforts to preserve remaining redwood forests or to protect the whooping crane from extinction as symbolic efforts to retain organic variety in our lives.[60]

Mumford's fear that men and women will become ensnared in a prison of sameness helps explain his severe criticism of Buckminster Fuller for advocating environmentally controlled geodesic domes and cities built on islands or submerged in seas. It also clarifies his distaste for behaviorism and especially for teaching machines. Mumford opposes any person, any institution, any device that threatens to rob man of variety and to increase monotony.

Unification and individuation must operate together for Mumford's utopian vision of One World to materialize. While seeking a world united, he seeks a world diversified. Ethnocentrism is deplored as it is by all contemporary anthropologists and local customs are encouraged. At the same time, cultural universals like cooperation, love, and friendship are emphasized and new universals for a future culture constructed. Mumford finds no inconsistency or contradiction in the continual process of individuation and universalization.

While in sympathy with some aspects of cultural relativism outlined by Herskovits and other anthropologists, the thrust of Mumford's philosophy is sharply in the direction of cultural universals elaborated by Kluckhohn and others. This is only natural for a world citizen who has attacked isolationism all his life. His dream of world unity does not suppress cultures and subcultures that contribute to the whole. Nor does it allow one belicose unit to overtake another. Mumford's conception of One World, like his total philosophy, is dynamically balanced and inclusive.

Implications for Education in Relativism and Universalism

Cultural relativism and cultural universalism have an important bearing on curriculum and the teaching-learning process. In recent years, ethnocentric attitudes have been expressed in catchy phrases like "My country, right or wrong" and "America, love it or leave it." How many schools tried to change these attitudes? For many, the Indochina war was a brutally real symbol of America's contempt for other peoples and other cultures, especially the non-white majority. How did schools deal with this and to what extent are they continuing to address it? For Mumford the war was a prime example of oppressive post-historic imperialism which stands in the way of a transformation to One World culture based on universal values like love, cooperation, and individual freedom. Are schools helping students become aware of other examples of American imperialism?

As a beginning, curriculum materials from textbooks to audio-visual aids must be freed of ethnocentric bias. Within this country, the shameful neglect of Afro-American history and black contributions to American culture by otherwise perceptive critics like Mumford cannot be condoned. Only recently has this deplorable situation begun to be rectified in schools and colleges, and then only under pressure from black activists. But even with increased attention being focused on Afro-American studies at present, the job has barely begun; many high school students have no better conception of black culture than their older brothers and sisters or their parents. Elementary and secondary curricula must include the black, Puerto Rican, Indian, Chicano, and Japanese-American experience in American life, as well as the experiences of various other ethnic groups.

Reaching beyond national borders, curricula on all levels should introduce students to the history, customs, myths and institutions of local cultures around the world. Admiration for the unique contributions of indigenous cultures could be accompanied by recognition of cultural qualities like childhood affection and community resource sharing which might assist in the search for universal understanding and brotherhood. Appreciation of distinct cultural values coupled by sensitivity to broad human needs and aspirations should be the aim of a curriculum dedicated to planetary cooperation in a world physically close.

Teaching-learning that encourages both categories of values requires open, informed, and dedicated teachers willing and able to grow with their students toward community: community on a small scale and community on a scale that reaches around the globe. Teachers themselves must have studied cultures and sub-cultures, from first-hand experience as well as from reading and discussion. In order to do so, their college preparation should include at least a year's experience as participant-observer in a culture other than their own. During this time familiarity with customs and language is gained but, most of all, appreciation for the values of a totally different way of life, of a different way of adapting to the environment, of a different historical tradition.

Person-to-person contact with others around the globe increases man's consciousness of his common humanity as well as his cultural differences. To make world cooperation a working reality, Mumford proposes an International Work Corps which would benefit teachers and students alike. Following the lead of Fourier and his conception of the work army for peace, later modified by William James in *The Moral Equivalent for War*, Mumford suggests forming peace armies to perform active services in the region. Many, preferably all, in the domestic corps would later become active in the International Work Corps and thus broaden face-to-face enounters. Mumford's enthusiasm for this world interchange, attempted to a limited extent by the Peace Corps ten years after his proposal, is apparent in a passage from *The Conduct of Life:*

> The result of such transmigrations would be to enrich every homeland with mature young men and women, who knew the ways and farings of other men, who would bring back treasures with them, songs and dances, technical processes and civic customs, not least, ethical precepts and religious insights, knowledge not taken at third hand from books, but through direct contact and living experience; thus, the young would bring back into every village and city a touch of the universal society of which they form an active part.[61]

For Mumford's idea to be successful, an international or world body would organize and administer the corps, and the interchange of great numbers of young people would always be two-way. Students — and teachers to learn and work alongside of them — would travel to countries in Latin America, Africa, and Asia for a period of a year (or more, ideally) and students-teachers from these areas would come to the United States to share their feelings and values with Americans. Though the emphasis might be placed on youth, adults of all ages could participate in what might become an exciting adult education program: a program combining travel, learning, work and, above all, social intercourse with fellow residents of the planet.

The opportunity for citizens of geographically distant lands to get to know each other on a personal basis as they live and work together could deepen appreciation for cultural diversity as well as sharpen awareness of man's universal humanity. Technologically, especially with the advent of jumbo jets, vast transmigrations are quite feasible. Financially, the program could begin immediately if every country earmarked ten percent of its current defense budget for the transportation and basic necessities of participants. The real question, as always, is whether or not individuals and governments are willing to make a commitment to shatter provincialism and expand horizons through international exchange on an unprecedented scale.

Mumford devotes less than two pages to his concrete proposal for an international corps but even then does so with "some misgivings," explaining that his use of a "deliberately eutopian illustration of the new doctrines and practices"[62] is simply meant to illustrate the rich potentialities open to us. It is unnecessary for Mumford to feel "misgivings" about this illustration since a good many of his other worthy ideas would have greater relevance if accompanied by similar examples. It is puzzling, too, that he seems rather skittish about providing a "eutopian" illustration and then finding it necessary to warn that it should not be dismissed "as a mere fantasy."[63] Mumford need not apologize for his suggestive design or for its "eutopian" nature; by doing so, he contradicts his own view of "eutopian" as desirable and realizable and his own definition of fantasy as frequently creative and constructive.

Most startling of all, however, is a comment that makes one wonder if Mumford is genuinely appreciative of at least some elements in every culture; a disturbing ethnocentric bias appears to slip into his statement that vast student interchange "will eventually irrigate the parched cultural soil of many lands."[64] He does not reveal which lands have a "parched cultural soil," but his comment does reveal a certain superiority over and condescension toward these unnamed cultures wherever they may be. Perhaps his use of "cultural" here is a reversion to culture as the refinement of taste; Mumford never clearly defines his concept of culture and there are certainly times like this in his writing when culture or "cultural" is considered synonymous with "enlightened" Western culture.

Mumford probably means that increased inter-cultural exchange will enrich all cultures, particularly those dominated by repressive leaders in totalitarian regimes or those suffering from restricted world views in the United States and Soviet Union. Though consistent with his philosophy, the fact remains this is not what is said; as a result, Mumford is left open to interpretation that could range from cultural insensitivity to elitism to bigotry. Certainly blacks would find his comment offensive because until recently black culture in the United States and in Africa was considered "parched" and therefore unworthy of much attention in American schools. His value judgment about "parched cultural soil" is no more justified than arbitrarily judging black cultural "soil" or any other cultural "soil" parched and, by implication, inferior.

Mumford further weakens his proposal by suggesting that the International Work Corps be "a democratic version of the grand tour that the favored classes of Europe gave their young heirs in the seventeenth and eighteenth centuries."[65] The grand tour as a system of education, purely in class terms of course, helped to unify Europe and even "to bring about a certain humane forbearance in the conduct of war and the settlements of peace that contrasts with our present unseemly practices.[66] The comparison is poor since the International Work Corps would involve all classes and all races, include all nations and cultures, not just the highly developed and Westernized. And the Corps would encourage involvements in as many aspects of the host culture as possible. Rather than a superficial "grand tour," albeit a democratic one, the corps would provide deep immersion in the cultures and a mutual sharing of experiences, knowledge, customs and hopes for the future.

If Mumford betrays an aristocratic bias in his suggestion for foreign travel, his basic idea to encourage world cooperation through cultural interchange remains valuable. The conception of an International Work Corps as a system of education that unites formal studies, civic responsibilities, and vocational interests is particularly constructive. Administered on a wide scale across the globe, the Corps' influence on peoples and cultures could be immense.

One World will not be created by books, constitutions, laws and technical devices alone, Mumford rightly concludes: "One of the ultimate aims of our lifetime education," he affirms, "will be to make us the sharers in and creators of this universal culture: out of that development will come balanced regions, balanced communities, balanced men."[67] The development of a global culture shaped by person-to-person contacts should be foremost in the plans of educationists, statesmen and individual world citizens.

Mumford: Philosopher-Citizen of the World
As he encourages others to do, Mumford dares to dream of One

World civilization. Sometimes his dreams are vague, sometimes abstract, sometimes sketchy. Often his proposals raise more questions than they answer and his utopian goals seem more and more unattainable as crises deepen throughout the world. But Mumford's ideas deserve sober reflection. He is a profound — if sometimes roundabout — thinker. His diagnosis of the ills of modern humanity and modern culture goes deep and his normative commitment to remedy these ills is unshakable.

Most of Mumford's suggestions for dealing with a person's sense of alienation have great validity. His continued call for self-renewal and for a cooperative social order to replace the one-sided dominance of despotic individuals, classes, races, and nations are worthy goals, even though the means to achieve these goals seem distant and evasive.

As late twentieth century residents of earth, "only a little planet,"[68] perhaps what we need most is a sense of purpose, a sense of meaning, in our own life and in our complex society. If we were to cultivate our potentialities to the fullest, as Mumford urges; if we were to center our life on imaginative, creative, loving endeavor; if we were to strive for a cooperative economy and political order, we might find significance and fulfillment in our life. In the end, Mumford's greatest contribution is his challenge to men and women — not the least to educators — to find meaning and purpose in the process of self-renewal and hope and sustenance in a democratic, ever-renewing world culture.

Educationally, Mumford would agree with educational philosopher Alexander Meiklejohn who wrote over three decades ago: "Every human being, young or old, should be taught, first of all, to be a citizen of the world, a member of the human fellowship. All other lessons are derivatives of that primary lesson."[69] And in a very real sense, all other lessons or themes of Mumford's life-work are derivatives of his earnest desire for world citizenship and world fellowship. If Mumford himself cannot be given any other label, certainly he can be justifiably called a world citizen because he exemplifies the kind of person Meiklejohn sincerely hopes education will encourage from childhood through adult life.

---

[1]Mumford, *The Transformations of Man*, pp. 117-21.
[2]*Ibid.*, p. 134.

3Mumford, *The Transformations of Man*, p. 143.

4*Ibid.*

5Mumford, *The Transformations of Man*, p. 149.

6*Ibid.*, p. 152.

7Brameld, *Education as Power* (New York: Holt, Rinehart and Winston, 1965), p. 32.

8Gunnar Myrdal, "The Necessity and Difficulty of Planning the Future Society," in *Environment and Change: The Next Fifty Years*, ed. by William R. Ewald (Bloomington: Indiana University Press, 1968), pp. 252-55. (Hereinafter referred to as "Planning the Future Society.")

9Mumford, "The Art of the 'Impossible'," in *Alternatives to the H Bomb*, ed. by Anatole Shub (Boston: Beacon Press, 1955), p. 17.

10Myrdal, "Planning the Future Society," pp. 252-55.

11Mumford, "The Art of the 'Impossible'," p. 29.

12*Ibid.*

13Erich Kahler, "Reality of Ut," in *Out of the Labyrinth*, (New York: George Braziller, 1967), p. 52.

14Chase, *The Most Probable World*, p. 191.

15*Ibid.*, pp. 180-81.

16Mumford, "Wardom and the State," *Dial*, LXVII (October 4, 1919), 304-5.

17Mumford, *The Culture of Cities*, p. 370.

18Mumford, *The Conduct of Life*, p. 10.

19Mumford, "Toward a Free World," p. 11.

20*Ibid.*, pp. 8-10.

21Mumford, *In the Name of Sanity*, p. 89.

22*Ibid.*, p. 8.

23Mumford, "Toward a Free World," p. 14.

24*Ibid.*, p. 5.

25Mumford, *Faith for Living*, p. 326.

26Mumford, *The Transformation of Man*, p. 158.

27Mumford, "The Art of the 'Impossible'," p. 12.

28Mumford, *Faith for Living*, pp. 324-25.

29Mumford, *The Transformations of Man*, pp. 156-57.

30Brameld, *Education as Power*, pp. 103-19.

[31]Brower, "A Proposal for Earth National Park," p. 30.

[32]*Ibid.*, p. 31.

[33]Theodore Brameld, "Social Consensus in Truth Seeking," address delivered at a meeting of the New England Philosophy of Education Society, North Andover, Massachusetts, October 25, 1969.

[34]*Ibid.*

[35]See Brameld, *Education for the Emerging Age* (New York: Harper and Row, 1950), p. 130 and Brameld, *Education as Power*, p. 131.

[36]Melville Herskovits, "Some Further Comments on Cultural Relativism," *American Anthropologist*, LX (April, 1958), 270.

[37]Clyde Kluckhohn, "Universal Categories of Culture," in *Anthropology Today*, ed. by A.L. Kroeber (Chicago: University of Chicago Press, 1953), p. 515.

[38]Felix M. Keesing, *Cultural Anthropology* (New York: Rinehart, 1958), p. 46.

[39]Melville Herskovits, *Man and His Works* (New York: Alfred A. Knopf, 1956), p. 78.

[40]*Ibid.*, p. 63.

[41]David Bidney, "The Concept of Value in Modern Anthropology," in *Anthropology Today*, p. 693. (Hereinafter referred to as "The Concept of Value").

[42]Robert Redfield, *The Primitive World and its Transformations* (Ithaca: Cornell University Press, 1953), p. 146.

[43]Bidney, "The Concept of Value," p. 698.

[44]George Peter Murdock, "The Common Denominator of Cultures," in Ralph Linton, ed., *The Science of Man in the World Crisis* (New York: Columbia University Press, 1945), p. 123.

Ibid., p. 125.

[46]Kluckhohn, "Universal Categories of Culture," p. 521.

[47]Mumford, private interview, November 14, 1967.

[48]Clyde Kluckhohn, "Values and Value-Orientations in the Theory of Action: An Exploration in Definition and Classification," in Talcott Parsons and Edward Shils, ed., *Toward a General Theory of Action* (Cambridge: Harvard University Press, 1945) p. 418. (Hereinafter referred to as: "Values and Value-Orientations.")

49Clyde Kluckhohn and A.L. Kroeber, *Culture: A Critical Review of Concepts and Definitions* (New York: Vintage Books, 1952), p. 349.

50Kluckhohn, "Values and Value-Orientations," p. 418.

51Clyde Kluckhohn, *Mirror for Man*, Premier Books (Greenwich: Fawcett Publications, 1944), p. 243.

52Kluckhohn, "Values and Value-Orientations," p. 418.

53*Ibid.*, p. 419.

54Mumford, *The Conduct of Life*, p. 165.

55*Ibid.*, p. 237.

56*Ibid.*, p. 240.

57Mumford, *The Culture of Cities*, p. 311.

58Mumford, "Prospect," *Man's Role in Changing the Face of the Earth*, p. 1151.

59Lewis Mumford, "Message from Lewis Mumford," *Menorah Journal*, XXVII (January-March, 1939), 100-101.

60Mumford, "Closing Statement," *Future Environments of North America*, p. 727.

61Mumford, *The Conduct of Life*, pp. 278-79.

62*Ibid.*, p. 279.

63*Ibid.*

64*Ibid.*

65*Ibid.*

66*Ibid.*

67*Ibid.*, p. 280.

68See *Only a Little Planet*, edited by David R. Brower (San Francisco: Friends of the Earth, 1972).

69Alexander Meiklejohn, *Education Between Two Worlds* (New York: Harper and Brothers, 1942), p. 286.

✿ postscript

LEWIS MUMFORD'S organic philosophy encompasses the balanced person, the self-governing group and the universal community. The balanced person honestly confronts himself or herself, has confidence in his/her creative powers, strives for self-actualization and takes in elements of all cultures. The self-governing group is small enough to encourage active participation, stimulates deeper I-thou relationships and respects individual rights while promoting group consensus and social planning. The universal community demands both personal and societal obligation in the quest for world order, requires sacrifice on the part of wealthier nations in the distribution of resources, and insists that cooperation on a global scale is the only hope for survival in a nuclear age. Education must never neglect individual, group, and world needs and aspirations. Education for creative selves must be joined by education for creative societies and education for a just and peaceful world.

In his dialectical approach, Mumford strives for synthesis between the one and the many, microcosm and macrocosm, past and future, rational and unrational, tool-making and symbol-making, stability and change, good and evil, participation and contemplation, self-renewal and cultural renewal. Mumford's whole life has been devoted to this dialectical process. Educators can learn from him to seek synthesis in curriculum building, the teaching-learning process, the control of schools and teacher education.

As Mumford is wary of fashionable panaceas or grandiose educational schemes based on extremes, educators should be wary of reliance upon one total system or another. Mumford's dialectical approach is of inestimable value because it rejects deceptively easy or contrived solutions in favor of solutions respecting wholeness, balance and growth.

In this volume, educators and others have been challenged to ask: What kind of a person and what kind of a world do we want to help create now and in the future? How can technology serve human needs? How can architecture provide a life-fulfilling environment? Why are cities choking, how can they recover, and what alternatives to cities are possible? Why is global cooperation imperative and world citizenship desirable? Throughout, we have argued for an education that probes to the roots of personal-social crises confronting humankind.

Mumford's ideas have served as a springboard for further development of many issues and ideas. His goal of a "biotechnic" or non-consumptive, ecologically sound, socially just society necessitates a biotechnic education which stresses development of political risk-taking and personal-social growth in students and teachers. An organic technology centering on human needs, feelings and desires promotes self-actualization instead of retarding it. Educators can and should explore the benefits of a healthful, decentralized technology and help students re-direct technology toward social ends.

As has been indicated, Mumford sees architecture not only fulfilling basic human requirements but also expressing our highest aspirations and most creative dreams. Educators have barely tapped the potential of architectural analysis as a means of critically examining our entire physical environment. While lamenting the extreme deprivation and exploitation of contemporary American cities, Mumford helps us realize that cities can become more human places to live and work. Educators might take his suggestion to focus upon the planning and designing of totally new communities as well as explore the problems and promises of present urban areas.

As an especially valuable educational tool, Mumford's notion of regional survey as an intensive study of one's region can be used by educators at all levels and in virtually all discipline areas. And his appeal for world community helps us realize that border-hopping is both necessary and unavoidable in today's world. Students and teachers can learn a vast amount from experiences in other cultures, but they can also attack ethnocentrism and isolationism in their home schools and communities. Conflict resolution, analysis of alternative world order models, and values clarification in the areas of social justice and economic well-being could become prominent.

We have seen how curriculum as well as educational strategies can be built upon the wide variety of ideas introduced by Mumford in his many books and articles. Considerable attention has been devoted to educational implications in Mumford's writings because schools and other institutions have an important, though often-neglected transforming as well as transmitting role to play. Mumford's ecohumanism points the way to a transformed society, transformed education, and a transformed world. Educators should seek nothing less.

✺ appendix
the life and work
of lewis mumford

WHO IS THIS MAN, Lewis Mumford, who has been called "the chief heir of Emerson in American moral philosophy,"[1] the author of the "best book about America if not the best American book I have ever read,"[2] and the prophet with "the moral force and the savage indignation of the prophets of the Old Testament, as of England and New England"?[3] Mumford the man and Mumford the "American Prophet," as Van Wyck Brooks has aptly titled him,[4] symbolizes those values deep in American culture which emphasize individual freedom, social cooperation, racial and ethnic equality, aesthetic sensitivity and love of humanity as opposed to the exploitation of man and nature, the priority of profits, unplanned-uncontrolled technology, and isolation from the world at large. Perhaps it is not surprising that Brooks has linked him to the humanistic tradition of Jefferson, Emerson, Thoreau, Whitman, and others.[5]

Born on October 19, 1895 in Flushing, Long Island, New York, Lewis Mumford grew up on the West Side of New York City in a middle-class neighborhood. Of his early public school education at P.S. 166 he once commented: "I remained a docile pupil, a model pupil, always an excellent pupil in the futile academic sense, until I entered high school, where my interests widened and my marks worsened."[6] From 1909 to graduation in 1912, he attended Stuyvesant High School which prepared students for engineering; when the time had come to choose a high school, Mumford was in the process of making crude model airplanes and a simple wireless radio so Stuyvesant seemed appropriate.[7] The young boy was suddenly faced with an entirely new part of the city and, in his own words, "boys who ate strange food whose flavors pervaded their breath and seemed to hang about their clothes; boys whose aggressive vitality left me feeling like a sick goldfinch among a flock of greedy sparrows."[8] Needless to say, this experience was profoundly educational, as were the boy's ceaseless wanderings about the city, observing and musing.

Many of Mumford's high school teachers, unlike the elementary, were young and enthusiastic. One English teacher's personality so impressed the boy that he later recalled the really important value of this, and other, classes: "Not the lesson itself, but the overflow — a hint, a pat on the shoulder, the confession of a secret ambition, a fragment of unposed life as someone had actually lived it."[9] This type of affective learning that frequently takes place outside the formal limits of a particular subject matter or classroom has been important to Mumford throughout his life. And he has continued to believe that the teacher as a full person with many life experiences, varied interests, and a friendly approach is far superior to the teacher who has mastery of a body of knowledge but fails to relate personally as a many-dimensioned human being.

After graduation from high school, young Mumford worked as a copyboy for the *Evening Telegram* and found time to read Plato and William James, even at 3:25 in the morning! At the same time, he took evening courses at City College of New York, skipping typical freshman courses and jumping to junior and senior courses in politics, philosophy, and English. Praising his professors — Morris Cohen, Alfred Compton, John Pickett Turner, and Earle Palmer — as "men of character," Mumford particularly singled out the latter instructor of poetry as "a frail but ageless figure, half pixie, half demon, with the sudden touch of one who had not lightly triumphed over terror and wrath and pain."[10] Once again it was the professor as a person that stood out; so important was this for Mumford that he has remarked, without meaning to exaggerate: "One touch of Palmer's ruthless sincerity was at least half a college education."[11]

Later studying at Columbia University and the New School for Social Research under Thorstein Veblen, the young student accumulated enough credits for a college degree but never obtained one, later explaining that since he did not intend to teach he did not feel the need for a degree.[12] After serving a short time as a radio electrician in the Navy, in 1919 Mumford became an associate editor of the *Dial*, a highly respected fortnightly review. John Dewey was an editor of the *Dial* at the same time, but the two never became friendly either at this time or in later years when they exchanged biting criticism in print.

One of Mumford's few articles dealing directly with education, "The Place of the Community in the School," appeared in the *Dial* the year he joined the staff. Arguing that the community itself was richer in educational resources than the school proper, that nowhere had the school taken full advantage of community institutions, that use of the community by the school implied active cooperation of the community *in* the school,[13] Mumford sounded very modern and half a century ahead of recent developments that intimately relate the school to the community. In the same article he suggested regional survey, an idea developed further in the twenties and thirties as an integrated, first-hand means of studying the total environment.[14]

Other articles in the *Dial* of 1919 criticized the current American situation — "the actual America of Security Leagues, espionage organizations, race riots, and compulsive militarism"[15] — and chided scholars for failing to question the state as a sovereign unit while attempting to provide constructive ways and means of achieving international cooperation.[16] At the age of twenty-four, Mumford was already committed to the concept of world community which became for him a stronger and deeper conviction over the years.

Mumford originally came across the writings of Patrick Geddes, the Scot biologist-sociologist, just a few years out of high school. And in 1920 Victor Branford, a colleague of Geddes, invited Mumford to come to Britain to serve as acting editor of the *Sociological Review*. Geddes' masterpiece, *Cities in Evolution*, had been concerned with education of the citizen toward a better understanding of the city and his active role in urban life. The book inspired Mumford to walk through the streets of New York and into outlying districts with a new purpose: "looking into its past, understanding its present, replanning its future became indissoluble parts of a single process: a task for all citizens, not merely for professionals."[17]

Strangely, since he spent half of 1920 in London, Mumford did not actually meet his mentor until years later in New York. When they did meet, the younger man acted as a kind of personal secretary to the man whose influence continued to grow on him. However, the two were very different in personality, and Mumford ruefully admitted that the collaboration they both hoped for did not become a reality. "I was overwhelmed by him," Mumford has commented, "our rhythms of work and thought were entirely different and I couldn't bear to be talked at for hours at a time."[18] But this did not diminish Mumford's respect for the old master and his critical reaction to machine-ridden civilization. In fact, one of Geddes' American students, Philip Boardman, has acknowledged that "the distinguished writer and critic who is responsible for making many of Geddes' ideas widely known in America was Lewis Mumford."[19]

For all his high regard for Geddes and his propagating of Geddes' ideas, Mumford today has some severe criticism of Geddes' life and work which he would have revealed in a biography if he had written one. Two chapters in a future autobiography, one already published in *Encounter* magazine, will discuss the relationship between the master and his disciple and appraise the master's work.[20]

In the early twenties, Mumford met Van Wyck Brooks who became one of his close friends. Brooks has said that of all his writing contemporaries Mumford "was always the one with whom I felt most sympathetic and closely allied, and from the moment I fell in with him he took for me the place that Randolph Bourne had left vacant."[21] Deep in the midst of literary and artistic movements thriving in New York during the twenties, Mumford became acquainted with and became a great admirer of Alfred Steiglitz, the pioneering photographer; Georgia O'Keefe, Steiglitz's wife and a great artist; and Waldo Frank, a leading author.

Early in the decade Mumford spent one summer teaching at a private school in Peterborough, New Hampshire and later at a well-known progressive school in New York, the Walden School, where he taught English. Though never considering himself a first-rate teacher in these schools, he felt that he was more successful in later years as a visiting college professor at Dartmouth, Stanford, the University of Pennsylvania, Massachusetts Institute of Technology, and Harvard.[22]

His first book was published in 1922 at the age of twenty-seven. *The Story of Utopias*, a study of classic utopias, was the beginning of an abiding and deepening interest in the utopian mood. In a preface to the paperback edition published forty years after the original, the author explained that he regarded utopian thinking as a young man and still as an older man as the opposite of "One-sidedness, partisanship, partiality, provinciality, specialism."[23] However, he did not hesitate to criticize classic utopias as too inflexible, too centralized, and too closed.[24] Summing up the utopian philosophy from which he has seldom strayed in over a half century of work, Mumford observed:

> He who practiced the utopian method must view life synoptically and see it as an interrelated whole: not as a random mixture, but as an organic and increasingly organizable union of parts, whose balance it was important to maintain — as in any living organism — in order to promote growth and transcendence.[25]

Two years after *The Story of Utopias* came *Sticks and Stones: A Study of American Architecture and Civilization*, an early and original interpretation of American architecture in cultural perspective. *Sticks and Stones*, translated a year later into German, introduced another long-standing interest: architecture as a home for man. In 1926, after a summer of lectures on "The Development of American Culture" at the Geneva School of International Studies, Mumford wrote *The Golden Day*, a landmark book in American literature and culture. Called an "uneven accomplishment" by one critic[26] and criticized by the author himself in the 1957 edition for its omissions, this small book nevertheless was influential at the time, according to the eminent Harvard historian F.O. Mathiessen.[27]

In *The Golden Day* Mumford spoke of "pragmatic acquiescence" in the face of unchecked industrial expansion and the resulting social ills. Praising John Dewey for his firm belief in democracy and severe criticism of conventional education, Mumford nonetheless criticized Dewey for lack of discrimination in his personal standards. Taking Dewey to task for justifying fine art by citing its instrumental quality and for speaking of the intrinsic worth of invention, he argued that the main weakness in Dewey's philosophy was a weakness in emphasis. Though recognizing the place of the arts, Dewey was preoccupied with science and technology in the instrumental sense.[28] Today Mumford believes that Dewey was quite nettled by his comments in *The Golden Day*, perhaps goading him to clarify his views on art eight years later in *Art as Experience*.[29]

Just as Mumford was often too quick to label Edward Bellamy a utilitarian thinker without adequately accounting for Bellamy's religious-spiritual interests, he was too quick to label Dewey's "utilitarian type of personality"[30] in *The Golden Day*. His criticism of Dewey's respect for the common man was quite unjustified; he implied that Dewey believed "what had been produced by the mass of men must somehow be right, and must somehow be more significant than the interests which occupy only a minority!"[31] Unjustified, too, was Mumford's extremely harsh judgment of Dewey's writing style. Although Dewey's style left something to be desired, Mumford's colorful condemnation seemed more than a bit exaggerated:

> Style is the indication of a happy mental rhythm, as a firm grip and a red cheek are of health. Lack of style is a lack of organic connection . . . Mr. Dewey's pages are as depressing as a subway ride — they take one to one's destination, but a little the worse for wear.[32]

Mumford continually oversimplified and underrated Dewey's achievements. However, late in life he admitted that because of his own strained relations with Dewey he did not follow the development of Dewey's ideas as closely as he might have.[33]

Dewey responded promptly to the accusations of the cantankerous young critic in an article in the *New Republic*. Defending himself, Dewey criticized Mumford for developing false myths about pragmatism. Defending William James, he denounced Mumford's misunderstanding and hasty dismissal of James' contributions to philosophy. Actually Dewey considered Mumford fairer to himself than to James.[34] Mumford quickly replied in the *New Republic* two weeks later. Admitting that he began as a pragmatist and stated that fact in an early article, Mumford said he would not renounce the claim now; he had learned much from James and Dewey and hoped to learn more. "But pragmatism as an approach to life," he continued, "must be judged by its own criterion; and as a complete philosophic orientation, it has come to seem to many of us, not false, but insufficient."[35] Mumford was looking for greater attention to the spiritual, aesthetic, unrational domains of life and more commitment to purpose and ends than Dewey and instrumentalism seemed to provide. In this he was seeking the very same change of emphasis that Theodore Brameld and other reconstructionist educators sought in the nineteen-fifties, sixties, and seventies: a shift toward the open but achieveable goals of social-self-realization and world community.

Mumford wrote a large number of articles in the twenties, many appearing in the *New Republic* of which he was a contributing editor. In one book review, he attacked the author of *The Children's Own Book of Letters and Stories* whose book was "typical of the pseudo-new education" because it preserved "all the old vices of the old methods by putting them in a bright contemporary dress, and by introducing numerous allusions to the marketplace and to practical life."[36] In contrast to this inferior volume, he highly praised Hugh Mearns' *Creative Youth: How a School Environment Set Free the Creative Spirit* which suggested imaginative ways to teach literature.[37]

Other reviews acknowledged the importance of Negro art,[38] raved about Charles Horton Cooley's *Life and the Student* while criticizing American sociology in general,[39] and considered Darwin not as a symbol and figure but as a *man* in critically reviewing four books on Darwin's life and work.[40] Of particular interest in light of the Mumford-Dewey interchange was a 1929 review of T.V. Smith's *The Philosophic Way of Life*. Mumford recommended Smith's work as a whole, but cited fallacies in his view of aesthetics. Mumford worried that the Chicago school, for all its attempts to humanize industry and improve the social order, showed contempt for the arts: "In their distrust of ends that are not instrumentally connected, the Chicago School has an inveterate tendency to abandon the search for relevant ends altogether, and to deify instruments."[41] Once again he called for a more dynamic balance between means and ends, even in Smith's otherwise "penetrating and sympathetic exposition."[42]

Like Ralph Waldo Emerson, Henry David Thoreau, Frank Lloyd Wright, and a host of other creative Americans, Mumford was largely self-educated. He has been proud of his style of education outside the formal structure of schools and colleges — education through extensive travelling, shrewd observation, careful reading and practical work — just as he has been pleased with this kind of education in great people like the landscape designer Frederick Law

Olmsted. When all the elements of this education were integrated as they were in Walt Whitman and Herman Melville, in Henry George and Olmsted, this was American education at its best, Mumford once commented.[43] Mumford is especially proud of the fact that he himself received no academic degree of any kind until 1965 when he accepted an honorary doctorate and it is interesting to note that he has never been attached to a college or university except as visiting professor or scholar. From the time he was a young man, Mumford has been wary of professional education and educators in spite of the fact that he has delved into, or skirted around, educational issues and problems all his life.

Practicing civic and regional surveying, inspired by Geddes, Mumford explored the towns and cities of the Eastern seaboard with notebook and camera and learned to use buildings as documents, very much as archaeologists use artifacts.[44] He contributed an article on "The City" to Harold Stearns' *Civilization in the United States*, an "adventure in intellectual co-operation" according to the editor.[45] The year before, at the age of twenty-six, he castigated suburbia as "that vast and aimless drift of human beings"[46] in an amazingly relevant and timely piece and criticized the failure to create a good life in modern cities.

Mumford's growing interest in cities brought him into contact with a group of men who incorporated themselves into the Regional Planning Association of America in the early nineteen-twenties. Two of the group's leaders, Clarence Stein and Henry Wright, pioneered in planning a successful housing project on Long Island for mixed-income families. Mumford moved with his wife Sophia, whom he had married in 1921, and his infant son Geddes to Sunnyside Gardens in September 1925.

Out of this community experiment grew Radburn, New Jersey, an innovative new town, and between 1935 and 1940 the abortive Greenbelt Towns in several different states which never became genuine balanced communities. Mumford was not boasting unjustifiably when he recently observed: "During the next twenty-five years Clarence Stein and I kept alive here, almost single-handed, the fundamental ideas of the New Towns movement."[47] In the late sixties and now in the seventies Mumford and Stein have much more company, including a number of government officials. But for all the flourish and political rhetoric it remains to be seen whether the kind of balanced, organic regional towns and cities Mumford advocates will actually be built. Most indicators point to the private and semi-private development of new towns and cities in name only and, with very few exceptions, not to the creation of radically different places to live, bring up children, mix with a variety of people, learn in a freeing atmosphere, and work without having to commute by automobile for hours.

Throughout the thirties Mumford continued to write for the *New Republic*, opening the decade with the award of "Booby Prizes for 1929" to such notables as Henry Ford, Calvin Coolidge, Herbert Hoover and other favorite targets in architecture, city planning, and business.[48] Later in 1930 he deplored housing conditions in the United States, pointing out that the period of "prosperity" from 1922 to 1929 marked a steady decline in the quality of housing. Arguing that the alternative to low-grade building was well-designed group housing — housing that no longer yielded to the sacredness of free-standing houses, a by-product of the Romantic movement — and community planning, he asked what thoughtful individuals should ask today: "Why should we deceive ourselves into thinking that these wretched slums we are creating are emblems of individual initiative or the pledge of a fine domestic life?"[49] After forty-five years, at least some architects and planners are becoming upset about the proliferation of single box-like houses across the land and are consequently increasing experimentation with cluster housing, town houses and other ways to build pleasant homes without obliterating the natural landscape.

Mumford was also ahead of his time in recognizing Charles Sanders Peirce as "one of the great seminal minds that America has produced"[50] in a letter to the *New Republic* pleading for two thousand dollars to assure publication of the voluminous Peirce notes and papers. Appreciating that many people were near starvation at the time because of the depression, he nevertheless concluded — quite characteristically — that "starvation of the spirit is as disastrous as starvation of the body; and in meeting one situation, let us not forget the other."[51] He was not one to forget the intellectual, aesthetic, and spiritual needs of people even when material, physical, and biological needs were desperate.

In a 1935 letter to the same magazine, Mumford asked the editors to leave behind "the stale liberalism of capitalist compromise" which did not seek to alter the goals and motives of capitalism, but not to leave behind the "revolutionary tradition of liberalism."[52]

Communism or collectivism was not the answer to capitalism; rather, the liberal tradition which depended upon informed consent of the citizens, freedom of criticism, and the rights of minorities should be supported.[53] All through the thirties, and into the next decade, Mumford continued his attack on liberals which began with "The Pragmatic Acquiescence" in the twenties and reached its most controversial point in "The Corruption of Liberalism" in 1940.

In an article in *Challenge to the New Deal*, Mumford made it clear that he was less than pleased with revolutionaries and radicals of the past who "prided themselves upon a defect in their education — the lack of concrete objectives."[54] Radicals were unprepared to run the state *if* they gained control over it, because farmer and worker radicals had "no concrete plans or goals apart from those dictated by capitalism or formulated by naive reaction against capitalism." [55] Mumford was generalizing, perhaps over-generalizing, as he had a tendency to do. But he might level the same criticism against some reformers today who do not have a clearly defined idea of the society and culture they want to create, let alone an effective strategy to achieve a good society. At the same time, he would be encouraged by the deep searching of youth and by the fact that many individuals have rejected capitalist goals in favor of more communal, cooperative ways of sharing and living.

In addition to writing a column of architectural criticism for the *New Yorker* — "The Sky Line" — which appeared irregularly for over thirty years, and articles in *The Nation, American History,* and *Freeman,* Mumford wrote *The Brown Decades: A Study of the Arts in America, 1865-1895* which was based on the Guernsey Center Moore lectures given at Dartmouth College in 1929. Later came *Technics and Civilization,* a critical history of the machine and its effects on civilization and the first in the "Renewal of Life" series which eventually reached four volumes.

Of *Technics and Civilization,* the British aesthetic educator Herbert Read once commented: "Too diffuse to be science, too disconnected to be history, too concrete to be philosophy, it is difficult to fit into any category. Might perhaps be classed as one of the prophetic books."[56] Another reviewer enthused about Mumford's subjecting "the modern industrial and social scene to such a ransacking and dissection as it has seldom if ever experienced before,"[57] and *The Times Literary Supplement* responded positively to his holistic approach.[58]

When first published, *Technics and Civilization* stood very much alone as a study of technology in historical-cultural perspective, but since then much has been written as Mumford himself acknowledged in an unusual self-criticism of the book written twenty-five years after the original.[59] Admitting certain weaknesses, he nevertheless concluded:

> Whatever the original defects of *Technics and Civilization*, whatever further shortcomings time has disclosed, it still unfortunately possesses its original distinction: it stands alone, an ironic monument if not an active influence.[60]

Perhaps Mumford was too modest. Certainly any book that almost forty years ago alerted us to the social limits of population growth, [61] the consequences of air pollution,[62] and the implications of automobiles and highways on community life[63] has already exerted some active influence and promises to exert more as the timeliness of his ideas becomes apparent.

The Culture of Cities (1938), Mumford's most influential volume and the second in the "Renewal of Life" series, established him as a world authority on urban culture, past, present, and future. The book was used by underground planners in Poland, the Netherlands, and Greece to help reconstruct cities after World War II. And it helped stimulate the British New Towns movement after that war. Chapters on regionalism and the social basis of a new urban order were especially valuable contributions to educational theory and practice.

When war began in Europe in the late thirties, Mumford spoke out vigorously against Hitler and fascism and urged the United States to involve itself in that colossal struggle. This country, he argued, could not retreat into isolationism, could not turn its back and watch Hitler engulf Europe, without sacrificing its moral fabric. In "Call to Arms," an article in the *New Republic* four months before the betrayal at Munich, Mumford vehemently exhorted his country-men to take up arms. Full of arousing emotion and patriotic zeal, crammed with flamboyant expressions like "Liberty Still Tastes Sweet,"[64] the article caused a strong reaction in editorials and letters-to-the-editor. As historian Merle Curti has observed, many American intellectuals remained indifferent or even apologized for Nazi fascism in the 1930's, [65] but Mumford was not among them. He grew so angry at the *New Republic* that in June 1940 he resigned a position as contributing editor in opposition to that liberal journal's neutral stand. By September of the same year, the editors had changed their minds. In a letter to the magazine, Mumford happily congratulated the *New Republic* for now favoring a declaration of war against the Axis powers.[66]

Just two months before his resignation, "The Corruption of Liberalism" had been printed. Like "Call to Arms," this denunciation of "pragmatic liberals" created a storm of controversy; some individuals writing to the editors defended Mumford's view of liberalism, but most correspondents were extremely critical. Mumford felt so deeply about what he considered the disintegration of liberalism and the vulgarization of pragmatism that he revised the same essay for publication in *Faith for Living* in 1940 and included a considerably revised though fundamentally consistent version in *Values for Survival* (1946). The inability of liberals to act forcefully on moral issues seemed to bother Mumford most. He found serious fault with their "incurable optimism,"[67] their lack of understanding the irrational element in fascism,[68] and their pervasive attitude: "too noble to surrender, too sick to fight."[69] He chided them for not recognizing the problem of evil and therefore for not being able to deal with evil men: "they look in vain for merely intellectual mistakes to account for the conduct of those who have chosen to flout man's long efforts to become civilized."[70] Mumford, profoundly influenced by men like Freud and Jung, was well aware of the irrational and non-rational dimensions of human behavior.

Contrasting "pragmatic liberalism" to "ideal liberalism," Mumford declared that he favored the humanist (or "ideal") tradition of liberalism going back to Confucius, Socrates, Plato, Aristotle, Rousseau, and Jefferson, but not the second element in liberalism, a by-product of inventors and industrialists, which he called "pragmatic liberalism."[71] "Pragmatic liberalism" avoided the normative disciplines, those dealing with purpose and value like aesthetics, ethics, and religion, which "ideal" liberals like Rousseau did not.[72] Moreover, "pragmatic liberals" were afraid to use force which sometimes, as in the late thirties and early forties, was absolutely necessary to halt the cancer of fascism. Revealing a tough-minded attitude uncharacteristic of many utopian humanists, Mumford asserted in "The Corruption of Liberalism":

> Force cannot be left behind, no matter how humane and
> rational our standards of conduct. He who under no

circumstances and for no human purpose will resort to force, abandons the possibility of justice and freedom.[73]

One critic of the attack on "pragmatic liberalism," philosopher Sidney Hook, was appalled by Mumford's charges and strongly criticized his advocating war against Hitler.[74] Hook, contending that "extremism, frantic and reckless extremism mars almost every page"[75] of Faith for Living, denounced Mumford's "metaphysical passion" as frightening "because it leads to an extremism which willfully sacrifices the power to make intellectual discriminations."[76] But it was just this passion, this commitment to moral ends which Hook derides, that Mumford knew was missing in pragmatic liberals. With his liberal hesitance, passivity and what Mumford has called the "ignoble notion of national security"[77] firm in his mind, Hook seemed to exemplify the "pragmatic liberal."

Involvement in Education

Throughout the nineteen-thirties Mumford took an active interest in education as a writer and visiting college professor. He was an occasional contributor to the Social Frontier, one of the authentic voices of this decade, according to Lawrence Cremin, and throughout the thirties "the only journal specifically addressed to teachers that openly and forthrightly discussed the ideological problems of an ideological age."[78] The Social Frontier published "The Social Significance of Contemporary Art" in 1935 and "Survey and Plan as Communal Education," included later in The Culture of Cities. For most of its five-year existence, Mumford was listed on the Board of Contributors of this journal and upon its change of name and takeover by the Progressive Education Association in 1939, he became an Associate Editor with Frank Baker, George Counts, and George Hartman of Frontiers of Democracy. In spite of his official titles, however, Mumford did not play an active role on either journal; the "progressivists," he claimed, simply enlisted him to serve on these periodicals and accordingly placed his name on the title of each.[79]

In 1931 Mumford took part in a lecture-discussion series at Columbia University and lectured on social planning and a planned economy at the Rand School of Social Science in New York. Later that year he was appointed lecturer for a semester at Union College and then became a visiting professor of art at Dartmouth College. In

1933 Mumford spoke to the New York City Association of Teachers of English on literature and its relation to life[80] and several years afterward returned to New York to address a luncheon meeting of the Association of Instructors of Hunter College. On that occasion, he replied to the President of Hunter who had asked if student participants in peace strikes disapproved by college authorities should be considered disorderly persons. Mumford maintained that participation by students in occasional peace demonstrations should not be viewed as cause for disciplinary action.[81]

From time to time in the thirties and early forties Mumford spoke before the Progressive Education Association. At a regional conference of several thousand representatives of public and private colleges held in 1934, he developed a theme which became a hallmark of his life-work:

> Technically, we at least have the means of a good life, not for a minority, but for the mass of mankind. But socially, we are surrounded by obsolete institutions and practices that are hostile to the new order. Blindly holding on to their privileges, the ruling castes prefer to face chaos rather than a fundamental change in the social order.[82]

In a speech concerned with social conditions in the United States delivered at the annual meeting of the PEA in February, 1940, Mumford outlined the need for a unit of common personal and political action — the region. Conscious development of regional units was essential, he stressed, and so was the uniting of student needs with community needs.[83] His deep interest in regionalism stemming from the twenties grew steadily throughout the thirties. In *The Culture of Cities*, and a year later in a speech before the Bennington Planning Conference of the Commission on Teacher Education of the American Council on Education, he developed the concept of regional survey as a means of educational synthesis, an idea which dated back to the 1890's when first devised by Patrick Geddes.

The latter address, one of Mumford's most important contributions to the field of education, appeared in October, 1939 in the *Educational Record* as "The Social Responsibilities of Teachers and Their Implications for Teacher Education." In January, 1940 the *Education Digest* printed the speech in abbreviated form and it was later published by the Commission on Teacher Education in a pamphlet entitled *Cultural and Social Elements in the Education of Teachers.* After the war, Mumford included "The Social Responsibilities of Teachers," an almost identical version of the Bennington speech, in *Values for Survival.*

Most of Mumford's views expressed in this address remained relevant during the intervening years and are germane today, especially those dealing with the active role of education in creating an emergent social order with greater attention to the expressive arts, the political and social roles of teachers, and regional survey as synthesis. Though a few of his ideas are dated and have in time proved false — the assertion, for instance, that disparities between region and region, class and class were growing smaller[84] when indeed they have continued to grow larger — most have retained a remarkable freshness.

Recently, Mumford seems to have abandoned some of his early faith in the ability of formal education and educators to solve social ills or help bring about a new social order. While originally sympathetic to George Counts' challenge in the thirties, he now believes Counts and others attempted to give a political task to schools which schools were unfit to perform.[85] This represents a departure from the confidence in education expressed in "The Social Responsibilities of Teachers and Their Implications for Teacher Education." Emphasizing that the schools are only one of many institutions that can bring about needed changes, revealing disillusionment with the educational establishment, and showing far less optimism than he did in 1939, Mumford lately has shown reluctance to put great hope or faith in any single institution and takes pains to note that educators are usually no better or no worse than any other group of people. He is careful not to pin the word "education" (which means schooling to many) on something which is more than "educational" just as he is careful not to credit "education" with achieving singlehandedly that which is the responsibility of many individuals and institutions.[86]

What especially troubles Mumford today about schooling is not the tendency to perpetuate the past and traditional methods of learning which he joined progressivists in opposing, but the opposite tendency: to become mesmerized by the novelty of teaching machines and all the latest gadgets pedalled by hardware-software hucksters. Mumford is not a romanticist unalterably opposed to technology in the classroom, but he is opposed to technology when it dominates or stands in the way of deeper I-thou relationships. What we need, he once declared, are more teachers not more machines.[87]

In 1935 Mumford was appointed a member of the Board of Higher Education of New York City, but within two years had resigned because he could not devote sufficient time to the Board's activities as well as to his writing.[88] When the Commission on Teacher Education of the American Council on Education was created in 1938 to encourage experimentation in teacher education and study teacher preparation institutions, Mumford became a member of the Commission. He also served on the Commission on Resources and Education of the National Education Association and the Progressive Education Association.

As the forties began, Mumford increased his attacks on fascism begun two years earlier in *Men Must Act* and in various essays. Active physical force was necessary to abolish slavery, a forerunner of fascism, and active physical force was needed in the current crisis.[89] He lauded Gandhi's non-violent methods, but said they would not work against a barbarous foe like fascism.[90] Paradoxically, Mumford deplored violence and loved reason but thought force and even coercion were occasionally necessary. He was generally open-minded and normally not fearful of alien theories or philosophies, but uncharacteristically proposed extreme repressive measures to obliterate fascist thought and action in the United States.[91]

Calling for a transfer of loyalty from an economics of comfort to an economics of sacrifice in the same volume, Mumford urged "the unqualified surrender of so-called national sovereignty to a higher authority, acting under a common constitution and law, in which all the states that participate shall have a part"[92] five years before the establishment of the United Nations. Tragically, his appeals for sacrifice in order to save democratic life culminated in a bitter personal sacrifice: the death of his only son, Geddes, in Italy during the war. Mumford's profound loss can be sensed in *Green Memories: The Story of Geddes Mumford.* During Geddes' childhood and youth, father and son had roamed the hills around their home in Amenia, New York, not unlike Thoreau in Concord; an intimate family life had always been important to the Mumfords. Geddes' tragic death at the age of nineteen left only one child, Allison Jane, to Lewis and Sophia.

In spite of continued opposition and resentment from liberals, one of whom wrote an irreverent poem mocking his anti-isolationist position,[93] Mumford argued doggedly for United States military involvement because all nations were interdependent and fascism had to be checked. "Isolation is suicide," he reiterated, "the isolated nation is a figment of pride: a base delusion."[94] Speaking before the American Philosophical Society in 1940, he claimed there was no hope for America in any doctrine of cultural isolation.[95] In a radio address broadcast a year before Pearl Harbor by the Canadian Broadcasting Corporation, Mumford affirmed the need for a world union of peoples organized on a democratic and cooperative basis,[96] and just three months before Japan struck he demanded a declaration of war in a debate on isolationism in his home town.[97] During and after the war he kept speaking and writing about the need for world unity, making specific proposals like a World Equalization Fund to eliminate economic disparities between nations and regions[98] and general proposals like a "doctrine of love" to provide the moral foundation for global equalization.[99]

In 1943 Mumford initiated a humanities program at Stanford University. In his own words, the first basic course, called "The Nature of Man," was intended as a:

. . . philosophical exposition of the nature of man as revealed in both the sciences and the humanities; it seeks to embrace both the objective and the subjective aspects of man's existence, the external and internal, the empirical and the transcendental.[100]

Later addressing the First Annual Conference held by the School of Humanities, Mumford defended the humanities as an indispensable part of the curriculum, even in wartime, but criticized the current mode of teaching humanities. He called for the education of political responsibility and the promotion of an "affectionate concern for the salvation of the common man."[101] Moreover, he assured his audience that a better postwar world would require more than improvement in political and economic organization; the creation of a humanistic philosophy and religion was necessary to give the emergent order unity and purpose.[102] In a forward-looking plea which was not heeded on a large scale by schools and universities for more than twenty years, and not even then in some institutions, Mumford urged his humanist colleagues as their first post-war duty to "understand and interpret the non-European cultures — not only the sophisticated cultures of the East, but the more primitive cultures of the South Seas and Africa."[103]

In December, 1942, Mumford spoke before the annual meeting of the Bay Region Teachers Association in San Francisco, an address later printed in *Values for Survival*. It was a tough speech, finding virtue in "army discipline, comradely cooperation, and combat" as a necessary part of education.[104] Revealing a stern Puritan streak, Mumford called for intense self-discipline, hard work whether one liked it or not, and "meaningful drill," whatever that might be, as distinguished from "old-fashioned drill" in the traditional school.[105] Criticizing educational pedagogy for its "over-elaboration of empty technique"[106] and teachers and administrators for sharing with businessmen a love for organizing, routinizing, and mechanizing to produce a uniform product,[107] Mumford never-theless insisted that the educational system did not deserve being singled out as a lonely scapegoat for the world crisis even if it did contribute by encouraging life-adjustment rather than independence and individual initiative. He had little use for those who favored adjusting to the current situation rather than acting to change it and to renew themselves in the process.

Post-War Optimism and Pessimism

The third volume in Mumford's "Renewal of Life" series, *The Condition of Man*, was published toward the end of the war. Continuing to interpret the development of Western man and to suggest needed changes in his outlook, Mumford's scholarly work ranged from ancient Greek civilization to a concluding chapter titled "The Basis of Renewal" which called for a reorientation to spiritual, life-fulfilling goals — to meaning, purpose, love, organic balance.[108]

The fourth and last volume, *The Conduct of Life*, appeared in 1951. In this, his most philosophical work, Mumford elaborated on the theme of reorientation to life, or self and social renewal. His deep respect for religion and symbolism, for language and art, became more apparent than ever; his moral philosophy was eloquently and passionately expounded in this profoundly human, existential volume. Only *The Transformations of Man* which followed in five years came close to developing Mumford's organic philosophy as thoroughly as *The Conduct of Life*. In succinct form,

The Transformations of Man presented his total outlook and concept of renewal from an historical perspective. Devoting at least some attention to education in this book, Mumford stated that education "will constitute the principal business of life"[109] in the transformation from an economy based on human exploitation and excessive consumption of goods to a life economy based on the satisfaction of basic needs and greater opportunities for leisure. Though discouraged after the war, Mumford had not lost his long-range hope for a new transformation of man.

Discouragement resulted not only from the quickening materialistic frenzy in the late forties and fifties but from atomic weapons which ushered in a potentially disastrous age. In 1946 he demanded that the United States government stop the Bikini bomb tests,[110] and the same year asked Americans to question their own barbarism in dropping atomic bombs on Japan.[111] An article entitled "The Social Effects of the Atom Bomb," reprinted in *In the Name of Sanity*, was required reading in 1946-47 in the National War College but Mumford's repeated exhortations generally fell on deaf ears.

In the fifties, Mumford continued to remind his fellow citizens of the horrors of nuclear warfare and asked scientists to assemble in a world congress to make a qualitative-quantitative assessment of the probable outcome of an atomic world war.[112] In "The Morals of Extermination" he blasted the United States and Britain for sanctioning the dehumanized techniques of fascism in what was politely called "obliteration bombing" during the war. When the atom bomb was invented, American authorities needed no special justification to use it, he averred, because mass extermination had become commonplace.[113] In conclusion, he returned to the theme of self-renewal:

> . . . the key to all practical proposals lies in a return to
> human feelings and sensitivities, to moral values, and
> to life-regarding procedures as controlling factors in the
> operation of intelligence.[114]

The conclusion to another essay on the threat of nuclear annihilation ended on very much the same self-renewing note:

> The first step toward creating such a world is for us to
> recover our human initiative and our moral grip. The

processes that will save us cannot be bargained for 'at the summit.' They must first be established at the base, in our souls.[115]

Mumford was angry in *In the Name of Sanity*, charging that secrecy, isolation and preoccupation with physical survival led to the sure disintegration of civilization. Calling for sanity, for reason and purpose, for rejection of automatic thinking, he challenged his fellow humans to dream of love and peace and then act with audacity "to rescue mankind from the compulsions and irrationalities that now undermine our whole civilization."[116] Unlike some intellectuals during the McCarthy era, Mumford spoke out courageously: "In the name of freedom we are rapidly creating a police state: and in the name of democracy we have succumbed, not to creeping socialism but to galloping Fascism."[117]

Fascism was still the real enemy of the United States, he observed in 1955, fascism in the form of a totalitarian political structure, an authoritarian ideological structure and a monolithic economic structure organized to assist the military.[118] Americans would have to demand the seemingly "impossible" of themselves and their leaders in order to exert moral leadership in the world and prevent the almost certain extermination of the human race.[119] "Not the least extraordinary fact about the postwar period," he noted, "is that mass extermination has awakened so little moral protest."[120] Not until the late nineteen-sixties when the Vietnam war stirred intense moral indignation at home and in the world at large did the protest against mass extermination, this time by napalm and indiscriminate destruction of villages and cold-blooded murder of innocent civilians, become loud and strong, though still not as loud or as strong as Mumford would have wanted.

Mumford's literary influence waned somewhat in the nineteen-fifties. *The Transformations of Man* was hardly noticed when it appeared in 1956, though in the sixties it became better known and respected. Some Mumford critics observed that his early books on literature, architecture, technology, and the city offered fresh inter-pretations, but that his later books had moved from criticism of society to sermons on "the condition of man" and "the conduct of life."[121] *Time* magazine often belittled him with epithets like "Preacher Mumford" and "Moralist Mumford" and furthermore was convinced that as his reputation had risen, his influence had declined.[122] But the editors of *Saturday Review*, on the other hand, hailed Mumford as "one of the most significant philosophers of our own day."[123]

The latter assessment was much more accurate than that of critics who railed about "staleness" and "preaching." True, Mumford's early interpretations were path-finding and his admonitions had a spiritual and poetic quality. But true, too, that many of his perceptions and ideas have proven prophetic and remain applicable to the human dilemma. In many ways, his interpretations of technology, city life, regional planning, and world culture, to suggest a few, are as pertinent and pregnant today as they were when first written; in fact, they are more relevant at the present critical time. Mumford's spiritual language and poetic style may be difficult for some readers, but his dramatic use of language does not deserve a "preaching" label unless one means by that a compassionate call to brotherhood and spiritual renewal. Mumford is a moralist and not ashamed of it, but he is above all a teacher who feels the commanding need to help develop individuals willing and able to live broader, more loving lives in secure yet dynamically balanced communities. As a teacher of the human condition, of the rich potential or cataclysmic horror of the future, he is unsurpassed.

In 1955 Mumford was co-chairman of the famous international symposium, "Man's Role in Changing the Face of the Earth," sponsored by the Wenner-Gren Foundation for Anthropological Research at Princeton University. As chairman of a session of the conference called "Man's Self-transformation," he explained that discussion would be devoted to dialectic — to conversation, argument, dialogue — and to human desires, dreams, and purposes more than to facts or to truth of a scientific order.[124] Emphasizing that the symposium was meant to consider the earth as modified by all forms of human action, he noted that this included modification by ethical principles, education, and art as well as by science and technology.[125] Mumford concluded the conference by an appeal for love in all its dimensions to counteract the powerful drive of post-historic (modern, industrial, dehumanized) man:

> Of every invention, of every organization, of every fresh
> political or economic proposal, we must dare to demand:
> Has it been conceived in love and does it further the
> purposes of love?[126]

In the nineteen-sixties, Mumford spent a year as rotating Ford professor of political science at the University of California, Berkeley, and in 1962 was lecturer at the City College of New York. Awarded the Presidential Medal of Freedom in 1964 and, most appropriately, the Emerson-Thoreau medal of the American Academy of Arts and Sciences in 1965, he then accepted his first degree, an honorary LL.D., from the University of Edinburgh and in 1967 an honorary Doctor of Architecture from the University of Rome. During the late sixties Mumford studied and wrote as visiting scholar at Leverett House, Harvard University.

In 1961, Mumford finished *The City in History: Its Origins, Its Transformations and Its Prospects*, a huge volume which recapitulated and updated interpretations of the historic city in *The Culture of Cities*. Symbolically, the author noted in a "Preface," the book reflected the historic growth of the city itself in that some material from the earlier book was retained to ensure an organic continuity and stability which might have been lost if he had, "like a speculative builder with a bulldozer, levelled the whole tract."[127] Though an exhaustive study of urban life and forms, like all of Mumford's works *The City in History* was impossible to classify into any single discipline or subject, as one reviewer acknowledged.[128] One critic called the author "the true reformer, the essential pessimist to whom the good exists and only as potential,"[129] because of his indictment of nineteenth century industrialism and twentieth-century urban-suburban deterioration. And *Time* caustically observed that "after 40 years of sermonizing his patience is growing thin. The gentle Job has become the raging Jeremiah as he casts his eyes upon signs of Rome reborn . . ."[130]

Dramatic and negative as some reviews were, *The City in History* pleased many critics, not the least the jury of the National Book Awards which presented the award for nonfiction to Mumford in March, 1962. The year the book was published Queen Elizabeth, on recommendation of the Royal Institute of British Architects, and in recognition of his contributions to city planning and architecture, presented the Royal Gold Medal for Architecture to Mumford.

Further developing his interest in technology in the sixties, Mumford served on the Executive Council of the Society for the History of Technology and then on the Advisory Council. The Society, an interdisciplinary organization concerned with the human-social implications and possibilities in technology, published the journal *Technology and Culture* to which he contributed several articles. During the tenth anniversary celebration of the Fund for the Republic in 1963, Mumford, then president of the American Academy of Arts and Letters, spoke on "Technology and Democracy." Excerpts from his address comparing "authoritarian" or system-centered and "democratic" or man-centered technics were printed in several periodicals.[131] At a conference commemorating the four-hundredth anniversary of the birth of Francis Bacon sponsored by the American Philosophical Society and the University of Pennsylvania, Mumford earnestly inquired:

> Has the time not come, then — in technology as in every other aspect of the common life — to reexamine our accepted axioms and practical imperatives and to release science itself from the humanly impoverished and underdimensioned mythology of power that Francis Bacon helped to promote?[132]

In a speech delivered at the Opening General Session of the Nineteenth National Conference on Higher Education in Chicago in 1964, Mumford directed educators to look searchingly and question intensively the current mass production of scientists, technicians, and engineers focused as it was on an obsolete model — a model based on the automation of knowledge, on mechanical quantification, on the rejection of human autonomy. Education, he insisted, should be addressed to larger and more central human purposes than to "automated" knowledge.[133] He feared that as the facilities of educational institutions expanded — with their nuclear reactors, computers, television equipment, learning machines, and standardized tests — the human content of the curriculum would necessarily shrink, "for the very presence of the human potentiality disturbs this complex mechanism which operates increasingly as a single unit and can be managed only by remote control under centralized direction."[134]

Mumford's interest in technology and culture reached its apex in *The Myth of the Machine: Technics and Human Development* of 1967, and in *The Myth of the Machine: The Pentagon of Power* three years later. Re-interpreting the whole development of humanity including pre-historic religion and myths, domestication, the cult of kingship, the "megamachine" (or over-bearing and monopolistic machine), and the growth of empires and complex inventions in the Middle Ages, the author paved the way in the first volume for a more profound understanding of contemporary technology and life. He developed the thesis that ritual and art, language and social organization, have historically been as or more important to man's development than tool-making or the taming of nature, necessary as these have been. Tools and more complex technics (material culture) could not have developed far without a corresponding concern with the fabrication of symbols of all sorts (non-material culture).

A reviewer aptly summarized Mumford's ability to use specific examples to build his case and yet maintain a broad heuristic scope when he observed that the author "peculiarly combines the qualities of the hard-headed alert reporter unshaken by the most bewildering evidence, and a bold penchant for generalization."[135] Peter Drucker, another reviewer, decided that Mumford made a good philosopher of history and historian of technology, concluding that "Mumford has written a book of great beauty — imaginative, hauntingly poetic, and harmonious in its organization."[136] Surprisingly, a review of *The Myth of the Machine* appeared in an educational periodical, a great rarity for any of Mumford's books. John G. Meitner gave the book a favorable, if not very profound, review in the *National Elementary Principal*. Meitner, too, was struck by his poetic language, but what would encourage Mumford most about this review was the fact that Meitner as a physical scientist — more specifically as manager of the Aerospace Program at Stanford Research Institute — reacted so sympathetically to Mumford's book:

> In this age of moral bankruptcy, Mumford's message is refreshing . . . for the sake of ourselves and that of our off-spring the time has come, first to slow the current with which we move — and, we hope with Mumford, to change its direction and its course in the future.[137]

If a space scientist could feel this way, surely there was hope that Mumford's ideas might have an impact on contemporary man and woman.

Interest in Mumford may have dwindled to some extent in the nineteen-fifties, but in the sixties it blossomed as evidenced by the critical success of *The City in History* and *The Myth of the Machine* which itself was a runner-up for the National Book Award in 1968, as well as by the publication and re-publication of other books: a revised edition of *Herman Melville*, an early biography of the author written in 1929; a group of far-sighted articles collected under the title *The Highway and the City* of 1964; a collection of essays selected by Harry T. Moore and Karl W. Deutsch, *The Human Prospect*, published in 1965. Paperback editions of *The Story of Utopias, Technics and Civilization, The Golden Day, The Culture of Cities,* and *The Condition of Man* all appeared in the past fifteen years. Most of his major books are still in print.

In addition to his own volumes, Mumford wrote introductions to a number of books of personal and/or philosophical friends. In an introduction to Benton MacKaye's *The New Exploration: A Philosophy of Regional Planning*, he claimed that MacKaye's work deserved a place on the same shelf that held Thoreau's *Walden* and George Perkins Marsh's *Man and Nature*, two other favorites which had to wait many years before proper appreciation was accorded.[138] An introductory essay to Ebenezer Howard's *Garden Cities of To-Morrow* was actually written in 1945, but was included in the popular paperback edition of Howard's classic book which appeared in 1965. The Introduction to *Toward New Towns for America* by Mumford's long-time friend, Clarence Stein, was written fifteen years before the first paperback issue of 1966, but in the mid and late sixties this book and its introduction received a warmer reception than in the early fifties.

In 1968 Mumford wrote an introduction to a selection of Emerson essays and journals. Most striking in his description and analysis of Emerson was the similarity between the two men. Both did extensive writing, but both also left their studies to become involved in the political and social crises of their time. Emerson denounced slavery and the Mexican-American war which Mumford called the Vietnam of Emerson's day.[139] Emerson was rooted in his community and region, as was Mumford, but neither was provincial or isolationist; both were at home not only in America but in Europe and, to a lesser extent for Mumford, in the Orient.

In 1969 *American Heritage* featured an adaptation of the introduction to Emerson's essays and journals preceded by an explanatory note demonstrating the editors' high regard for Mumford and his achievements, a regard shared by the late Van Wyck Brooks, Erich Fromm, Theodore Brameld, and a growing number of young people. The editors called Mumford "one of the true savants of the twentieth century."[140] What finer compliment could have been paid to this man whose views frequently have been called "old fashioned?"

Published in the late sixties, *The Urban Prospect* included a number of articles and addresses written over a period of forty-odd years, but the final chapter, "Postscript: The Choices Ahead," was prepared expressly for this book. The "Preface" especially delighted the author because it originally appeared in the *Survey Graphic* in May 1925, but years later it seemed just as timely. Only the discussion of radio rather than television dated it, he mused. [141]

In one chapter of *The Urban Prospect*, a speech delivered in California in 1962, Mumford expressed hope for the new generation of college students, hope that they "will overcome our passivities, overthrow our regimentations, and place the guardians of life once more in command."[142] But in the "Postscript" of a few years later he expressed less hope in young people, disregarding the New Left and modern radical movements altogether. Rather, he continued his persistent claim that urban problems whether concerned with housing, population, congestion, racial strife, welfare, or poverty "could not be treated by purely temporizing local remedies, since they were symptomatic of deeper organic defects in our civilization."[143]

Mumford was right to probe for the deeper causes of urban unrest and deterioration and to inspire others to do likewise; he was wrong to let this painstaking search stand in the way of immediate and massive financial support for the big cities which by 1968 had become depressingly ugly and starved of services, particularly to the black population. He did not seem to recognize the gravity of the situation in American ghettoes; he did not grapple with "Black Power" or appreciate the need for black identity and black culture; he did not recognize the extent of white racism in America and failed to comprehend the difficulties encountered by black children growing up in a predominantly white society that ostracized and condemned them to inferior status. These are serious omissions in Mumford's life and work and cannot be dismissed. But they do not negate the lasting value of his overall philosophy which, at least in general terms, has always deplored prejudice and has consistently treated men and women of whatever nationality, color, or religion as members of one race — the human race.

An early critic of the Vietnam war, Mumford sent an open letter to President Johnson in 1965 opposing American intervention. Though not accepted for publication by any Eastern newspaper, the letter was printed in the *San Francisco Chronicle* and Mumford believes it influenced the teach-in movement on the West Coast. [144] In *Authors Take Sides on Vietnam* he called for unconditional withdrawal of all American forces from Vietnam and a public admission of military and political defeat which would be an assertion of moral strength in the tradition of Jefferson and Emerson, Whitman and James.[145] His position was unequivocal:

> The intervention of the United States in Vietnam is entirely without justification in either law, politics, or morals, and the progressive brutalization of American methods there has placed the United States Government in the infamous category of collective aggressors and exterminators.[146]

In 1968 Mumford expressed his disappointment on not receiving the National Book Award for *The Myth of the Machine*. Actually, he felt that books by three able people — Suzanne Langer, Theodosius Dobzhansky, and himself — should have been favorably considered in the final selection. But he correctly predicted that Jonathan Kozol would win the award for *Death at an Early Age*. Not begrudging Kozol the honor, Mumford nonetheless admitted candidly that the award would have been a much-needed stimulus for his own work at a discouraging time to write. He seemed to gain consolation from placing as runner-up in the competition, and from one judge who favored his book.[147] With all his honors and a distinguished career mostly behind him, Mumford's human need for recognition, and recognition of his ideas, revealed itself in this frank desire for a psychological boost.

As he worked on his autobiography, Mumford found that the last thirty to thirty-five years were extremely distasteful. Everyone's life had been crippled by them to one extent or another and he did not feel in a hurry to finish this last part of the autobiography. Wanting to complete other work before his faculties faded, he sensed this was his last chance to put ideas together in a meaningful form. The second volume of *The Myth of the Machine: The Pentagon of Power* was written to offer both a dark and a happy look at the future; increasingly pessimistic, however, Mumford wondered if anything other than a terrible shock would turn humanity from its present reckless course. In his own words, he felt "optimistic about possibilities, pessimistic about probabilities."[148]

One optimistic possibility Mumford considered was that his books may have the effect on people several hundred years from now that Francis Bacon's had on people several hundred years after Bacon's life.[149] If this should happen, and Mumford would be the first to acknowledge it is a big "if," perhaps the future of humankind will be bright. But that will all depend upon our humanity toward each other in the interim.

The Pentagon of Power of 1970 proved to be a powerful successor to the first volume of *The Myth of the Machine*. Continuing where he left off, Mumford further developed his concept of the "megamachine" and its influence since the age of exploration at the end of the fifteenth century. In forcefully written chapters with titles like "The Mechanized World Picture," "Political Absolutism and Regimentaton," and "The Megatechnic Wasteland," he exposed the historic exploitation of man and nature. No one can read *The Pentagon of Power* without being stirred in some way by Mumford's persuasive arguments. At the end, he remained as convinced as ever that human beings can make a choice:

> But for those of us who have thrown off the myth of the machine, the next move is ours: for the gates of the tech-nocratic prison will open automatically, despite their rusty ancient hinges, as soon as we choose to walk out. [150]

Mumford's recent book, *Interpretations and Forecasts: 1922-1972*, is a collection of writings from various periodicals and books. In a brief preface, the author explained that some of his "more valuable contributions appeared in periodicals of limited circulation, now vanished or difficult to consult."[151] Mumford concentrated on five main themes in this volume, planning a later book of selections on additonal themes. One chapter features articles on Melville, Audubon, and Emerson among others; another examines personalities like Bacon, Rousseau, Darwin, and Marx; two chapters deal with technology and civilizations; and a final chapter centers on "Transformations of Man."

In a contemporary article in *Interpretations and Forecasts*, Mumford gave credit to contemporary young people for reminding us of the vitality and creativity of flowers and other living things. In the early seventies he was heartened by the concern of youth to maintain and create a living environment, not a dying environment which technocrats would have us accept as normal. As he observed accurately, the environmental revolution has been enhanced by the young and by educators who appreciate the value of environmental studies in Mumford's broad humanistic sense. It is appropriate that Anne Chisholm, interviewing "philosophers of the earth," chose Mumford to open her series of conversations with ecologists. "Of all the wise men whose thinking and writing over the years has helped to prepare the ground for environmental revolution," she wrote, "Lewis Mumford . . . must be pre-eminent."[152] It is certainly time for educators and others to recognize this pre-eminence.

[1]Allan Temko, "Which Guide to the Promised Land: Fuller or Mumford?" *Horizon*, X (Summer, 1968), 26.

[2]George Santayana, in reference to *The Golden Day* by Lewis Mumford, quoted in Edward Duff, S.J., "Lewis Mumford: The Post-Christian in an Anti-Christian World," *The Commonweal*, XXXVII (October 30, 1942), 38.

[3]Van Wyck Brooks, "Lewis Mumford: American Prophet," *Harper's Magazine*, June, 1952, p. 50.

[4]*Ibid.*, pp. 6-7, 46-53.

[5]*Ibid.*, p. 53.

[6]Lewis Mumford, quoted in Charles Moritz, ed., *Current Biography Yearbook* (New York: H.W. Wilson Company, 1963-64), p. 290.

[7]Mumford, *The Human Prospect*, p. 54.

[8]*Ibid.*, p. 55.

[9]*Ibid.*, p. 59.

[10]*Ibid.*, p. 63.

[11]*Ibid.*

[12]Lewis Mumford, quoted in Moritz, ed., *Current Biography Yearbook*, p. 290.

[13]Lewis Mumford, "Place of the Community in the School," *The Dial*, LXVII (September 20, 1919), 244-46.

[14]*Ibid.*, p. 245.

[15]Lewis Mumford, "Mr. Ransom's Facts and Mr. Russell's Fancies," *The Dial*, LXVII (August 23, 1919), 153.

[16]Lewis Mumford, "Wardom and the State," *The Dial*, LXVII (October 4, 1919), 303.

[17]Mumford, "Mumford on Geddes," p. 84.

[18]Lewis Mumford, quoted in Philip Boardman, *Patrick Geddes: Maker of the Future* (Chapel Hill: The University of North Carolina Press, 1944), p. 412.

[19]Boardman, *Patrick Geddes: Maker of the Future*, p. 412.

[20]Mumford, private interview, March 29, 1968.

[21]Van Wyck Brooks, *An Autobiography*, (New York: E.P. Dutton, 1965), p. 406.

[22]Lewis Mumford, private interview, November 14, 1967.

[23]Lewis Mumford, *The Story of Utopias*, Compass Books (New York: The Viking Press, 1962), p. 5.

[24]Mumford, *The Story of Utopias*, p. 4.

[25]*Ibid.*, pp. 5-6.

[26]David R. Weimer, "Anxiety in The Golden Day of Lewis Mumford," *The New England Quarterly*, XXXVI (June, 1963), 188.

[27]Mumford proudly cited Mathiessen's recognition of *The Golden Day's* influence in his introduction to the 1957 edition of this book, p. viii.

[28]Lewis Mumford, *The Golden Day: A Study in American Literature and Culture* (4th ed. (New York: Dover Publications, 1968), p. 135.

[29]Mumford, private interview, November 14, 1967. It should be noted that Dewey's *Art as Experience*, published in 1934, was based on ten lectures given at Harvard University in the winter and spring of 1931.

[30]Mumford, *The Golden Day*, p. 134.

[31]*Ibid.*, p. 131.

[32]*Ibid.*

[33]Mumford, private interview, March 29, 1968.

[34]John Dewey, "The Pragmatic Acquiescence," in Kennedy, ed., *Pragmatism and American Culture*, p. 50.

[35]Mumford, "The Pragmatic Acquiescence: A Reply," in Kennedy, ed., *Pragmatism and American Culture*, p. 54.

[36]Lewis Mumford, "'Teaching' English Literature," *New Republic*, November 10, 1926, p. 351.

[37]*Ibid.*, pp. 351-52.

[38]Lewis Mumford, "Art, Modern and Primitive," *New Republic*, December 1, 1926, p. 49.

[39]Lewis Mumford, "A Sociologist's Roadside Notes," *New Republic*, April 4, 1928, pp. 226-27.

[40]Lewis Mumford, "The Criticism of Darwin," *New Republic*, February 1, 1928, pp. 301-2.

[41]Lewis Mumford, "Metaphysics and Art," *New Republic*, December 18, 1929, p. 118.

[42]*Ibid*.

[43]Mumford, *The Brown Decades*, p. 85.

[44]Mumford, "Preface: 1954," in *Sticks and Stones*, p. 3.

[45]Harold E. Stearns, ed., *Civilization in the United States* (New York: Harcourt, Brace and Company, 1922), p. 111.

[46]Lewis Mumford, "The Wilderness of Suburbia," *New Republic*, September 7, 1921, p. 45.

[47]Mumford, *The Urban Prospect*, p. 211.

[48]Lewis Mumford, "The Booby Prizes for 1929," *New Republic*, January 8, 1930, pp. 190-91.

[49]Lewis Mumford, "The Chance for Civilized Housing," *New Republic*, September 17, 1930, pp. 115-16.

[50]Lewis Mumford, "Toward the Publication of Peirce's Works," letter to the editors of *New Republic*, December 30, 1930, p. 195.

[51]Mumford, "Toward the Publication of Peirce's Works," p. 195.

[52]Lewis Mumford, "On the Road to Collectivism," *New Republic*, February 6, 1935, p. 361.

[53]*Ibid*.

[54]Mumford, "The Need for Concrete Goals," in Alfred M. Bingham and Selden Rodman, eds., *Challenge to the New Deal*, p. 226.

[55]*Ibid*., p. 224.

[56]Herbert Read, "A Prophetic Book," review of *Technics and Civilization*, by Lewis Mumford, in *The Yale Review*, XXIV (1934), 173.

[57]Case, "Closing in on the Machine," p. 211.

[58]"Man and the Machine," review of *Technics and Civilization*, by Lewis Mumford, in *The Times* (London) *Literary Supplement*,

October 11, 1934, reprinted in Allan Angoff, ed., *American Writing Today* (New York: New York University Press, 1957).

59Lewis Mumford, "An Appraisal of Lewis Mumford's *Technics and Civilization* (1934)," *Daedulus*, LXXXVIII (Summer, 1959), 527-36.

60*Ibid.*, p. 535.

61Mumford, *Technics and Civilization*, pp. 261-62.

62*Ibid.*, p. 167.

63*Ibid.*, p. 237.

64Lewis Mumford, "Call to Arms," *New Republic*, May 18, 1938, p. 42.

65Curti, *The Growth of American Thought*, p. 749.

66Lewis Mumford, "Letter to the Editors," *New Republic*, September 8, 1940, pp. 311-12.

67Mumford, *Faith for Living*, p. 116.

68*Ibid.*, p. 117.

69*Ibid.*, p. 56.

70Mumford, *Values for Survival*, p. 31.

71*Ibid.*, pp. 25-6.

72Mumford, *Faith for Living*, p. 70.

73Lewis Mumford, "The Corruption of Liberalism," *New Republic*, April 29, 1940, p. 571.

74Sidney Hook, "Metaphysics, War and the Intellectuals," *Menorah Journal*, XXVIII (October-December, 1940), 329.

75*Ibid.*, p. 330.

76*Ibid.*, p. 329.

77Mumford, "The Corruption of Liberalism," p. 573.

78Lawrence Cremin, *The Transformation of the School*, Vintage Books (New York: Random House, 1964), p. 232.

79Mumford, private interview, November 14, 1967.

80*New York Times*, February 23, 1933, p. 19.

81*New York Times*, April 5, 1936, p. 35.

82Lewis Mumford, quoted in "Youth Stagnating, Educator Warns," *New York Times*, Nov. 24, 1934, p. 17. ©1934 by The New York Times Company. Reprinted by permission.

83W. A. MacDonald, "Regional Growth Urged on America," *New York Times*, Feb. 24, 1940, p. 11.

84Mumford, "The Social Responsibilities of Teachers," p. 476.

85Mumford, private interview, March 29, 1968.

86*Ibid.*

87*Ibid.*

88*New York Times*, June 15, 1937, p. 25.

89Mumford, *Faith for Living*, pp. 95-98.

90*Ibid.*, p. 103.

91Mumford, *Faith for Living*, pp. 106-7.

92*Ibid.*, p. 325.

93"Correspondence," *New Republic*, May 13, 1940, p. 644.

94Mumford, *Faith for Living*, pp. 180-81.

95*New York Times*, April 20, 1940, p. 34.

96Mumford, *Values for Survival*, p. 54.

97*New York Times*, August 28, 1941, p. 15 and August 31, 1941, p. 20.

98Mumford, "Toward a Free World: Long-Range Planning under Democratic Control", p. 12.

99*Ibid.*, p. 13.

100Lewis Mumford, "The Making of Men," in *The Humanities Look Ahead: Report of the First Annual Conference held by the Stanford School of Humanities* (Stanford: Stanford University Press, 1943), p. 140.

101Mumford, "The Making of Men," p. 136.

102*Ibid.*, p. 132.

103Lawrence E. Davies, "Humanities Urged as Armor of War," *New York Times*, May 9, 1943, p. 8.

104Mumford, *Values for Survival*, p. 174.

105Mumford, *Values for Survival*, p. 175.

106*Ibid.*, p. 173.

107*Ibid.*, pp. 172-73.

108Mumford, *The Condition of Man*, pp. 391-423.

109Mumford, *The Transformations of Man*, p. 178.

110*New York Times*, February 28, 1946, p. 12.

111Mumford, *Values for Survival*, p. 97.

112Lewis Mumford, "Anticipations and Social Adjustments in Science," *Bulletin of the Atomic Scientists*, X (February, 1954), 34-36.

113Lewis Mumford, "The Morals of Extermination," *Atlantic Monthly*, October 1959, pp. 39-40.

114*Ibid.*, p. 44.

115Lewis Mumford, "The Moral Challenge to Democracy," *Virginia Quarterly Review*, XXXV (Autumn, 1959), p. 576.

116Mumford, *In the Name of Sanity*, pp. 8-9.

117*Ibid.*, p. 155.

118Lewis Mumford, "The Art of the 'Impossible!' " in *Alternatives to the H Bomb*, ed. by Anatole Shub (Boston: Beacon Press, 1955), p. 22.

119*Ibid.*, pp. 28-29.

120*Ibid.*, p. 16.

121Van R. Halsey, "Lewis Mumford's *Golden Day*," *New Republic*, August 12, 1957, p. 21.

122*Time*, October 1, 1951, p. 106; *Time*, April 28, 1961, p. 103.

123The Editors, *Saturday Review*, September 22, 1951, p. 11.

124Lewis Mumford, "Man's Self-transformation," in *Man's Role in Changing the Face of the Earth*, ed., by William L. Thomas, p. 1088.

125*Ibid.*, p. 1090.

126Lewis Mumford, "Prospect," in *Man's Role in Changing the Face of the Earth*, p. 1152.

127Mumford, *The City in History*, p. xi.

128Geoffrey Bruun, "Metropolitan Strait Jacket," review of *The City in History*, in *Saturday Review*, April 15, 1961, p. 36.

129Henry S. Churchill, "Lewis Mumford's New Work About the Culture of Cities," *Scientific American*, July 1961, p. 175.

130"Necropolis Revisited," review of *The City in History*, in *Time*, April 28, 1961, p. 103.

131Lewis Mumford, "Now Let Man Take Over," *New Republic*, February 16, 1963, pp. 12-15; Lewis Mumford, "Are We Selling Our Souls for Progress?" *Science Digest*, July 1963, pp. 85-89.

132Lewis Mumford, "Science as Technology," in *Proceedings of the American Philosophical Society*, CV (October, 1961), p. 511.

133Lewis Mumford, "The Automation of Knowledge," *Vital Speeches of the Day*, XXX (May 1, 1964), 444.

134Lewis Mumford, "The Automation of Knowledge," *Vital Speeches of the Day*, 443.

135Edward T. Chase, "Man, Machines, and Mumford," review of *The Myth of the Machine*, in *Commonweal*, March 8, 1968, p. 694.

136Peter F. Drucker, "Review of *The Myth of the Machine*," in *Technology and Culture*, IX (January, 1968), 98.

137John G. Meitner, "Technics and Human Development," review of *The Myth of the Machine*, in *National Elementary Principal*, XLVII (April, 1968), 66.

138Lewis Mumford, "Introduction" to *The New Exploration: A Philosophy of Regional Planning*, Illini Books (Urbana: University of Illinois Press, 1962), p. vii.

139Lewis Mumford, "Introduction" to *Ralph Waldo Emerson: Essays and Journals* (Garden City: Doubleday and Company, 1968), p. 18.

140Editors, *American Heritage*, XX (February, 1969), 104.

141Mumford, private interview, March 29, 1968.

142Lewis Mumford, *The Urban Prospect*, p. 23.

143*Ibid.*, p. 233.

144Mumford, private interview, November 14, 1967.

145Lewis Mumford in *Authors Take Sides on Vietnam* (New York: Simon and Schuster, 1967), p. 56.

146*Ibid.*, pp. 55-56.

147Mumford, private interview, March 29, 1968.

148*Ibid.*

149*Ibid.*

150Lewis Mumford, *The Myth of the Machine: The Pentagon of Power*, p. 435.

151Lewis Mumford, *Interpretations and Forecasts: 1922-1972* (New York: Harcourt Brace and Jovanovich, 1973), p. vii.

152Anne Chisholm, *Philosophers of the Earth: Conversations with Ecologists* (New York: E.P. Dutton, 1972), p. 1.

✦ bibliography
books

Barrett, William. *Irrational Man*. Garden City: Doubleday Anchor, 1962.

Bellamy, Edward. *Looking Backward*. Foreword by Erich Fromm. New York: The New American Library, 1960.

Berkson, I. B. *Ethics, Politics and Education*. Eugene, Oregon: University of Oregon, 1968.

_____ . *The Ideal and the Community*. New York: Harper and Row, 1958.

Bidney, David. "The Concept of Value in Modern Anthropology." *Anthropology Today*. Edited by A. L. Kroeber. Chicago: University of Chicago Press, 1953.

_____ . *Theoretical Anthropology*. New York: Schocken Books, 1967.

Boardman, Philip. *Patrick Geddes: Maker of the Future*. Chapel Hill: The University of North Carolina Press, 1944.

Brameld, Theodore. *Cultural Foundations of Education*. New York: Harper and Row, 1957.

_____ . *Education as Power*. New York: Holt, Rinehart and Winston, 1965.

_____ . *Education for the Emerging Age*. New York: Harper and Row, 1950.

_____ . *Patterns of Educational Philosophy: Divergence and Convergence in Culturological Perspective*. New York: Holt, Rinehart and Winston, 1971.

_____ . *The Teacher As World Citizen — A Scenario of the 21st Century*. Palm Springs, CA.: ETC Publications, 1976.

_____ . *Toward a Reconstructed Philosophy of Education*. New York: Holt, Rinehart and Winston, 1956.

_____ . *The Use of Explosive Ideas in Education*. Pittsburgh: University of Pittsburgh Press, 1965.

Branford, Victor. *Science and Sanctity*. London: LePlay House Press and Williams and Norgate, 1923.

Brooks, Van Wyck. *An Autobiography*. New York: E. P. Dutton and Company, 1965.

Brower, David, ed. *Only a Little Planet*. San Francisco: Friends of the Earth, 1972.

Buber, Martin. *Between Man and Man*. New York: Macmillan, 1965.

Burnett, Whit. "A Philosopher of Renewal." *This is My Philosophy*. Edited by Whit Burnett. New York: Harper and Brothers, 1957.

Burtt, E. A. *In Search of Philosophic Understanding*. New York: The New American Library, 1965.

Chase, Stuart. *The Most Probable World*. Baltimore: Penguin Books, 1968.

Chisholm, Anne. *Philosophers of the Earth: Conversations with Ecologists*. New York: E. P. Dutton, 1972.

Counts, George S. *Dare the Schools Build a New Social Order?* New York: John Day, 1932.

Cox, Harvey. *The Secular City*. New York: The Macmillan Company, 1965.

Creese, Walter L. *The Search for Environment, The Garden City: Before and After*. New Haven and London: Yale University Press, 1966.

Cremin, Lawrence A. *The Transformation of the School*. New York: Vintage Books, 1964.

Curti, Merle. *The Growth of American Thought*. 2nd ed. New York: Harper and Brothers, 1951.

_____ . *The Social Ideas of American Educators*. Rev. ed. Patterson, New Jersey: Littlefield, Adams and Company, 1965.

DeBell, Garrett. *The Environmental Handbook*. New York: Ballantine Books, 1970.

Dewey, John. *Art as Experience*. Capricorn Books. New York: G. P. Putnam's Sons, 1958.

_____ . *Democracy and Education*. New York: The Free Press, 1966.

_____ . *Experience and Education*. New York: Collier Books, 1963.

_____ . "The Pragmatic Acquiescence.." *Pragmatism and American Culture*. Edited by Gail Kennedy. Boston: D.C. Heath, 1950.

Divoky, Diane, ed. *How Old Will You Be in 1984? Expressions of Student Outrage From the High School Free Press.* Discus Books. New York: Avon Books, 1969.

Ehrlich, Paul R. *The Population Bomb.* New York: Ballantine Books, 1968.

Falk, Richard A. *This Endangered Planet: Prospects and Proposals for Human Survival.* New York: Vintage Books, 1972.

Fischer, John H. "Schools for Equal Opportunity." *The Schoolhouse in the City.* Edited by Alvin Toffler. New York: Frederick A. Praeger, 1968.

Frank, Lawrence K. *The School as Agent for Cultural Renewal.* Cambridge: Harvard University Press, 1959.

Fromm, Erich. *Marx's Concept of Man.* New York: Frederick Ungar Publishing Company, 1961.

_____ . *The Revolution of Hope: Toward a Humanized Technology.* New York: Bantam Books, 1968.

Galbraith, John Kenneth. *The New Industrial State.* New York: The American Library, 1967.

Geddes, Patrick, "A Suggested Plan for a Civic Museum (or Civic Exhibition) and Its Associated Studies." *Sociological Papers.* Vol. III. London: Macmillan and Company, 1907.

_____ . *Cities in Evolution.* London: Williams and Norgate, Ltd., 1949.

_____ . "Civics: As Concrete and Applied Sociology." *Sociological Papers.* Vol. II. London: Macmillan and Company, 1906.

Gerzon, Mark. *The Whole World is Watching: A Young Man Looks at Youth's Dissent.* New York: Paperback Library, 1969.

Goodman, Paul. *Growing Up Absurd.* New York: Vintage Books, 1960.

_____ . *Utopian Essays and Practical Proposals.* New York: Vintage Books, 1962.

_____ . and Goodman, Percival. *Communitas: Means of Livelihood and Ways of Life.* New York: Vintage Books, 1960.

Goodman, Robert. *After the Planners.* New York: Simon and Schuster, 1973.

Hanna, Paul R. *Youth Serves the Community.* New York: D. Appleton Century, 1936.

Herskovits, Melville. *Man and His Works*. New York: Alfred A. Knopf, 1956.

Howard, Ebenezer. *Garden Cities of To-Morrow*. Edited, with a preface, by F. J. Osborn. Introductory essay by Lewis Mumford. Cambridge: M.I.T. Press, 1965.

Huhns, William, *The Post-Industrial Prophets*. New York: Harper and Row, 1971.

Huxley, Aldous. "The Politics of Ecology." *The Triple Revolution: Social Problems in Depth*. Edited by Robert Perrucci and Marc Pilisuk. Boston: Little, Brown and Company, 1968.

Huxley, Julian. *Essays of a Humanist*. New York: Harper and Row, 1964.

_____. *Evolution in Action*. A Signet Book. New York: New American Library, 1953.

Inlow, Gail M. *The Emergent in Curriculum*. New York: John Wiley and Sons, 1966.

Jacobs, Jane. *The Death and Life of Great American Cities*. New York: Random House, 1961.

Jaeger, Werner. *Paideia: The Ideals of Greek Culture*. Trans. by Gilbert Highet. New York: Oxford University Press, 1939.

James, William. *Pragmatism and Other Essays*. New York: Washington Square Press, 1963.

Jaspers, Karl. *Man in the Modern Age*. Anchor Books. Garden City: Doubleday and Company, 1957.

Josephson, Eric and Mary, ed., *Man Alone: Alienation in Modern Society*. New York: Dell Publishing Company, 1962.

Jung, G. C. *The Undiscovered Self*. A Mentor Book. New York: The New American Library, 1957.

Kahler, Erich. *Man the Measure: A New Approach to History*. New York: G. Braziller, 1956.

_____. *Out of the Labyrinth*. New York: G. Braziller, 1967.

Kardiner, Abram and Preble, Edward. *They Studied Man*. New York: The New American Library, 1963.

Karier, Clarence J. *Man, Society, and Education*. Glenview: Scott, Foresman and Company, 1967.

Keesing, Felix M. *Cultural Anthropology: The Science of Custom*. New York: Rinehart and Company, 1958.

Keniston, Kenneth. *Young Radicals: Notes on Committed Youth*. A Harvest Book. New York: Harcourt, Brace and World, Inc., 1968.

Kennedy, Gail, ed., *Pragmatism and American Culture*. Boston: D. C. Heath, 1950.

Kilpatrick, William H. "The Underlying Philosophy of Co-operative Activities for Community Improvement." Introduction to *Youth Serves the Community* by Paul R. Hanna. New York: D. Appleton-Century, 1936.

Kluckhohn, Clyde. *Mirror for Man*. Greenwich: Fawcett Publications, 1944.

_____ . "Universal Categories of Culture." *Anthropology Today*. Edited by A. L. Kroeber. Chicago: University of Chicago Press, 1953.

_____ . "Values and Value Orientations in the Theory of Action: An Exploration in Definition and Classification." *Toward a General Theory of Action*. Cambridge: Harvard University Press, 1954.

_____ . and Kroeber, A.L. *Culture: A Critical Review of Concepts and Definitions*. New York: Vintage Books, 1952.

Krutch, Joseph Wood. *Human Nature and the Human Condition*. New York: Random House, 1959.

Kubie, Lawrence S. *Neurotic Distortion of the Creative Process*. New York: The Noonday Press, 1965.

Kulski, Julian Eugene. *Land of Urban Promise, Continuing the Great Tradition: A Search for Significant Urban Space in the Urbanized Northeast*. South Bend, Indiana: Notre Dame Press, 1967.

Lens, Sidney. *Radicalism in America*. New York: Thomas Y. Crowell, 1969.

Little, Charles E. and Mitchell, John G. *Space for Survival: Blocking the Bulldozer in Urban America*. Richmond Hill, Ontario: Simon and Schuster of Canada, 1971.

Lubove, Roy. *Community Planning in the 1920's: The Contribution of the Regional Planning Association of America*. Pittsburgh: University of Pittsburgh Press, 1963.

MacKaye, Benton. *From Geography to Geotechnics*. Urbana: University of Illinois Press, 1968.

_____ . *The New Exploration: A Philosophy of Regional Planning*. Introduction by Lewis Mumford. Urbana: University of Illinois Press, 1962.

McHarg, Ian L. *Design With Nature*. Introduction by Lewis
    Mumford. Garden City, New York: The Natural History
    Press, 1969.

Mairet, Philip. *Pioneer of Sociology: The Life and Letters of Patrick
    Geddes*. London: Lund Humphries, 1957.

"Man and the Machine." Review of *Technics and Civilization* by
    Lewis Mumford. *American Writing Today*. Edited by Allan
    Angoff. New York: New York University Press, 1957.

Mannheim, Karl. *Man and Society in an Age of Reconstruction*.
    London: Routledge and Kegan Paul Ltd., 1949.

Marcuse, Herbert. *An Essay on Liberation*. Boston: Beacon Press,
    1969.

————— . *One Dimensional Man*. Boston: Beacon Press, 1964.

Marsh, George Perkins. *Man and Nature*. Edited by David
    Lowenthal. Cambridge: Harvard University Press, 1965.

Maslow, Abraham. *The Farther Reaches of Human Nature*. New
    York: Viking Press, 1972.

Mayer, Albert. *The Urgent Future*. New York: McGraw Hill, 1967.

Meiklejohn, Alexander. *Education Between Two Worlds*. New
    York: Harper and Brothers, 1942.

Mitchell, John G. ed., *Ecotactics: The Sierra Club Handbook for
    Environmental Activists*. New York: Pocket Books, 1970.

Montagu, Ashley. *Education and Human Relations*. New York:
    Grove Press, 1958.

————— . *The Humanization of Man*. Cleveland and New York:
    The World Publishing Company, 1962.

Morgan, George W. *The Human Predicament: Dissolution and
    Wholeness*. Providence: Brown University Press, 1968.

Moritz, Charles, ed., *Current Biography Yearbook*. New York:
    H. W. Wilson Company, 1963-64.

Morris, William, ed., *The American Heritage Dictionary of the
    English Language*. New York: American Heritage Pub-
    lishing Company, 1971.

Mumford, Lewis. *Architecture*, Chicago: American Library Asso-
    ciation, 1926.

————— . "The Arts." *Whither Mankind: A Panorama of
    Modern Civilization*. Edited by Charles A. Beard. New
    York: Longmans, Green and Company, 1928.

————— . *Art and Technics*. New York: Columbia University
    Press, 1952.

Mumford, Lewis. "The Art of the 'Impossible'." *Alternatives to the H Bomb*. Edited by Anatole Shub. Boston: Beacon Press, 1955.

_____ . *The Brown Decades: A Study of the Arts in America, 1865-1895*. New York: Dover Publications, 1955.

_____ . "The City." *Civilization in the United States*. Edited by Harold E. Stearns. New York: Harcourt, Brace and Company, 1922.

_____ . *City Development: Studies in Disintegration and Renewal*. New York: Harcourt, Brace and Company, 1945.

_____ . *The City in History: Its Origins, Its Transformations, and Its Prospects*. New York: Harcourt, Brace and World, Inc., 1961.

_____ . "Closing Statement," *Future Environments of North America*. Edited by F. Fraser Darling and John P. Milton. Garden City: The Natural History Press, 1966.

_____ . *The Condition of Man*. New York: Harcourt, Brace and Company, 1944.

_____ . *The Conduct of Life*. New York: Harcourt, Brace and Company, 1951.

_____ . *The Culture of Cities*. New York: Harcourt, Brace and Company, 1938.

_____ . *Faith for Living*. New York: Harcourt, Brace and Company, 1940.

_____ . "From Revolt to Renewal." *The Arts in Renewal*. Edited by Sculley Bradley. New York: A.S. Barnes, 1951.

_____ . *From the Ground Up*. New York: Harcourt, Brace and World, 1956.

_____ . "The Garden City Idea and Modern Planning." Introductory essay in *Garden Cities of To-Morrow* by Ebenezer Howard. Cambridge: M.I.T. Press, 1965.

_____ . *The Golden Day: A Study in American Experience and Culture*. 4th ed. New York: Dover Publictions, 1968.

_____ . *Green Memories, the Story of Geddes Mumford*. New York: Harcourt, Brace and Company, 1947.

_____ . *Herman Melville*. New York: The Literary Guild of America, 1929.

_____ . *The Highway and the City*. New York: The New American Library, 1964.

Mumford, Lewis. "How War Began." *Adventures of the Mind.* New York: Vintage Books, 1960.

_____ . *The Human Prospect.* Edited by Harry T. Moore and Karl W. Deutsch. Carbondale and Edwardsville: Southern Illinois University Press, 1965.

_____ . "I Believe." *I Believe: The Personal Philosophies of Certain Eminent Men and Woman of Our Time (Living Philosophies, Revised).* Edited by Clifton Fadiman. New York: Simon and Schuster, 1939.

_____ . *In the Name of Sanity.* New York: Harcourt, Brace and Company, 1954.

_____ . *Interpretations and Forecasts: 1922-1972.* New York: Harcourt, Brace, Jovanovich, 1973.

_____ . "Introduction" to *The New Exploration* by Benton MacKaye. Urbana: University of Illinois Press, 1962.

_____ . "Introduction" to *The New Towns: The Answer to Megalopolis* by Frederick J. Osborn and Arnold Whittick. New York: McGraw-Hill Book Co., 1963.

_____ . "Introduction" to *Patrick Geddes: Maker of the Future* by Philip Boadman. Chapel Hill: University of North Carolina Press, 1944.

_____ . "Introduction" to *Ralph Waldo Emerson: Essays and Journals.* Garden City: Doubleday and Company, 1968.

_____ . in *Living Philosophies.* New York: Simon and Schuster, 1931.

_____ . "Looking Forward." *Science and Man.* Edited by Ruth Nanda Anshen. New York: Harcourt, Brace and Company, 1942.

_____ . "The Making of Men." *The Humanities Look Ahead: Report of the First Annual Conference Held by the Stanford School of Humanities.* Stanford: Stanford University Press, 1943.

_____ . *Men Must Act.* New York: Harcourt, Brace and Company, 1939.

_____ . *The Myth of the Machine: Technics and Human Development.* New York: Harcourt, Brace and World, 1967.

_____ . *The Myth of the Machine: The Pentagon of Power.* New York: Harcourt, Brace, Jovanovich, 1970.

Mumford, Lewis. "The Napolean of Notting Hill." *Toynbee and History, Critical Essays and Reviews.* Edited by M.F. Ashley Montagu. Boston: Porter Sargent, 1956.

_____ . "The Natural History of Urbanization." *Man's Role in Changing the Face of the Earth.* Edited by William L. Thomas, Jr. Chicago: University of Chicago Press, 1956.

_____ . "The Need for Concrete Goals." *Challenge to the New Deal.* Edited by Alfred W. Bingham and Seldon Rodman. New York: Falcon Press, 1934.

_____ . "A New Kind of Teacher." *The Humanities Look Ahead.* Stanford: Stanford University Press, 1943.

_____ . "Patrick Geddes, Victor Branford and Applied Sociology in England: The Social Survey, Regionalism and Urban Planning." *An Introduction to the History of Sociology.* Edited by Harry Elmer Barnes. Chicago: University of Chicago Press, 1948.

_____ . "Foreword" to *Planned Society: Yesterday, Today, Tomorrow.* Findlay Mackenzie, editor. New York: Prentice-Hall, 1937.

_____ . "The Pragmatic Acquiescence: A Reply." *Pragmatism and American Culture.* Edited by Gail Kennedy. Boston: D. C. Heath, 1950.

_____ . "Prospect." *Man's Role in Changing the Face of the Earth.* Chicago: University of Chicago Press, 1956.

_____ . ed., *Roots of Contemporary American Architecture.* New York: Reinhold Publishing Corp., 1952.

_____ . "The Significance of Back Bay Boston." *Back Bay Boston: The City as a Work of Art.* Boston: Museum of Fine Arts, 1969.

_____ . *The South in Architecture.* New York: Harcourt, Brace and Company, 1941.

_____ . *Sticks and Stones: A Study of American Architecture and Civilization.* 2nd Rev. Ed. New York: Dover Publications, 1955.

_____ . *The Story of Utopias.* Compass Books. New York: The Viking Press, 1962.

_____ . *Technics and Civilization.* Harbinger Books. New York: Harcourt, Brace and World, 1963.

_____ . "Technics and the Nature of Man." *Knowledge Among Men.* New York: Simon and Schuster, 1966.

Mumford, Lewis. "Technology and Democracy." *Challenges to Democracy: The Next Ten Years.* Edited by Edward Reed. New York: Frederick Praeger, 1963.

_____ . *The Transformations of Man.* New York: Collier Books, 1962.

_____ . "The Unified Approach to Knowledge and Life." *The University and the Future of America.* Stanford University: Stanford University Press, 1941.

_____ . "University City." *City Invincible: A Symposium on Urbanization and Cultural Development in the Ancient Near East.* Chicago: University of Chicago Press, 1960.

_____ . *The Urban Prospect.* New York: Harcourt, Brace and World, Inc., 1968.

_____ . *Values for Survival: Essays, Addresses, and Letters on Politics and Education.* New York: Harcourt, Brace and Company, 1946.

Munk, Arthur W. *A Synoptic Philosophy of Education: Toward Perspective, Synthesis, and Creativity.* Nashville: Abingdon Press, 1965.

Murdock, George Peter. "The Common Denominator of Cultures." *The Science of Man in the World Crisis.* Edited by Ralph Linton. New York: Columbia University Press, 1945.

Myrdal, Gunnar. "The Necessity and Difficulty of Planning the Future Society." *Environment and Change: The Next Fifty Years.* Edited by William R. Ewald. Bloomington: Indiana University Press, 1968.

Nash, Roderick. *Wilderness and the American Mind.* New Haven: Yale University Press, 1967.

Perloff, Harvey S. *Education for Planning: City, State, and Regional.* Baltimore: Johns Hopkins Press, 1957.

Redfield, Robert. *The Primitive World and its Transformations.* Ithaca: Cornell University Press, 1953.

Reiser, Oliver L., and Davies, Blodwen. *Planetary Democracy: An Introduction to Scientific Humanism and Applied Semantics.* New York: Creative Age Press, 1944.

Riesman, David. *The Lonely Crowd: A Study of the Changing American Character.* New Haven and London: Yale University Press, 1961.

Ripley, S. Dillon. "Introduction" to *Knowledge Among Men.* New York: Simon and Schuster, 1966.

Roszak, Theodore. "Introduction: The Human Whole and Justly Proportioned." *Sources*. Edited by Theodore Roszak. New York: Harper and Row, 1972.

──────── . *The Making of a Counter Culture*. Garden City: Anchor Books, Doubleday and Company, 1969.

Royce, Joseph E. *The Encapsulated Man*. Princeton: D. Van Nostrand Company, 1964.

Schneider, Kenneth R. *Autokind vs. Mankind: An Analysis of Tyranny, A Proposal for Rebellion, A Plan for Reconstruction*. New York: Schocken Books, 1971.

Schwartz, Alvin. *Old Cities and New Towns: The Changing Face of the Nation*. New York: E. P. Dutton and Company, 1968.

Seidenberg, Roderick. *Posthistoric Man*. Boston: Beacon Press, 1957.

Seligman, Ben B. *Most Notorious Victory: Man in an Age of Automation*. Foreword by Robert L. Heilbroner. New York: The Free Press, 1966.

Shepard, Paul and McKinley, Daniel. *The Subversive Science: Essays Toward An Ecology of Man*. Boston: Houghton Mifflin Company, 1969.

Shimahara, Nobuo, ed. *Educational Reconstruction: Promise and Challenge*. Columbus: Charles E. Merrill, 1973.

Sommer, Robert, *Tight Spaces: Hard Architecture and How to Humanize It*. Englewood Cliffs, N.J.: Prentice-Hall, 1974.

Starr, Roger. *The Living End: The City and its Critics*. New York: Coward-McCann, Inc., 1966.

Stein, Clarence S. *Toward New Towns for America*. Introduction by Lewis Mumford. Cambridge: The M.I.T. Press, 1966.

Stein, Maurice R. *The Eclipse of Community: An Interpretation of American Studies*. Princeton: Princeton University Press, 1960.

Terry, Mark. *Teaching for Survival*. New York: Ballantine Books, 1971.

Thayer, V. T. *Formative Ideas in American Education*. New York: Dodd, Mead and Company, 1966.

Theobald, Robert. "Planning with People." *Environment and Change: The Next Fifty Years*. Edited by William R. Ewald. Bloomington: Indiana University Press, 1968.

Thomas, William L., ed. *Man's Role in Changing the Face of the Earth*. Chicago: University of Chicago Press, 1956.

Ulich, Robert, ed., *Education and the Idea of Mankind.* New York: Harcourt, Brace and World, 1964.

Von Eckardt, Wolf. *A Place to Live: The Crisis of the Cities.* New York: Delacorte Press, 1967.

Wagar, W. Warren. *Building the City of Man.* New York: Grossman, 1971.

————— . *The City of Man.* Baltimore: Penguin Books, 1967.

Wegener, Frank C. *The Organic Philosophy of Education.* Dubuque: William C. Brown Company, Publishers, 1957.

West, Thomas Reed. *Flesh of Steel: Literature and the Machine in American Culture.* Nashville: Vanderbilt University Press, 1967.

White, Morton and Lucia. *The Intellectual Versus the City: From Thomas Jefferson to Frank Lloyd Wright.* A Mentor Book. New York: The New American Library. 1962.

Whitehead, Alfred North. *The Aims of Education and Other Essays.* London: Ernest Benn Ltd., 1932.

————— . *Science and the Modern World.* New York: The Macmillan Company, 1926.

Whyte, Lancelot Law. *The Next Development in Man.* A Mentor Book. New York: The New American Library, 1950.

Whyte, William H. *The Last Landscape.* Garden City: Doubleday and Company, 1968.

Wood, Robert C. "The Development of Administrative and Political Planning in America." *Environment and Change: The Next Fifty Years.* Bloomington: Indiana University Press, 1968.

✿ journals and magazines

Agne, Russell M.; Conrad, David, and Nash, Robert J. "The Science Teacher As Energy Analyst and Activist." *The Science Teacher,* 41 (November, 1974), 12-17.

"Balancing Act." Review of *The Condition of Man. Time.* June 5, 1944, pp. 100-104.

Berkeley, Ellen Perry. "Environmental Education from Kindergarten
    Up." *Architectural Forum*. CXXX (June, 1969), 46-53,
    110.
Bing, Alexander M. "Can We Have Garden Cities in America?" *The
    Survey, Graphic Number*, May 1, 1925, pp. 172-73.
Boardman, Philip L. "An Adventure in Education." *Progressive
    Education*, XII (February, 1935), 75-84.
————— . "Sir Patrick Geddes." *The Social Frontier*, III (June,
    1937), 273-74.
Brameld, Theodore. "The Quality of Intellectual Discipline in
    America." *The Annals of the American Academy of
    Political and Social Science*, CCCLXXVIII (July, 1968),
    75-82.
————— . "Reconstructionist Theory: Some Recent Critiques
    Considered in Perspective." *Educational Theory*, XVI
    (October, 1966), 33-43.
Bronowski, J. "Strategy for the Next Plateau." *Nation*, July 14,
    1956, pp. 41-3.
Brooks, Van Wyck. "Lewis Mumford: American Prophet." *Harper's
    Magazine*, June, 1952, pp. 6-7, 46-53.
Bruun, Geoffrey. "Metropolitan Strait Jacket." *Saturday Review*,
    April 15, 1961, p. 17, 35-36.
Case, Clarence Marsh. "Closing in on the Machine." Review of
    Technics and Civilization. *Sociology and Social Research*,
    XIX (February, 1935), 210-17.
Chase, Edward T. "Man, Machines and Mumford." Review of *The
    Myth of the Machine. Commonweal*, March 8,
    1968, pp. 694-95.
Churchill, Henry S. "Lewis Mumford's New Work About the Culture
    of Cities." *Scientific American*, July, 1961, pp. 175-80.
Conrad, David; Nash, Robert; Shiman, David. "Foundations of
    Education: The Restoration of Vision to Teacher Prep-
    aration." *Educational Theory*, XXIII (Winter, 1973),
    42-55.
Cooke, Alistair. "A Diary of Civilization: Review of *The Culture of
    Cities*." *The Spectator*, August 26, 1938, p. 341.
Cowley, Malcolm. "Shipwreck." Review of *Faith for Living. New
    Republic*, September 9, 1940, pp. 357-58.
Dewey, John. "Education and Social Change." *The Social Frontier*,
    III (May, 1937), 238.

Drucker, Peter F. "Review of *The Myth of the Machine.*" *Technology and Culture,* IX (January, 1968), 94-98.

Duff, Edward, S.J. "Lewis Mumford: The Post-Christian in an Anti-Christian World." *Commonweal,* October 30, 1942, pp. 38-41.

"Form of Forms." *Time,* April 18, 1938, pp. 40-43.

Frank, Waldo. "Toward a New Radicalism." *Nation,* September 3, 1955, pp. 196-201.

————— . "Views on Human Nature." Review of *The Conduct of Life. Saturday Review,* September 22, 1951, pp. 11-12.

Glicksberg, Charles I. "Lewis Mumford and the Organic Synthesis." *Sewanee Review,* XLV (January-March, 1937), 55-73.

Goodman, Paul. "The Human Uses of Science." *Commentary.* December, 1960, pp. 461-72.

————— . "The Pragmatism of his Boyhood." Review of *The City in History. Hudson Review.* XIV (Autumn, 1961), 443-45.

Halsey, Van R. "Lewis Mumford's Golden Day." *New Republic,* August 12, 1957, p. 21.

Harrington, Michael. "Cities to Live In." Review of *The Urban Prospect. New Republic,* May 25, 1968, pp. 23-24.

Herskovits, Melville J. "Some Further Comments on Cultural Relativism." *American Anthropologist,* LX (April, 1958).

Hook, Sidney. "Metaphysics, War, and the Intellectuals." *Menorah Journal,* XXVIII (October-December, 1940), 326-37.

Kauffmann, Stanley. "Mind Over Matter." Review of *The Myth of the Machine. New Republic,* April 29, 1967, p. 18, 29-30.

Kluger, Richard. "Pathology of a Sad, Urban Animal." Review of *The Urban Prospect. Book World,* II (June 9, 1968), 4.

Lynd, Staughton. "Urban Renewal — For Whom?" *Commentary,* January, 1961, pp. 34-45.

Madge, Charles. "Megalopolis Revisited." *New Statesman,* LIX, (April 23, 1960), 596-97.

Meitner, John G. "Technics and Human Development." Review of *The Myth of the Machine. National Elementary Principal,* April, 1968, pp. 61-66.

Mumford, Lewis. "Anticipations and Social Adjustments in Science." *Bulletin of the Atomic Scientists,* X (February, 1954), 34-36.

Mumford, Lewis. "Apology to Henry Adams." *Virginia Quarterly Review*, XXXVIII (Spring, 1962), 196-217.

_____ . "An Appraisal of Lewis Mumford's *Technics and Civilization* (1934)." *Daedalus*, LXXXVIII (Summer, 1959). 527-36.

_____ . "Architecture as a Home for Man." *Architectural Record*, CXXXXIII (February, 1968), 113-16.

_____ . "Are We Selling Our Souls for Progress?" *Science Digest*, July, 1963, pp. 85-89.

_____ . "Art, Modern and Primitive." *New Republic*, December 1, 1926, p. 49.

_____ . "Authoritarian and Democratic Technics." *Technology and Culture*, V (Winter, 1964).

_____ . "The Automation of Knowledge." *AV Communication Review*, XII (Fall, 1964), 261-76.

_____ . "The Automation of Knowledge." *Vital Speeches of the Day*. XXX (May 1, 1964), 441-46.

_____ . "Bernard Shaw's Case for Equality." *New Republic*, July 4, 1928, pp. 177-78.

_____ . "The Bolshevist Revolution." *New Republic*, April 11, 1928, pp. 250-51.

_____ . "The Booby Prizes for 1929." *New Republic*, January 8, 1930, pp. 190-91.

_____ . "Botched Cities." *American Mercury*, XVIII (October, 1929), 143-50.

_____ . "Break the Housing Blockade!" *New Republic*, May 17, 1933, pp. 8-11.

_____ . "The Builder's Art." *New Republic*, November 16, 1927, p. 361.

_____ . "Call to Arms." *New Republic*, May 18, 1938, pp. 39-42.

_____ . "The Case Against Time." *New Republic*, March 7, 1928, pp. 102-3.

_____ . "The Chance for Civilized Housing." *New Republic*, September 17, 1930, pp. 115-17.

_____ . "The Corruption of Liberalism." *New Republic*, April 29, 1940, pp. 568-73.

_____ . "The Criticism of Darwin." *New Republic*, February 1, 1928, pp. 301-2.

Mumford, Lewis. "The Decline of Spengler." *New Republic*, March 9, 1932, p. 104.

———. "Does Growth Doom Big Cities?" *Science Digest*, January, 1942, pp. 15-20.

———. "The Fallacy of Systems." *Saturday Review of Literature*, October 1, 1949, pp. 8-9.

———. "The Fate of Garden Cities." *Journal of the American Institute of Architects*, XV (February, 1927), 37-39.

———. "The Flowers of Progress." *New Republic*, September 6, 1933, pp. 106-7.

———. "Function and Expression in Architecture." *Architectural Record*. CX (November, 1951), 106-12.

———. "Garden Cities and the Metropolis: A Reply." *Journal of Land and Public Utility Economics*, XXII (February, 1946), 66-69.

———. "The Group Mind." *Sociological Review*, XIII (1922), 184-86.

———. "Have Courage!" *American Heritage*, XX (February, 1969), 104-111.

———. "The Hour of Disintegration." *New Republic*, February 21, 1934, pp. 51-52.

———. "If I Were Dictator." *Nation*, December 9, 1931, pp. 631-33.

———. "Irrational Elements in Art and Politics, Part I." *New Republic*, April 5, 1954, pp. 16-18.

———. "Irrational Elements in Art and Politics, Part II." *New Republic*, April 12, 1954, pp. 17-19.

———. "Leisure to Replace Work?" *Science Digest*, February 1942, pp. 5-8.

———. "A Letter to the President." *New Republic*, December 30, 1936, pp. 263-65.

———. "Letter to the Editors." *New Republic*, September 8, 1940, pp. 311-12.

———. "A Long-Term View of the War." *Progressive Education*, XIX (November, 1942), 358-60.

———. "The Machine and Its Products." *American Mercury*, January, 1927, pp. 64-67.

———. "Man the Finder." *Technology and Culture*, VI (Summer, 1965), 375-81.

Mumford, Lewis. "The Menace to the American Promise." *New Republic*, November 8, 1939, pp. 64-65.

_____ . "Message from Lewis Mumford." *Menorah Journal*, XXVII (January-March, 1939), 100-1.

_____ . "Metaphysics and Art." *New Republic*, December 18, 1929, pp. 117-18.

_____ . "A Modern Synthesis." *Saturday Review of Literature*, April 12, 1930, pp. 920-21.

_____ . "Monumentalism, Symbolism, and Style (Part One)." *Magazine of Art*, XXXXII (October, 1949), 202-7, 227-28.

_____ . "Monumentalism, Symbolism, and Style (Part Two)." *Magazine of Art*, XXXXII (November, 1949), 258-63.

_____ . "The Moral Challenge to Democracy." *Virginia Quarterly Review*, XXXV (Autumn, 1959) 560-76.

_____ . "The Morals of Extermination." *Atlantic Monthly*, October, 1959, pp. 38-44.

_____ . "Mr. Lippman's Heresy Hunt." *New Republic*, September 29, 1937, pp. 219-20.

_____ . "Mr. Ransome's Facts and Mr. Russell's Fancies." *Dial*, LXVII (August 23, 1919), 152-54.

_____ . "Mr. Santayana's Philosophy." *Freeman*, VII (May 23, 1923), 258-60.

_____ . "Mumford on Geddes." *Architectural Review*, CVIII (August, 1950), 81-87.

_____ . "The New Tractarians." *New Republic*, March 26, 1930, p. 162.

_____ . "The New History." *New Republic*, May 11, 1927, pp. 338-39.

_____ . "Not Segregation But Integration." *Architectural Record*, CCXXXIV (May, 1956), 192-93.

_____ . "Now Let Man Take Over." *New Republic*, February 16, 1963, pp. 12-15.

_____ . "Old Forms for New Towns." *New Yorker*, October 17, 1953, pp. 124-32.

_____ . "On the Road to Collectivism." *New Republic*, February 6, 1935, pp. 361-62.

_____ . "Orozco in New England." *New Republic*, October 10, 1934, pp. 231-35.

Mumford, Lewis. "A Philosopher of History." Review of *The Decline of the West*, by Oswald Spengler, *New Republic*, March 20, 1929, pp. 140-41.

——. "Place of the Community in the School." *Dial*, LXVII (September 20, 1919), 244-46.

——. "Reflections: European Diary." *New Yorker*, July 6, 1968, pp. 30-43.

——. "Reflections on Modern Architecture." *Twice a Year*, II (Spring-Summer, 1939), 135-41.

——. "Regions — To Live In." *The Survey, Graphic Number*, May 1, 1925, pp. 151-52.

——. "The Restoration of Sex." *New Republic*, April 15, 1936, pp. 281-82.

——. "Science as Technology." *Proceedings of the American Philosophical Society*. CV (October, 1961), 506-11.

——. "The Significance of Herman Melville." *New Republic*, October 10, 1928, pp. 212-14.

——. "Social Purposes and New Plans." *The Survey, Graphic Number*, February, 1940, pp. 119-21, 128-30.

——. "The Social Responsibilities of Teachers and Their Implications for Teacher Education." *Educational Record*, XX (October, 1939), 471-99.

——. "A Sociologist's Roadside Notes." *New Republic*, April 4, 1928, pp. 226-27.

——. " 'Teaching' English Literature." *New Republic*, November 10, 1926, pp. 351-52.

——. "Technics and the Future of Western Civilization." *Perspectives U.S.A.* XI (Spring, 1955), 77-94.

——. "Technics and the Nature of Man." *Technology and Culture*, VII (Summer, 1966), 303-17.

——. "The Theory and Practice of Regionalism." *The Sociological Review*, XX (April, 1928), 131-41.

——. "Thorstein Veblen." *New Republic*, August 5, 1931, pp. 314-16.

——. "Toward Civilization." Review of *Toward Civilization*, edited by Charles Beard. *New Republic*, May 28, 1930, pp. 49-50.

——. "Toward a New Regionalism." *New Republic*, March 25, 1931, pp. 157-58.

Mumford, Lewis. "Toward the Publication of Peirce's Works." *New Republic,* December 31, 1930, p. 195.

_____ . "Toward a Unitary Philosophy." Review of *The Next Development in Man,* by L. L. Whyte. *Saturday Review of Literature,* April 24, 1948, pp. 22-24.

_____ . "Towers." *American Mercury,* IV (February, 1925), 193-96.

_____ . "Trend is Not Destiny." *Architectural Record,* CXXXXII (December, 1967), 131-34.

_____ . "Utopia, The City and the Machine." *Daedalus,* LXXXXIV (Spring, 1965), 271-92.

_____ . "The Voice of Despair." Review of *The Modern Temper,* by Joseph Wood Krutch. *New Republic,* May 22, 1929, pp. 36-38.

_____ . "Voting the Humanist Ticket." *New Republic,* January 14, 1931, pp. 249-50.

_____ . "Wardom and the State." *Dial,* LXVII (October 4, 1919), 303-5.

_____ . "The Waste Land." *New Republic,* July 10, 1935, p. 258.

_____ . "What is a City?" *Architectural Record,* LXXXXII (November, 1937), 59-62.

_____ . "The Wilderness of Suburbia." *New Republic,* September 7, 1921, pp. 44-45.

_____ . "World Assize: Yes or No?" *Bulletin of the Atomic Scientists,* X (May, 1954), 159-61, 168.

_____ . "Writers' Project." *New Republic,* October 20, 1937, pp. 306-7.

"Mumford's 'Good Life,' " *Newsweek,* May 22, 1944, pp. 98-101.

Nash, Robert J. "Accountability — The Next Deadly Nostrum in Education?" *School and Society,* 99 (December, 1971), 501-4.

Nash, Robert J. and Agne, Russell M. "Careers, Education, and Work in the Corporate State." *School Review.* LXXXII (November, 1973), 67-78.

"Necropolis Revisited." Review of *The City in History. Time,* April 28, 1961, p. 103.

"The New Craftsmen." *Newsweek,* February 16, 1970, p. 72.

"Planning in House and City." *Nature,* June 10, 1939, pp. 953-55.

Read, Herbert. "A Prophetic Book." Review of *Technics and Civilization. Yale Review*, XXIV (Autumn, 1934), 173-76.

Savelle, Max. "The Flight from Reason." *Journal of Modern History*, XVII (June, 1945), 153-62.

Smith, Robert. "Id Over Superego." Review of *In the Name of Sanity. Nation*, November 20, 1954, pp. 447-48.

Tankel, Stanley. "Review of *The City in History.*" *Architectural Forum*, CXIV (June, 1961), 171, 173, 176.

Tead, Ordway. "Man in Search of Himself." Review of *The Condition of Man. Saturday Review of Literature*, May 20, 1944, pp. 8-9.

Temko, Allan. "Lewis Mumford at Seventy-two." *Harper's Magazine*, October, 1967, pp. 106-11.

————— . "Which Guide to the Promised Land: Fuller or Mumford?" *Horizon*, X (Summer, 1968), 24-31.

Von Eckardt, Wolf. "A Great Mover of Our Times." Review of *The Urban Prospect. The American Scholar.* XXXVII (Autumn, 1968), 688-92.

————— . "New Towns in America." *New Republic*, October 16, 1963, pp. 16-18.

Weimer, David R. "Anxiety in the Golden Day of Lewis Mumford." *New England Quarterly*, XXXVI (June, 1963), 172-91.

Wertime, Theodore A. "Culture and Continuity: A Commentary on Mazlish and Mumford." *Technology and Culture*, IX (April, 1968), 203-12.

Zinn, Howard. "The Academic Revolution: The Case for Radical Change." *Saturday Review*, October 18, 1969. pp. 81-82, 94-95.

✺ pamphlets and addresses

Mumford, Lewis. *The Human Way Out.* Wallingford, Pennsylvania: Pendle Hill Pamphlet No. 97, 1958.

————— . *Man as Interpreter.* New York: Harcourt, Brace and Company, 1950.

————— . "Toward a Free World: Long-Range Planning under Democratic Control." Address delivered at a Conference on World Order, Rochester, New York, November 13, 1951.

❖ index